A Different Road

Two roads diverged in a wood, and I –
I took the one less travelled by,
And that has made all the difference.

– Robert Frost
From "The Road Not Taken"

Shirley Brickenden
    Bradgate Arms
       416 515 1013

ARTHUR LABATT

A Different Road

A MEMOIR

Shirley and George
Thanks so much for
your input.
Arthur

BPS
books

Toronto and New York

Published by
BPS Books
Toronto and New York
www.bpsbooks.com
A division of Bastian Publishing Services Ltd.
www.bastianpubserv.com

Publisher's note:
A limited-number hardcover edition with colour photographs was produced in 2012 for private use; printed in Canada by Webcom Ltd.

Hardcover and paperback editions with black-and-white photographs published in Canada, the United States, the United Kingdom, and Australia in 2012 by BPS Books, under the ISBNs 978-1-927483-28-2 (hardcover) and 978-1-927483-24-4 (paperback).

Cataloguing-in-Publication Data available from Library and Archives Canada.

Editor: Eloise Lewis of LifeTales, Toronto, Ontario, www.lifetales.ca
Cover design: Gnibel
Cover photo by Matt Barnes
Interior design and typesetting: Daniel Crack, Kinetics Design, www.kdbooks.ca

Material quoted from *Snatched! The Peculiar Kidnapping of Beer Tycoon John Labatt*, Copyright © Susan Goldenberg 2004. Printed with permission of Dundurn Press Limited.

Contents

Acknowledgements

I could not have succeeded in publishing this book without the help of countless individuals who took the time to reminisce with me about days gone by.

My sister, Mary Lamb, and I have stayed close during our lives, and she was critically important in reminding me of some of our early experiences. She was also the only one I could reminisce with when writing about our youthful relationships with Mother and Father. Also, my sister-in-law, Lori Labatt, the widow of my brother, Jack, was very helpful regarding his life. Jack's former partner, Ian Taylor, and his wife, Irene, spent considerable time filling me in on Jack's exploits in the British Virgin Islands.

A high-school friend from London, Ontario, Dr. Bruce Feaver, gave me some interesting insights into my teenage years at Central Collegiate. A double first cousin (once removed), Shirley Brickenden, supplied me with a great deal of detailed background on the Labatt and Browne family ancestry. My last surviving first cousin on the Labatt side of the family, Kathleen Patton, has given me a number of original oil paintings of my great grandmother, Eliza Kell Labatt. Also, Sam McLeod, a long-term loyal employee of Labatt's, gave me a number of framed photographs of senior management of the company. John Frankel discussed with me at length our days at camp as well as our travel adventures in Europe.

I would also like to thank Bill Crawford of Clarkson Gordon and Graham Weeks of McLeod Young Weir for their time in reviewing our careers together; also a number of individuals from Trimark/Invesco, including Bob Krembil, Brad Badeau, Bill Harker, Phil Taylor, Peter Intraligi, David Warren, and Jamie Kingston, who were very helpful on my years at Trimark.

I owe a debt of gratitude to many people who helped me research my father's kidnapping, the history of the brewery, and the history of the Labatt family. Nellie Swart, the former archivist at Labatt's, was very helpful; with the permission of management, she made available to me *A History of Labatt's*, written in the late 1980s by Professor Albert Tucker of York University. Western Archives, Western University assisted with some research and original historical material. I gained considerable knowledge of my father's kidnapping from various sources, including: *Snatched! The Peculiar Kidnapping of Beer Tycoon John Labatt*, by Susan Goldenberg; "The Labatt Snatch," by Alice Gibb for the London & Middlesex Historical Society's *Historian*; *The Kidnapping of John Labatt*, by Frank Crowe, the detective assigned to the case; and *Who Said Murder?* in which Charles W. Bell, the lawyer who represented wrongly convicted member of the kidnapping gang David Meisner, chronicles the case.

Kathii Benn was equally helpful as she researched the history of my travels and confirmed my recollections of visits to all corners of the globe.

Special recognition is in order for my executive assistant, Odette Goodall, who helped me immeasurably with names, as well as with the stories themselves. Odette and I have worked together for thirty-five years, and she knows nearly everyone I have written about.

Many thanks to my good friend Stuart MacKay, who so kindly gave me his model of the Labatt's Streamliner truck, pictured on the cover, from his extensive collection of model trucks.

I must also acknowledge my editor, Eloise Lewis, for her wise counsel and excellent organizational skills. Her encouragement and keen perspective were significant over the three years that I sent her scattered anecdotes and reminiscences. Her skill in putting them together cohesively was indispensable. Nor can I underestimate the value of Rod McQueen's encouragement in getting me started. I'd also like to convey my appreciation to Don Bastian of BPS Books for his publishing expertise and meticulous attention to detail in preparing this book for publication.

A special thanks also to my wife, Sonia, who is an author and much more organized than I could ever hope to be. Sonia carefully reviewed my drafts, which I randomly passed on to her. We often had a hard time seeing how these unrelated stories would ever fit together. I appreciate all her help and patience – and her lessons in the many functions of a computer.

My three children, Sheila, Jacquie, and John, were incredibly supportive in recalling their childhood experiences and encouraging me to keep going. And I am pleased that their children – my six wonderful grandchildren, Fraser, Jessica, Dylan, Courtney, Kinder, and Christopher – were happy to contribute their youthful experiences to the book.

I thank you all for the support, patience, and assistance that you have given me. You have enhanced my anecdotal material and my writing experience immensely.

PREFACE

WHEN I was three months old, my father was kidnapped and my mother's hair turned white. Despite that rather dramatic beginning, I enjoyed a very happy life. As she was getting on in years, my mother said to me, "Arthur, you have led a charmed life." This is so true, even though I have had my share of disappointments and failures, which were very real and sometimes depressing. I have therefore tried to keep most of the anecdotes and reminiscences in this book on a lighter note.

It had never occurred to me to record the story of my life until I met Rod McQueen in 2007, during my tenure as chancellor of the University of Western Ontario. Rod had just received an honorary PhD in recognition of his outstanding career as a journalist and author. I sat beside him at a dinner given in his honour by Paul Davenport, the president of the university. Rod is a very warm individual, and we chatted about everything under the sun. At the end of the evening, after I had recounted many personal anecdotes, he asked me if I had ever considered writing my memoirs. I replied that I didn't think anyone would be interested in my life story. He countered by saying he was sure that my children and grandchildren would be interested in some family history.

I asked Rod how one would go about this monumental task, and his answer was that a great deal of discipline would be required. He told me that he has set a personal goal of writing five hundred words a day and mentioned that Graham Greene's practice in later life was three hundred and fifty daily. "However," he added, "Greene's words were better. I have to throw a lot of mine out."

I discovered that writing is a very solitary undertaking. My wife, Sonia, who has co-authored two books on the environment and has written dozens of learned papers, agrees wholeheartedly. I haven't been as disciplined as I would have liked. I now realize that when rain or sleet are pounding away outdoors, one can be happy writing, tucked into some cozy little nook. However, it's much harder when beautiful weather beckons. I remember someone telling me that most of the world's great writers have lived in zones where bad weather prevails. I now understand why.

In 2010, I ran into Rod and his wife at the opera in Toronto and mentioned that I was deep into putting my anecdotes to paper. He seemed pleasantly surprised and told me that although he has suggested this idea to a number of people, less than one percent ever did anything about it.

I wish to stress that my purpose in writing the stories in this book is to record a piece of family history for future generations. Some chapters may also be of interest to family friends, and others, to my business colleagues. It is not a commercial venture or a scholarly work rather, it is the story of a genuinely happy life.

My father, John Sackville Labatt.

I MY PARENTS

IN twentieth-century London, Ontario, the Labatt name – the history and the local resonance attached to it – had a great influence on my upbringing. The name itself can be traced back to seventeenth-century France. (The Labatt genealogy is detailed in Appendix 2.)

As part of the fourth generation in the Labatt brewery, I had my own expectations of a career in the family business, but my life took a different course. Before launching into my own story, I must introduce my parents along with some rather dramatic events that painted the backdrop of my early years.

My Father

I remember my father, John Sackville Labatt, as a kind and caring man who taught me by example to treat others with respect. He spoke to the maintenance man at the brewery the same way he spoke to the master brewer. He was born in 1880 in London, Ontario, the eldest child of John Labatt and Sophia Browne. Sophia was my grandfather's second wife. His first, Catherine Biddulph, had died in 1874 of measles, leaving him with three very young daughters. Sophia was from Montreal, the sister of Dr. Arthur Browne, a distinguished obstetrician who had married John's sister, Jane. In fact, it was at their wedding that John met Sophia. Of the twelve children from John's two marriages, nine survived – seven girls and two boys. Sophia died in 1906, the result of an accidental poisoning by a pharmacist who mixed too much strychnine into her prescription.

Father attended McGill University, where he joined the Kappa Alpha

Society. Founded in 1825 at Union College in Schenectady, New York, and organized as a "literary society," it is the oldest general fraternity. My older brother Jack was a Kap, and so was my father's brother, Hugh, who was initiated into the fraternity when he was in his fifties. (Not having attended university, but with a brother who was a Kap, he felt it was about time he became one, and the fraternity was happy to welcome another Labatt into its fold.) I joined the fraternity when I attended McGill University. Father always wore his Kap Key.

After earning his science degree from McGill, Father spent two years at the Brewers Academy in New York City and became a qualified brewmaster. That may seem an odd itinerary for a McGill graduate, but it wasn't in my father's case. He was the son of John Labatt, the sole owner of John Labatt Limited, and the grandson of the brewery's founder, John Kinder Labatt.

John Labatt brought his two boys – my father, and my uncle, Hugh Francis Labatt – into the company in 1900. When he died in 1915, Father became president, and Uncle Hugh became vice president and secretary. The two brothers were close and assumed joint management of the company.

My grandfather wanted to ensure the continuity of the company as a family business. A scrupulously fair man, he did something unusual for the times: He left the brewery in equal parts to all nine of his children. Not only did he give his daughters a financial interest in the business, but he also granted them a voice. Under the terms of his will, the brothers had to obtain the consent of their seven sisters for any change in ownership. Remarkably, there were never any disputes among the nine siblings. Two of John's daughters were elected to the five-member family board of directors, which was also unusual, and served from 1915 to 1945, when the company went public.

The brothers' early days in managing the firm were challenging, due to the First World War, Prohibition, and the Great Depression of the 1930s. Just fifteen of Ontario's sixty-four breweries survived this difficult period, and only Labatt's remained under the same ownership. There were many occasions when John, Hugh, and their sisters considered selling the company for a pittance, but they always decided to hang on.

John and Hugh felt they didn't have enough money to consider

Top: *My father's brother, Hugh Labatt.*
Bottom: *Father and Uncle Hugh. The two brothers obviously got along well.*

marriage during that time; they shared an apartment, and, according to Mother, did their own laundry. They both married in the 1920s and remained at the helm of the company. Before Father's marriage in 1926 to my mother, Bessie Lynch, he took a Mediterranean cruise with forty widows on board. Mother told me she could never figure out how he escaped their clutches.

During the 1920s and '30s, breweries in Ontario were fairly small organizations and were run by a general manager. During and after the prohibition years, Mr. E. M. Burke was the general manager at Labatt's. He was formal, disciplined, and proper and was always called Mr. Burke, even by my father and Uncle Hugh. He was a good manager, but he also made sure he looked after himself. He negotiated an annual remuneration – a combination of salary, commission, and bonus – that was equal to the salary and dividend that Father and Uncle Hugh received.

Hugh Mackenzie, the first person outside the Labatt family
to be given the title of vice president of John Labatt Limited.

In 1930, Mr. Burke reached the age of sixty-seven but had no wish to retire. That same year, a young man named Hugh Mackenzie was hired as comptroller. He was a chartered accountant from Toronto-based Clarkson, Gordon & Company and was recommended by Colonel Lockhart Gordon, a senior partner at the firm. Mackenzie had become familiar with the auditing of breweries during his work for the Royal Commission on Customs and Excise, in 1926–27. Mackenzie's professional training foreshadowed a new phase in the history of the company's leadership.

In 1935, Burke finally retired, and Hugh Mackenzie succeeded him as general manager. Father got along very well with him, and the company maintained a steady pattern of growth. In addition to being general manager, Mackenzie was given the title of vice president, the first use of this title outside the family. Effectively, Hugh Mackenzie was the chief executive officer of Labatt's.

In 1945, Labatt's became a public company and continued to grow at a very fast pace by acquiring breweries in Toronto and Manitoba, and establishing one in Montreal. Many new professional managers were hired during this period. Two of my cousins – John Cronyn and Alex Graydon – joined the company, followed, in 1950, by my brother Jack.

When he was in his thirties, Father was the Master of the Hunt at the London Hunt Club. On one hunt, he had lent his own horse to another member of the club and was riding a borrowed one that, unbeknownst to Father, was just getting over distemper and was therefore quite weak. As Father guided him over a stone wall, the horse missed by a foot and flipped over, landing on one of Father's legs, breaking it in nine places. He was lucky to have escaped with his life, but underwent multiple operations in Canada and was on crutches for more than two years. When the First World War broke out in 1914, he was at sea travelling to England to have yet another operation. He ended up with limited movement of his knee and one leg two inches shorter than the other. As a result, he wore an elevated boot, walked with a cane, and had a pronounced limp. The kidnapping of my father in 1934, the year I was born, made headlines everywhere and I have devoted a later chapter to this dramatic and difficult period in his life.

Father was in his mid-fifties when I was born. Because of his riding accident and the fact that he had suffered a major heart attack in his

Father with our dog Queenie.

forties, sports were out of the question. He described his condition as having a "game leg" and said that was why he couldn't play sports. I never gave it a second thought.

I didn't really see much of Father in my younger years, nor, for that matter, did I see a lot of Mother. I was brought up by nurses, housekeepers, and chauffeurs – all of them wonderful people. In no way did I feel deprived or left out. I called my father "Pop," a name I probably picked up from comic books I was reading.

I have a scattering of cherished memories of Father. I used to help him get dressed when he wore his formal attire. I also made him his favourite drink, Scotch and soda, using the big pressurized seltzer bottles of those days. Father used to tell me that he felt obliged to have a sip of beer when greeting visitors at the brewery, but what he really looked forward to was coming home and having a Scotch. He loved listening to Gilbert and Sullivan on the old 78 records and could recite at length the poetry of Lewis Carroll from *Alice's Adventures in Wonderland* and *Alice Through the Looking-Glass*. When the weather was rainy or blustery, he always told me, "This is no day for a boy in short pants."

He loved recounting stories about the brewery, including one about a dog that lived in the brew house. The dog was always a little tipsy and one day fell against a steam radiator and burned the hair on one side of his body. Father said the dog never touched another drop after that.

I was taken to my father's office, as a child, by a wonderful chauffeur named Harry Yott. When I was driven anywhere in London by a chauffeur, I always asked him to take off his cap, and I made sure I sat in the front seat. I didn't want to be seen being driven by a chauffeur. We usually took our dog Queenie to my dad's corner office. Queenie was a very friendly, overweight cocker spaniel. On the way home, we stopped at a smoke shop, and I ran in to buy the *London Free Press*, the *Globe and Mail*, and two packs of Sweet Cap cigarettes for Father.

The Second World War was all encompassing when I was growing up. We all gathered around our big Rogers Majestic radio set to listen to the evening news read by Lorne Greene and later by Earl Cameron. During the final days of the war, Father often said that he felt it was nearly over. I told him that if this did happen, the newspapers would have nothing to write about. He told me not worry, assuring me they would always be able to find car accidents or other disasters.

During the period right after the war, Father's health deteriorated. He retired in 1950, and he and Mother rented a house in Bermuda called Gay Shadows, during the winter. I remember Father as a very kind and quiet man. He was somewhat shy and lived a simple life. There was not a trace of arrogance in his being. He suffered from heart disease and lung problems from a lifetime of smoking. In those days, emphysema and heart disease were not directly attributed to smoking. Although he had given up cigarettes ten years before his death, he used to tell me he was living on borrowed time, and that a drug called digitalis was keeping him alive.

Father died of a heart attack at our cottage in Port Stanley, Ontario, on July 8, 1952. I had just turned eighteen and was working as a counsellor at Camp Ahmek in Algonquin Park.

The funeral service was held at our home on Central Ave. in London. (In London, we always said "Ave."– never "Avenue.") There was an open casket, and many people filed through the house to pay their respects. Relatively few people were in the living room for the service, but outside, in Victoria Park across from our house, hundreds (perhaps thousands) of people, many of them long-term employees of Labatt's, stood silently, paying their respects to a man they admired and loved.

My father had been president of Labatt's for thirty-five years. The *Labatt News* of August 1952 showed a photograph of Father, smiling, under which was written:

JOHN SACKVILLE LABATT.

The tributes that are paid to men after the hour of their passing need not be made for Mr. John Labatt. Too often these tributes are born out of the selfish declarations of our individual loss in the passing of a friend.

Mr. Labatt's full life was its own tribute to him when his days among his fellow-men were lived. In his living room there was modesty and quiet; dignity and thoughtfulness of others were a natural part of him.

To have known this man well or slightly; to have mingled life with him in business, at holiday greeting time, as a fellow–partner in a square dance or simply in quiet talking was to be enriched with the simplicity and rightness of the spirit that was in him.

His life has left its mark in the life of each of us who knew and loved him as one loves a just and good man. Some of the goodness we shall pass on to others in our meeting together.

And always we shall bear within us a warm remembering of "Mr. John" as a gentle and kindly man, a man of quiet honour.

After father's death, the headmaster of Trinity College School in Port Hope, where Father and Uncle Hugh were educated, mentioned him in The Headmaster's Report to the annual meeting of the Governing Body at the school, on October 15, 1952.

Mr. John Labatt was at T.C.S. from 1891 until 1896; he went on to McGill and graduated in 1900 with a BSc degree. For thirty-five years he was President of the family business, retiring in favour of his brother Hugh in 1950. Throughout his life he did everything in his power to increase the amenities of his home city, London, and the story of his benefactions would fill many pages. If all companies in Canada were led by men as public spirited as John and Hugh Labatt there would be no criticism of free enterprise. He always took a deep interest in his old School and helped us in countless ways.

My Mother

MOTHER'S name was Elizabeth Ann, but she was known to everyone as Bessie. Born in 1893, she grew up in Ottawa, one of nine children of William J. Lynch, a career civil servant who rose through the ranks to become the head of the Patent Office. Mother's early years in Ottawa were very important to her, and, even in her eighties, she always referred to herself as an "Ottawa girl."

Her large Irish Catholic family was very much a part of the Ottawa scene, which included visits to Government House, skating on the Rideau Canal, entertaining cabinet ministers, and attending tea parties. Her brothers and sisters were characters. Unlike my father's relatives, who were somewhat reserved, members of the Lynch clan were outgoing and great storytellers. There was Uncle Billy and Uncle Arthur, and Aunts Mamie, Josie, Flossie, Daisy, and Bebe (this is what everyone called them). These wonderful individuals visited London often, and for extended periods. This fact alone probably drove my father to escape to the London Club on more than one occasion.

When Mother was in her early eighties, she told me that she had only recently learned that her father was a lifelong closet Conservative. In the first half of the twentieth century, civil servants never divulged their political leanings. Mother had just assumed that he was a Liberal because someone had told her that all Catholics were Liberals. She then told me that had she known *her* father voted Conservative she would never have cancelled *my* father's vote during all those years of their marriage by voting Liberal.

After high school, Mother studied Library Science at McGill University and was an accomplished figure skater. She loved telling stories of famous people she knew. When I was a little boy, she told me that she had waltzed with the infamous Count Joachim von Ribbentrop at the Minto Skating

My mother, Bessie.

Club in Ottawa. Von Ribbentrop was the son of a German Army officer and had been educated in Switzerland. A charming fellow, he was fluent in English and French and represented the Minto Skating Club in competitions. He returned to Germany when war broke out in 1914 and later worked closely with Hitler in senior political positions before and during the Second World War. Although he claimed he was only following orders, he was found guilty during the Nuremberg War Crimes trials and was executed in October 1946.

Mother also met most of the politicians, diplomats, and religious figures of the day. Mackenzie King spoke at my parents' wedding in 1926, and, as we now know, he was a bit of a strange character. He led Canada for a total of twenty-two years, through half of the Depression and all of the Second World War. He was not an orator, nor did he espouse a radical platform, but as a master of compromise and conciliation, he was a consummate politician.

On more than one occasion, Mother was a guest at Government House of her close friends, Georges and Pauline Vanier. A First World War hero, Georges Vanier was Canada's first French-Canadian Governor General. During his time in office, he focused on young people, seniors, and the disadvantaged and worked hard to bring Canadians of English and French origin closer together.

Mother also became good friends with Emmett Cardinal Carter, who was Bishop of London from 1964 to 1978. He often dropped by for a visit and a drink. My mother, when offered an alcoholic beverage, always claimed, "No, I don't drink … Well, maybe a little glass of sherry." After downing it in one gulp, she readily accepted a refill. And sometimes, another. Then, feigning surprise, she would announce, "God's teeth, this has gone right to my head!"

Mother and Father met in Bermuda in the early 1920s, and the country became their second home. After he retired, Father spent his last three winters there. After his kidnapping in 1934, he never wanted to spend time in the United States, as some of the kidnappers were American, and he was afraid they were still out to get him.

My parents set up house in London in 1926 and my mother became a well-known figure around town. She was a founding member of the Family Service Bureau and became Lady District Superintendent of the St. John Ambulance Association (now known simply as St. John Ambulance). For these and other activities, she was named a Dame of the Order of Malta. Her devotion to the Catholic Church was boundless. She went to mass nearly every day and often brought home all kinds of lost and lonely people she met there.

During my high-school years at Central Collegiate, I arrived home one day and was introduced to Romero Lopez, a young man from Quito, Ecuador. Romero had been sent to Canada by his father to learn all he could about Massey-Harris farm equipment. Mother befriended him at mass because he looked so nervous and frightened. The principal reason for his anxiety was the fact that he was about to have his tonsils out the next day. All went well with the tonsillectomy, and Romero lived with us for three months. One day, at the cottage, when my sister, Mary, walked through the living room in her short shorts, Romero commented, "What a lovely body." Mother scolded him furiously, saying, "You never say that in polite company!" Thirty years ago, Sonia and I visited Ecuador and tried very hard to find Romero, to no avail.

While Mother could embrace anyone, she did not easily forgive those who took advantage of her. When I was in grade school, I told her that a man we called Stinky Davis owned the convenience store across the street from the school. She told me not to buy anything there because he had played a dirty trick on her years before. When she arrived alone from Toronto by train and was still very new to London, Stinky Davis, who was then a taxi driver, drove her all around town and charged her an exorbitant fare. She realized later that her new home on Central Ave. was only three blocks from the station.

While she never forgot Stinky's name, she wasn't above getting more important names wrong. I met Sonia, my bride-to-be, in the summer of 1957. That fall, Sonia and I drove from Toronto to London so I could introduce her to Mother. Mother's brother, Willie, and three of her sisters were visiting at the time, so the introduction of Sonia Armstrong took on an air of some importance. We arrived as lunch was being served, and Mother introduced Sonia as Connie Anderson. To this day, I have no idea where that name came from. Sonia didn't correct her, and one of mother's sisters started calling her Connie. This was soon straightened out. Sonia got along famously with the Lynch clan. She enhanced her acceptance into the family by helping Mother sew badges onto her beret for a Saint John Ambulance parade taking place later that afternoon.

Some years later, Sonia and I went to London to help Mother prepare for a three-month visit to Indonesia. Mother had packed far too much for the trip, including pillows, toilet paper, and heaven knows what else. Sonia and I had to do a complete repack, during which we realized that she was months behind in paying her bills. We found invoices stuffed behind light switches and under mattresses; some were fourth and fifth notices. When we pointed out that the Public Utilities Commission was threatening to cut off her power, Mother responded by calling them and stating that if they ever did such a thing she would leave London and never come back! We gathered up all of the bills and found someone to help her look after her business affairs.

Mother was taking the trip because she had donated a fully equipped ambulance to an Indonesian charity and was being accompanied by an old friend, Wilfred Grange, who had retired from the United Nations and knew the region well. Mother's nephew, Eddie Galbraith, was a navigator with Canadian Pacific Airlines, and Mother arranged to have him on board the trans-Pacific portion of the flight leaving from Vancouver. Sonia and I drove her to the Toronto Airport to help her board for the Toronto to Vancouver leg.

In a rather loud voice, she told the CP staff at the check-in counter in Toronto that she had led a long and happy life and was prepared to "go down in the drink" if an emergency occurred. She then introduced me and asked where she could buy the biggest insurance policy possible, naming me as the beneficiary. At the end of this conversation, which rattled the staff, the senior person on duty said it would be quite all right if I took Mother on board – right away.

Mary and I remember Mother as a wonderfully warm, cozy, and comforting mommy when we were very young children. Her nurturing ways filled us with security, especially in times of high fevers, sore throats, and such. Later on, however, she could be a strict disciplinarian dealing with rebellious teenagers.

Growing up with Mother was not always easy. Let's just say it was an experience. She could also be lots of fun. She had a great sense of humour and loved to laugh and tease. She enjoyed young people, and they related very well to her. She had her own abbreviations: "P"s were Protestants, and "H"s were homosexuals. And when the Women's Christian Temperance Union knocked on the door one day, collecting funds, she thought it was just a wonderful cause, and, much to my father's annoyance, donated $15.

Mother enjoyed good health until she turned eighty, and then a series of strokes diminished her quality of life. She had had some radiation treatments for breast cancer in her seventies but came through these with the help of Marie Shales, a good friend of my brother, Jack. Marie remained a great help to Mother in the latter years of her life.

When Mother became seriously ill, Mr. Postian, who owned the major rug company in London, and had laid the carpeting in our house, made a special visit to let us know where Mother hid her jewelry. He told us we would find it under the fifth stair runner from the first floor landing.

Mother wanted to stay at home on Central Ave. until she died. Mary and I made a solemn pledge to her that this would be the case, so we hired round-the-clock nursing help. Her mind remained remarkably alert, and she said she almost couldn't wait to die so she could go to heaven. Mother believed fervently in the afterlife. When I was young, she used to tell me that many millions of people on earth endured a miserable existence, and some had nothing to live for in this life. They could, however, look forward to a happier experience in the next life. On February 19, 1975, Mother died peacefully at home, just as she had wanted, no doubt ending up exactly where she expected to go.

In 2001, I made a donation to King's College for a new academic centre to be named the Elizabeth A. "Bessie" Labatt Hall. At both the announcement of this donation on June 5, 2001, and the official opening of the building in October 2003, I made some remarks that I feel sum her up pretty well. The following is taken from these two presentations.

Mother certainly was compassionate, inclusive, comforting, generous, warm, etc. We can all acknowledge these traits – she also had the common touch and was not at all pretentious. But when you add the fact that Mother was a bit eccentric – this magnifies and accentuates these qualities.

My sister, Mary, here with us today, my brother, Jack (who many of you knew and who died at far too young an age), would agree with me that growing up with Mother was an experience. Mother was unique. She certainly was a character. Despite the fact that she had the common touch, she was not a shrinking violet. She had lots of spunk – lots of nerve. At home, we used to say that "she had the nerve of a canal horse."

She loved royalty – prime ministers, governors general, church leaders, and captains of industry. If Mother wanted something, she would go right to the top – to one of the leaders she knew. Sometimes, this worked, but sometimes it didn't ...

There are lots of funny stories in this area. Certainly one I recall is the time she called the President of the Canadian Pacific Railway, Buck Crump, to ask if the Toronto to Montreal train could make a special stop for her in Dorval so that she could visit a sick friend. This is one that didn't work!

Another anecdote pertains to one of Mother's visits when Sonia and I were living in Paris. We knew that Mother loved the opera and we had tried everywhere to get tickets to the Saturday-evening performance. We had called ticket offices, concierges, scalpers, etc. Mother took charge – she immediately called the Vatican and got house seats – for that evening. This one worked.

Despite the fact that Mother was not pretentious and was always "Bessie" to her friends, she loved being Mrs. John Labatt. As my sister, Mary, used to say, "Mother was such a name dropper, she even dropped her own name." For example, she couldn't understand, when travelling in Spain and wishing to make a reservation in the dining car, why nobody on board had ever heard of Mrs. John Labatt.

I could go on for hours with amusing little stories, but in a more serious vein, I can say that Mother was very kind and very generous with her time. She really cared for people, from the blue-collar worker to the CEO.

We're here to honour Mother and I guess the second question is: Why King's College? There are many reasons:

One is the fact that Mother's life revolved around the Church – and she loved bright young people. She also had a strong social conscience. Mother's religious values, her inclusiveness, and her desire to help people go hand in hand with the values held by the school.

We were never a political family, but my strong sense is that Mother's leanings were to the left of centre – she just happened to marry a capitalist. I use this word in the very best sense. Seriously, both Mother and Father were caring people, concerned with social justice and ethics – values shared by King's.

Another fact is that it's nice to be able to do something in London. I had a wonderful and happy childhood growing up here, as did my sister, Mary, and brother, Jack.

About a year ago, I received a letter from Joan Smith [wife of Don Smith, founder of the construction company EllisDon]. This letter was

At the announcement of King's College's new academic centre to be named the Elizabeth A. "Bessie" Labatt Hall. I'm flanked by my sister, Mary, and Gerry Killan, the principal of King's.

on behalf of the King's College Campaign, but it was much more than that. It was about Mother and how she and my father had welcomed Joan's family to London in the 1930s. It was truly touching and was the catalyst behind this donation.

In closing, I would like to say that the whole family is proud to be honouring Mother at this great institution. This includes my father, who would have been delighted, because he knew how much Mother loved the Church, although he continued to hold his pew at St. Paul's, London's Anglican Cathedral.

Our generation is represented by my sister, Mary, and me. Three of her five grandchildren are here today – my son, John, and daughter Jacquie, and Mary's daughter, Jennifer. My eldest daughter, Sheila, and her family live in the Far East and this would have been a bit of a long flight. My wife, Sonia, and I are delighted that we are in a position to be able to support King's. I would also like to say that Mother's eleven great-grandchildren are very proud of their great-grandmother.

The London Evening Free Press

WESTERN ONTARIO'S FOREMOST NEWSPAPER

THE WEATHER: Probabilities—Cloudy and Cool   LONDON, ONTARIO, TUESDAY, AUGUST, 14, 1934—22 PAGES   THREE CENTS

J. LABATT KIDNAPPED

GANG SEIZES PRESIDENT OF BREWERY
ASKING PAYMENT OF $150 000 RANSOM
BEFORE GIVING CAPTIVE HIS RELEASE

St. Joseph's Hospital Where Kidnapped Man's Car Was Found

Wealthy Brewer Taken From Automobile While Driving From Summer Home at Sarnia to Office in London; Motor Car Is Later Found Abandoned on Street Near St. Joseph's Hospital, This City; Prominent London Business Man Held Under Threat of Death According to Meagre Information Available on Crime; Note Tells of Kidnapping of Labatt Company Official.

Mysterious Telephone Call to Family Residence Tells of Gang's Capture

John S. Labatt, prominent business man of this city, was held by kidnappers this afternoon for ransom believed to be $150,000.

He was captured by kidnappers on his way to London from Sarnia sometime during the morning, and his car was abandoned in London.

He is being held under threat of death, if any notification of the kidnapping is given to police authorities.

Whereabouts the ransom note was found is not known, but it was located in his automobile, when it was discovered near St. Joseph's Hospital.

Labatt and his family have been spending the summer in Sarnia, and the wealthy brewer was apparently on his way to his office in this city when kidnapped.

There are meagre details of the affair, for members of the

MYSTERY TELEPHONE CALL

II   THE KIDNAPPING

MY father's kidnapping had a significant effect on my upbringing. When I was growing up, my family never discussed it, but as a child, I was aware that something bad had happened. Our house on Central Ave. had steel bars on the basement windows, and all of the ground-floor windows and doors were wired with an alarm – a level of protection that was unheard of in those days.

The kidnapping, which happened in the summer of 1934, was discussed so rarely by my family that only in the past few years have I gained any knowledge of the crime and the four trials that ensued. Researching the event and the publicity surrounding it has proved to be fascinating. I summarize the story here based on information from the publications mentioned in my Acknowledgements.

HITTING THE HEADLINES

THE incident made headlines in Canada as well as the United States, including on the front page of the *New York Times*. Father was the victim of Canada's first publicized kidnapping. Earlier, two other businessmen from the London area had been kidnapped and later released. In those cases, ransom had been paid, but the details of the crimes had never been made public. One victim was Charles Burns, head of Carling Breweries, also based in London, and the other was Sam Low, a liquor company executive associated with Carling, who had been taken by force while driving to London from his home in Windsor.

The kidnapping of my father took place about two years after the

As a baby, with my siblings, Jack and Mary, in Bermuda,
where we stayed during the kidnapping trials.

kidnap-murder of Charles Lindbergh's baby son, and there had been a number of copycat kidnappings in the U.S. Until my father's abduction, Canadian law enforcement agencies had considered kidnapping a typically American crime. Indeed, kidnapping for ransom had reached epidemic proportions south of the border. The *New York Times* actually kept a "box score" on those who had been kidnapped and which of them had been freed.

Father remained in London while the trials took place, but the rest of the family and a nanny were sent off to Bermuda. Our group boarded one of the Canadian National Steamships' "Lady Boats" in Quebec City by special tender, which made our family more conspicuous than we intended. Jack was told not to mention the name Labatt, and to use the surname Sackville, my father's middle name, instead. Whenever he failed to get his way while on board the ship, he threatened my mother with, "La-La-La … I'll tell I'm a Labatt." We spent two years in Bermuda.

My mother's hair turning white, mentioned at the beginning of this book, wasn't the only outcome of the trauma. My cousin Eddie Galbraith told me that my first words were, "What's that noise?" Because of Mother's fears, my sister, Mary, wasn't allowed to walk to school alone until she was twelve years old.

Jack showed me where the handguns in our house were hidden. One day, in my early teens, I was alone in the house and thought I heard a noise. I crept down the stairs, armed with one of the loaded guns, even though I had only a vague idea how to shoot it. Luckily, it was a false alarm. Our chauffeur, Somerville, who was hired as my father's bodyguard after the kidnapping, told me that neither my father nor my uncle Hugh could hit the broad side of a barn door. Fortunately, we didn't keep these weapons around for long.

PROHIBITION AND ITS EFFECTS

IT'S important to know something about what transpired during the decades of the 1920s and 1930s in order to understand the mentality and motivation of the kidnappers. "The Roaring Twenties" is a phrase used to describe the vibrant decade of the 1920s in North America, with the Wall Street Crash of 1929 signalling its end. The 1930s were marked by the Great Depression, which lasted until the declaration of war, in September 1939.

The 1920s were seen as a period of prosperity and progress, especially in the United States. The decade truly did roar, thanks to the Model T, bathtub gin, the movies, and the first solo transatlantic flight by Charles Lindbergh. Anything seemed possible through modern technology. Mass-produced automobiles and appliances became affordable to the middle class. Jazz music became increasingly popular, spread by radio stations across North America. Speakeasies were everywhere during Prohibition and led to the rise of gangsters such as Al Capone.

In 1918, prohibition of the sale, manufacture, and transport of alcohol became the law of Canada in all provinces except Quebec. In the United States, the National Prohibition Act of 1919 covered every state. The law was repealed by many of the provinces in Canada during the 1920s – though not in its entirety in Ontario – so Canadian distillers and brewers resumed production. As my father explained it to me, Labatt's could brew full-strength beer and sell it to other provinces and the U.S. – as long as it did not touch Ontario soil.

There was a brisk business transporting beer from London to Port

Stanley on the London & Port Stanley Railroad bound for the U.S. Father told me that a number of cases were deliberately pushed off the conveyor belts running from the train cars to the holds of fishing boats every day. These cases were then "confiscated" by Canadian Customs personnel for their own enjoyment.

London was very well situated for beer sales to the United States. The New York Central Railroad, which ran from New York City to Chicago, had a major refuelling station in St. Thomas, eighteen miles from London. Boxcars loaded with beer were put on the trains and taken to Buffalo and Western and Upstate New York as well as to Detroit and the American midwest. In addition to rail transport, considerable quantities of "product" were trucked to Windsor and sold to Americans standing at the ready to transport them across the Detroit River.

The repeal of the Volstead Act in the U.S. in 1934 ended Prohibition and forced many underworld characters to look for other means of "employment." The gangsters knew the beer and the liquor business; it was logical that they would look at brewery and distillery executives if they chose kidnapping as their new profession.

As mentioned earlier, two executives of Carling Breweries of London had been kidnapped and released. A much wealthier liquor executive, Sam Bronfman of Seagram's, in Montreal, was the original, preferred target of Father's kidnappers. However, the gang didn't know Montreal; on a scouting trip to the swinging city they decided that a kidnapping there was way over their heads. Most of them were country boys from the Ontario/Michigan region, to which they returned after a few exciting days, completely broke. They decided to focus on the Labatt brothers.

The Labatt name was well known to the bootleggers in Ontario and Michigan, and my father had been warned by the police to be cautious. He had rented a different cottage than usual that summer to be a bit farther from the U.S. border and still be able to commute to London. He had also hired guards to protect his children.

A Fateful Drive

ON the morning of August 14, 1934, Father was driving from our cottage at Brights Grove, on the shores of Lake Huron, to a meeting at his office in London. I was just three months old at the time. Mary was three years old, and Jack was six. Running late, he took a short cut down a secluded stretch of gravel road. A car that had passed him earlier turned around and now was headed directly toward him. Father pulled over to the side of the road to avoid a collision. The other car stopped, and while the driver waited in the car, two men leapt out and ran toward him, brandishing guns. They were not wearing masks.

"Stick 'em up quick – this is a kidnapping," the leader shouted.

While one of the gang pocketed $99 from my father's wallet, leaving him with $1, the other men ordered him to write a short note to his brother. The note said simply:

Dear Hugh: Do as these men have instructed you to do and don't go to the police. They promise not to harm me if you negotiate with them. Your affectionate brother, John.

Father, who was fifty-four at the time, had suffered a couple of serious heart attacks, a fact that was known to the kidnappers. Although they were initially quite rough, they eventually calmed down. They taped Father's eyes and put sunglasses over the tape so anyone who saw him wouldn't be suspicious.

The gang's leader, Michael Francis McCardell, was a handsome, sharp-featured man of forty; he dubbed himself Three Fingered Abe in all of his dealings with the family. He was a Canadian who had been raised on a farm near the small Ontario town of Seaforth and had left at sixteen to find work in the States. McCardell's cohorts included Albert Pegram, a rather sullen, two-hundred-pound resident of Tennessee with connections to Ontario's illegal liquor trade, and Russell Knowles, a college-educated engineer.

After forcing Father to write to Uncle Hugh, McCardell and Pegram hustled him into their car. Knowles then drove Father's eight-cylinder Reo to London, where he left it, with the note inside, conspicuously parked on Grosvenor Street, in front of St. Joseph's Hospital.

The other two gang members, with their blindfolded captive in the back seat, headed north to a cottage in Muskoka that they had rented on Wildwood Lake, outside Bracebridge. During the drive, McCardell proved particularly companionable, chatting with father on a variety of subjects. He even asked him if he knew of any other potential ransom subjects around London or cash payrolls they could target. Father told him that the brewery paid by cheque and would not be a candidate.

By noon, Hugh Labatt and his uncle, Major-General Sydney Mewburn of Hamilton, were wondering why Father had failed to show up for their scheduled meeting. They had just arrived at Hugh's apartment on Waterloo Street for lunch when Hugh was called to the phone.

The caller, Russell Knowles, who borrowed McCardell's nickname of Three Fingered Abe, told Hugh, "You are doing business for export with the United States and we have your brother and we are holding him for

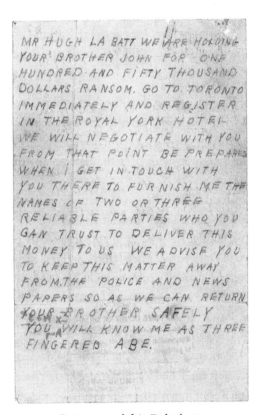

Ransom note left in Father's car.

ransom." After being cautioned to keep the "snatch" quiet, Hugh was told that he would find the ransom demand in his brother's Reo.

Despite the kidnapper's demand for secrecy, Hugh, on the advice of his uncle, immediately alerted the London police. The note that London Detective Thomas Bolton found under the Reo's rubber floor mat read:

> *Mr. Hugh Labatt: We are holding your brother John for one hundred and fifty thousand dollars ransom. Go to Toronto immediately and register in the Royal York Hotel. We will negotiate with you from that point. Be prepared when I get in touch with you there to furnish me the names of two or three reliable parties who you can trust to deliver this money to us. We advise you to keep this matter away from the police and news papers so as we can return your brother safely. You will know me as Three Fingered Abe.*

Any hope of keeping the crime out of the public eye immediately vanished when an anonymous caller tipped off a *London Free Press* reporter. The kidnapping soon turned into a media circus, despite attempts by the police to impose a blackout on information concerning the investigation. Several newspapers competed furiously to scoop one another on one of the most spectacular stories of the Depression. (In fact, the Labatt case would remain front-page news for over two years.) Once the kidnapping story broke, hungry newspaper reporters descended on both Toronto and London. Even the *New York Times* sent staff to the "wilds" of Ontario for first-hand accounts of any developments. An electronic billboard on the *Times'* office building in the heart of Manhattan flashed bulletins about the kidnapping in five-foot-high letters.

As soon as Mitchell Hepburn, Ontario's flamboyant farmer-turned-premier, heard of Father's disappearance, he called all of the province's police forces into action, cancelling their holiday leave. "We don't want an Americanized Ontario," the premier declared, a warning that kidnapping would not be tolerated north of the border.

While the provincial force set up roadblocks in the Sarnia area, the Royal Canadian Mounted Police started contacting American law enforcement agencies to compile a list of suspects. To this day, the Federal Bureau of Investigation has hundreds of pages of material on the kidnapping in its files.

A Hasty Exit

MEANWHILE, for three days and two nights, the gang kept Father in the secluded cottage, blindfolded and chained to the iron bedstead. The fact that he apparently never once tried to escape led many people to conclude later that the kidnapping was nothing more than a well-organized publicity stunt to advertise Labatt products. These false accusations were very hurtful to our family. Considering his physical condition, and his generally retiring nature, Father's failure to act is understandable. Also, like other Canadians, he would have read of the many kidnappings south of the border and of the tragic consequences suffered by their victims in failed rescue attempts.

During the days of my father's ordeal, however, the relationship between captive and kidnapper was somewhat unusual. When McCardell and Pegram arrived with Father, they helped guide him through thick brush and up the stairs of the rented cottage. McCardell then ordered Pegram to patrol the area around the cottage during the night. They left Father's blindfold on and secured him by the wrist to the bed with a dog leash. McCardell cooked a dinner of pork chops and beans, did the dishes, and he and Father slept the rest of the night in their respective rooms.

In the morning, McCardell, who had asked Father to call him Charlie, while he called my father John, inquired solicitously whether Father had slept well.

"Fairly well," he replied. "How about you?"

They then discussed how they both had suffered a touch of indigestion, with Charlie saying that he could have given him some bicarbonate of soda.

Next, McCardell sat on the edge of the bed and gave Father a shave with a safety razor. McCardell also offered to remove the tape and to bathe his eyes if Father would promise not to look at him. Father did not attempt a single peek. Later, during the trial, Father explained his rationale: "My guard was doing me a favour, so I felt honour bound not to look at him."

McCardell then brushed his hair, fed him breakfast, and offered him one of Father's cigarettes before lighting one for himself. They chatted about the taxable income of U.S. millionaire J.P. Morgan, and McCardell picked Father's brain again about other possible London targets for himself and

LOT D. PART OF LOT 20. CONCESSION 6. TOWNSHIP OF MONCK 28·8·34

INTERIOR OF COTTAGE ON LOT D PART OF LOT 20. CONCESSION 6. TOWNSHIP OF MONCK 28·8·34

Cottage in Muskoka where Father was held captive.

his "boys." Father replied that he didn't know of any. McCardell explained that things were getting tougher in his "business." He told Father that he didn't like kidnapping because it required planning, took too long, and was dangerous. He said he preferred holdups.

Throughout the day, McCardell plied Father with food – eggs, sweet biscuits, coffee, honey, bread and butter, pretzel sticks, oranges, and meat. The solicitous behaviour continued throughout his captivity. So did the daily ritual of shaving him, bathing his eyes, and chatting.

That first morning, Pegram was sent to Toronto to pick up fellow gang member Russell Knowles. After dropping off Father's Reo in London, Knowles had gone to Toronto to try to arrange the ransom pickup with Hugh Labatt. However, the combination of the blaring headlines about the snatch, reports of my father's dubious health, and the tightening police dragnet apparently panicked Pegram. He decided to flee back to familiar territory south of the border with their only car and was never seen again by police or his fellow gang members. This left Russell Knowles stranded in Toronto.

The attitude of the kidnappers changed after Knowles wearily struggled into the Muskoka cottage at two-twenty a.m. on Thursday, August 16. He had taken a bus from Toronto to Bracebridge, where he arrived around midnight, and then had walked the fifteen miles to the cottage. He had plenty of time during this moonlit hike to stoke his anger over Pegram's hasty exit. He vented his frustrations on McCardell, who told Knowles to be quiet so as not to awaken their hostage. However, Father was wide awake and heard their voices from his room.

THE TRAIL GOES COLD

AFTER being briefed by Knowles, McCardell tried to think of a way to salvage the situation. "We've got to get Labatt off our hands as quick as we can," he whispered urgently. "The coppers may be here any minute. We don't know but what Pegram may be leading them to trap us for some big reward that has been offered. First, though, we should try to drive the best bargain we can with Labatt so that we at least make some money."

With his anger spilling over to Father, Knowles shook him awake, yelling, "You're lucky to be alive. The boys wanted to do away with you. You're only a source of trouble. We can't collect the ransom because the Royal York Hotel is full of detectives and newspaper reporters. I spoke to your brother twice on the telephone and he said he was willing to pay a $50,000 ransom."

This was a lie, but Father had no way of knowing.

"What we should do is tie a stone to your feet and throw you into the lake," Knowles went on. "Your brother double-crossed us and notified the police and the press."

"That's no fault of mine," Father responded.

"The chief [McCardell] will let you go if you promise to pay us after you get free. Will you pay us $25,000?"

Under duress, and afraid of being shot if he refused, Father agreed.

Knowles then promised Father that he would be driven to Toronto and freed.

There was some confusion in Father's mind as to how many men were discussing his fate that night in the Muskoka cottage, although it was probably just Knowles and McCardell. He later asked his guard, Charlie (McCardell), "These fellows would not shoot me in my sleep, would they?"

"Oh no, don't worry, John," he answered. "Have a good sleep."

On one of the few occasions that my father discussed his kidnapping with me, he said he overheard the men talking about getting him out of Ontario and into the state of Michigan. When I was a teenager, Father told me that he believed capital punishment was a deterrent in the case of certain crimes, such as kidnapping. Michigan had no capital punishment; this was why they wanted to get him out of Ontario, Father thought. However, in researching the many articles and books on the kidnapping, I haven't found any mention of a discussion on the part of the kidnappers about taking Father to Michigan.

How to get Father to Toronto was now the immediate problem. Gerald Nicholson, a friend of McCardell's, from his bootlegging days, was visiting his brother in Bracebridge. McCardell walked the fifteen miles into town and convinced his friend to lend him his car. He did not tell Nicholson the reason.

When McCardell and Knowles led my father out of the cottage to the car, Nicholson immediately realized who he was. Driving him to Toronto would make him an accessory to the crime, yet he did not protest. The men waited for nightfall before departing and warned Father that they might have to shoot their way through some potential "bad spots." If that happened, he should drop to the floor of the car to avoid being hit.

They took back roads and arrived in Toronto after midnight, then drove down Yonge Street, the city's main north/south artery. Although there were roadblocks and motorcycle police were racing about, they were never stopped and questioned. Nicholson pulled up near the intersection of St. Clair and Bathurst streets, pointed Father in the direction of the Royal York Hotel, and handed him $1 out of the $99 that had been taken from him earlier.

Father walked for a couple of blocks and then hailed a cab.

The driver did not recognize him, even though his picture had been plastered on the front page of every newspaper for days. When Father arrived at the Royal York, he walked past dozens of police and reporters to the reception desk.

"I am John Labatt," he told the night clerk. "Where is my brother's room?"

Hugh and my father were not only related but also close friends and colleagues, so it was a particularly joyous reunion. Almost immediately, they slipped out of the hotel with R.G. (Dick) Ivey, their lawyer and close friend, who drove them to London. Unfortunately, they failed to notify either the Toronto or the Provincial Police. The police were very upset because by the time they knew Father was safe, the kidnappers' trail had gone cold.

A Tearful Reunion

THE brothers arrived at Uncle Hugh's apartment at four a.m. for a tearful reunion with Mother. Our family physician, Dr. W.J. Tillman, hurried over to examine Father. The doctor was a genial gentleman who looked after me when I was a boy. (He was so overweight that when I was in bed and waiting for him to arrive, Mother always placed a chair close to the bed and instructed everyone not to let Dr. Tillman sit on the bed because it might break.)

Dr. Tillman returned later in the day to check on Father again and announced to the press gathered outside our home: "Mr. Labatt has suffered a nervous collapse, but he is rational. He is very fatigued. He apparently suffered no violence at the hands of his captors. They seem to have looked after him well, and obviously, he was fed satisfactorily. His eyes are inflamed from wearing a bandage a long time. His heart is all right and he is in no danger. His condition is better than when I saw him this morning. It is difficult to say how long he must remain in bed after all the hardship he went through."

At this stage of the crime, there was little to report, and Father refused to speak publicly about his ordeal.

When reporters asked his lawyer, Dick Ivey, for comments, he replied, "If you were confronted with a matter that involved life and death to your family, what would you do?"

The answer was, "Probably keep quiet," to which Ivey responded, "Exactly."

The newspapers were full of speculation and manufactured headlines. The *Toronto Star*, for example, ran the headline AFTER WE TURN YOU LOOSE IN TORONTO – AND YOU TALK – AND ANY OF OUR GANG ARE ARRESTED – WE WILL COME BACK AND KILL YOU, implying that this was the death threat given to John Labatt by his abductors when they dropped him off on Thursday night in Toronto.

The *New York Times* ran a story on its front page on August 18 under the headline LABATT IS FREED, SUFFERS COLLAPSE, RANSOM IN DOUBT – *Brewer is Released in Toronto and Goes Home with Brother before Police Learn of It.*

The Aftermath

THE years following the kidnapping were very difficult ones for Father and the family. While the actual kidnapping and Father's days in captivity had been extraordinarily frightening, the search for the perpetrators and two years of jury trials were debilitating. According to police reports, Father was subjected to conflicting advice from the nine different Canadian and American police departments involved. Each department wanted to grab the glory in breaking the case. Lies were told, insinuations were made, and petty jealousies abounded. Father was harassed by publicity seekers and by supposed friends and advisors.

It turned out that there had been co-conspirators inside the brewery, and even Father's close friends and relatives were suspected of being in league with the kidnappers.

Although the original ransom note had been written to Hugh, Father had been instructed by Knowles and McCardell, on the drive from the Muskoka cottage to Toronto, to make contact with them through two Labatt employees, Lou McCaughey and Alex Colvin. McCaughey, the sales manager, was a long-time employee and a former London policeman. Colvin was Labatt's Windsor sales agent. Both men were suspects but were never charged. McCaughey later admitted that he had heard of plans to kidnap Father as far back as 1931, but said he had been too afraid for his safety and that of his family to come forward with the information.

In subsequent years, McCaughey continued to claim that he had no direct role in the actual kidnapping. However, he was involved with rumrunners and did a bit of personal bootlegging. He got to know a variety of seedy characters on the Windsor waterfront. One of them was John Bannon, who had been born on a farm near London. He was a rumrunner, who, as business started to decline at the end of the 1920s, had turned to the business of kidnapping. Bannon acted as a pick-up man in an earlier kidnapping in the region and sounded McCaughey out on the prospects of kidnapping Father. For three years, he kept the idea alive by keeping in touch with McCaughey and studying Father and Uncle Hugh's daily routines. He saw his role as the contact man for the collection of the ransom. Although McCaughey was never charged, he was let go by the brewery. Bannon was eventually convicted and sentenced to fifteen years.

Among those "in the racket," as Bannon described his business, was another Canadian who came from the same part of Ontario as Bannon and McCardell. His name was David Meisner. Bannon, whose involvement in the kidnapping was particularly dubious, acted as a police informant, and gave false information to Father about his guard, leading him to mistakenly point the finger at Meisner.

Meisner had moved to Covington, Kentucky, across the Ohio River from Cincinnati. Covington was a pretty wild town, and Meisner made his living there as a bookmaker. He admitted at his trial that he had been in discussions with Bannon, Knowles, McCaughey, and others in 1931, regarding kidnapping John Labatt, but claimed that he had backed out in 1934. He felt that Father was in bad health and that the Ontario Provincial Police had a strong detachment in the London area.

Adding to Father's testimony, however, several witnesses in Muskoka agreed that Meisner was undoubtedly one of three men who had rented the cottage. As a result of this combined testimony, Meisner was sentenced to fifteen years in prison.

The case might have ended with Meisner serving out his sentence had it not been for Bannon's greed. In July, he heard that McCardell had been caught in a gunfight and was being held in an Indiana jail. Bannon went to the police, hoping that if he identified the man in Indiana he would be able to collect a $5,000 reward being offered by the Ontario Attorney General.

Bannon told the police that McCardell was the brains behind the Labatt kidnapping and was the man that the police really wanted. McCardell and an accomplice had robbed a produce truck heading to Chicago. In a wild chase, his car was riddled with thirty bullets and he lost a finger on one hand. He now truly was Three Fingered Abe. McCardell was being held at Crown Point Jail in Indiana where John Dillinger, the notorious gangster, was once imprisoned. When McCardell realized that fellow gang member Bannon had ratted on him to the police, he decided to tell all. McCardell also felt that he would receive a more lenient sentence in a Canadian court.

Father was driven to Indiana and immediately recognized McCardell as his guard. McCardell greeted Father like an old friend and proceeded to recount their many conversations at the cottage and during the long drive to Muskoka. Father admitted that he had been mistaken in his identification of Meisner and was extremely upset about having to change his testimony.

McCardell also implicated the long-time sales manager at the brewery, Lou McCaughey. However, at later trials, Knowles and Bannon testified that McCaughey was not one of the partners in the kidnapping venture. McCardell was anxious to implicate the informer, Bannon, who had been planning the kidnapping since 1931. He also revealed that his two accomplices in the actual "snatch" were Leonard Pegram and Russell Knowles. Pegram was never found; there were rumours that he had been killed for running out on the gang. The search for Knowles continued.

During his trial, McCardell proved to be a very entertaining character, to the delight of the press. He said that he confessed because "it seemed logical that if the courts could convict an innocent man [Meisner], they wouldn't have much trouble convicting a guilty one." He told police that the "little Kentucky gambler" (Meisner), had tried to persuade the other men to abandon the idea.

Having spent over a year in prison, Meisner was freed, following the trials of the actual kidnappers, and left London with $10 given to him by his lawyer. Father, who was distressed by Meisner's plight, paid him a settlement of $5,500 and sent a letter of regret for his mistaken identification. The money enabled Meisner to have a cataract operation and subsequently open the Yo-Kum-In restaurant with his wife in Windsor. The restaurant was inspired by the Lil' Abner comic strip.

The last member of the gang, Russell Knowles, was arrested in December 1935, near Chicago. He was in poor health and was drinking heavily. He was with a tavern owner, who was also charged in the kidnapping but later was acquitted. The tavern owner went on to become a well-known enforcer for Teamsters Union boss Jimmy Hoffa.

David Meisner's lawyer, Charles Bell, in his book *Who Said Murder*, described Father's appearance during Meisner's second trial as

> *a positive shock. Torn as he was by anxiety in the winter, today he looks a wreck. Wrangling detectives, police officials who are keeping the stiletto ever handy for use on each other, wire-pullers and grafters galore looking for personal kudos and 'sugar' have made John Labatt's life a hell on earth during all the summer and autumn down to now.*

In addition, Father suffered stress and remorse over his promise to pay the kidnappers $25,000 in ransom. The kidnappers had threatened revenge not only on him but also on his family. For several years after the gang members were released after serving half of their fifteen-year convictions, Father received threatening letters bearing U.S. postmarks, demanding that he pay up. This is why he never wished to visit the States again and all of our family holidays from that point on were spent in Canada or Bermuda.

Although Father was not harmed during the kidnapping, the trauma of the event left its mark on him. Whenever the family was out of town, he had trusted employees live at our house in London. His office was something of a fortress. The executive offices were behind a locked door that required buzzer entry – which was uncommon in those days. A bodyguard/chauffeur drove him and the family on most occasions.

The stress of the kidnapping on both Mother and Father was enormous. Indeed, all of our lives were turned upside down, and the effect on the entire family can be felt to this day. I have always worried that our children and grandchildren could be targets. We still have an unlisted phone number.

Father had always been somewhat quiet and unassuming, but four jury trials over a two-year period and the extraordinary publicity made him even more reclusive. While he went on to achieve success in business, he felt haunted and hounded and was never the man he might have been. When crimes occur, it's not just the guilty who are punished.

My first studio photo.

III MY EARLY YEARS

Growing Up in London

ONE of my most vivid childhood memories was being taken to the CPR station to see King George VI and Queen Elizabeth, parents of our current Queen, Elizabeth II. This was the 1939 Royal Tour of Canada by their majesties, shortly before the start of the Second World War. I stood about twenty feet away from them as they waved from the rear platform of the Royal Train and was most impressed to see a king and queen.

I was born on May 11, 1934, and enjoyed an upbringing that was far from average. Our house at 256 Central Ave. is still standing, although it is now used as a wellness clinic for pregnant women. Built in 1890, it is a three-storey brick house with ten-foot ceilings that overlooks Victoria Park. As a boy, I watched workers install a Second World War tank in the park as a memorial just after the war ended in 1945.

Our house was about seven blocks from the centre of town – Dundas and Richmond Streets – and the Canadian Pacific Railway station was only three blocks away in the other direction. One of my nannies, Mrs. Foot, used to walk me to a store near the station to buy a gingerbread man.

I was somewhat shy and was always looked after by nurses, nannies, and a chauffeur. They were all very kind. Although I didn't see too much of my mother, I knew she was there if I needed her. In some ways, although I didn't realize it at the time, I was a bit of a forgotten child.

I often amused myself by riding my tricycle in a big circle on the main floor of the house: living room, dining room, in and out of the kitchen,

Our house on Central Ave. in London.

down the hall to the front door, and back into the living room. During those early years in London, and at our summer house at Port Stanley on Lake Erie, I didn't see much of my sister, Mary, or my brother, Jack. They were four and six years older, respectively. I was just Little Arthur.

I was quite a sickly kid, even to the extent once of being given the last rites of the Catholic Church. I have never been certain of the nature of my childhood illnesses. Mary remembers that the renowned Toronto paediatrician Dr. Alan Brown, who was one of the inventors of Pablum at the Hospital for Sick Children (SickKids), came to examine me in London when I was two years old, and diagnosed my condition as a "failure to thrive."

I definitely remember being given sulfa drugs. My friend, George DeVeber, who is a doctor, tells me that these drugs were the first antibiotics developed to treat infections, such as pneumonia, strep throat, and rheumatic fever. My memory is that the doctors said I did not have rheumatic fever. George asked if I remember the doctors listening to my heart, because I might have had a heart murmur. I do now recall the words "heart murmur" being bandied about. In those days, doctors often prescribed bedrest as the best cure. As for the last rites of the Catholic Church, my mother was absolutely convinced that I started getting better after I received this sacrament from the priest.

My Early School Days

I went to primary school at St. Angela's, a Catholic girls' school that Mary attended and that took boys up to grade three. I remember embarrassing Mary at a parents' night by putting up my hand when on the stage to ask my mommy to take me to the bathroom.

I have no recollection of attending regular school in grades four and five, most likely due to ill health. This void in my schooling was filled by Mother de Chantal, a French-Canadian Ursuline nun. No more than five feet tall, she was a wonderful woman who looked after me as if I was her own son. I went regularly to her quarters at St. Angela's, where she taught me the violin and piano, as well as reading and arithmetic. She never actually played the violin for me, because she was restricted by the broad, heavily starched white collar of the habit worn by nuns in the Ursuline order. She mothered me, washing my hands and face in the morning, and gave me presents at Christmas. Perhaps we filled a void in each other's lives. I was the son she never had, and she looked after me more than my own mother ever did.

Our family, circa 1937.

Season's Greetings
From the John Labatt Family
London, Christmas 1948

Our 1948 Christmas card of the family playing gin rummy.

If I could do it all over again, I would have suggested that she teach me piano as my first instrument rather than the violin, and that all instruction be in French. I have struggled to learn French all my life; I believe it would have made a big difference if I had started at a young age.

Because of Mother's profound Catholic faith, my schooling left a lot to be desired: Religion drove which schools I could attend. When I re-entered the school system, it was for grade six, at Sacred Heart Convent. Two rooms were devoted to classrooms, with grades four, five, and six in one room. Since this school went to grade six only, I spent my next two years at St. Peter's Separate School.

St. Peter's was a tough inner-city school. I think a high percentage of the boys there had been to reform school or at least were heading in that direction. Looking back, I think the nuns wisely kept a protective eye on me at recess. The principal, Sister Irenita, who was also the grade-eight teacher, was a tough disciplinarian and the one assigned to give the strap. Although I was never punished with it, I clearly remember hearing it being administered. I do believe it was a deterrent; it certainly was for me. What the Sisters couldn't control, however, were off-premise fights, and, as a result, I was beaten up on a number of occasions on my way to and from school.

By the time I finished elementary school, my brother and sister had talked Mother into letting me go to London Central Collegiate. I believe both Mary and Jack felt that they had been compelled to go to Catholic schools and that I should be free to choose a high school. Fortunately, two of the teachers at Central were women Mother knew from her church. This made a big difference; it probably comforted her to think that with these two looking out for me, I wouldn't lose all of my Catholic upbringing.

Central was quite a good school, and I enjoyed my four years there. I kept up the violin, playing first violin in the London Secondary School Symphony, made up of students from the four public high schools in London. I also joined the army cadets and played a number of B-flat instruments over the years. I started with the baritone horn, then switched to the sousaphone (a tuba for marching band) and ultimately the trumpet. The sousaphone was just too heavy.

Had I not been born a Catholic, I probably would have been sent to an exclusive private school such as Upper Canada College, or Trinity College School, which my father and Uncle Hugh attended. Of course, those were the days when the public school system was much better than it is today. Some kids were sent to private schools because they couldn't hack it in the public system.

My father, who felt too much religion had been foisted on him at TCS, left the choice of my religious education to Mother.

I have no idea how different I'd be if I'd gone to a private boarding school. I'm sure my grades would have been better. Perhaps I would have been more driven. I am certain that I would have been a better athlete. On the other hand, I might have had the sense of entitlement adopted by some private school boys, and might not have developed the common touch that I feel I have always possessed. As I attempt to analyse all this, it's possible that the answer is simply that I'm a bit shy and withdrawn.

When I was in grade eleven, my father retired, and he and Mother moved to Bermuda for most of the winter. Unfortunately, they left me in the care of a housekeeper who had little control over me. Consequently, after finishing grade twelve, I was sent off to be a boarder at St. Michael's College School, a Catholic school in Toronto where they hoped the supervision would be more rigorous. Whereas in fact, in grade thirteen, our final year, we boarders were given a lot of latitude. On weekends, the oldest-looking boarder would buy a case of beer and we would play poker, drink beer, and play boogie-woogie on the pipe organ.

I played the trumpet in the band at St. Mike's and got to know the Four Lads, who were all graduates of the school. They had graduated a few years ahead of me and went on to become big stars but still returned to St. Mike's to perform in a special concert just for us that included hits such as "Moments to Remember" and "Standin' on the Corner." I had two girlfriends (not at the same time, of course) who were both daughters of leading undertakers in Toronto. My father found this quite unusual, and, I have to admit, as I look back on it, so do I.

At that time, St. Mike's had a great Junior A hockey team, and I became friends with some of the players who went on to play in the National Hockey League, such as Dave Keon, Dick Duff, and Marc Reaume. The school provided a great advantage to promising young hockey players, especially ones from northern Ontario. Parents were promised that their sons would complete high school, and the school, in turn, did its best to make this happen. The boarders used to joke that the hockey guys ate T-bone steaks while the rest of us were served gruel, but the Basilian Fathers who ran the school did a good job.

SUMMERS AT PORT STANLEY

WHEN I was two or three years old, my father bought a summer cottage at Port Stanley, on the north shore of Lake Erie, about thirty miles south of London. After his kidnapping, he wanted a summer place well removed from the U.S. border and within an hour's drive of his

Amusing myself at Port Stanley.

office. He always had a driver, because of his fear of retaliation by the kidnappers. The cottage was in a well-treed area called Orchard Beach. It was about an hour's walk to the main beach, which was a bustling place with hot dog stands, a famous dance hall called the Stork Club, and a cement pier that extended about a quarter of a mile into the lake.

Lake Erie is sizeable, more than two hundred miles long and about sixty wide, but very shallow. The western section of the lake is only eighteen feet deep in places, and the deepest spot in the entire lake is just sixty feet. Foul weather could arrive without notice. We were never allowed to have a boat because of severe storms and enormous swells. I often watched spectacular lightning over the lake and huge waves smashing into the piers and the beach. The house had many lightning rods that I'm sure were hit on a number of occasions.

The cottage was a two-storey affair of a very unusual Chinese design, with all of the corners turning up in a pagoda style. The second floor had a large sitting room full of dragon tapestries and rattan furniture. As a boy, I was afraid of this oriental motif and avoided this room when I was alone.

One summer I was encouraged to grow watermelons. It was explained to me that the sandy soil in the region and the hot summer weather were ideal for this enterprise. I planted the seeds and dutifully watered the plants every day. Gradually, vines started growing along the ground and there were green leaves all over my little plot. One day, I was greatly encouraged to discover baby watermelons about the size of elongated walnuts. The next day, Father asked me how the watermelons were doing and I told him about their progress. He suggested I get my wagon and go take another look. He and Mother followed me to the garden – and there were four huge watermelons in the patch. These melons didn't seem to be attached to anything, and I needed help getting them into my wagon. I was very pleased with myself but even at my young age was skeptical of their twenty-four-hour growth spurt.

I had lots of playmates at Port Stanley. During the Second World War, we played commandos with homemade wooden rifles. I am still in touch with some of these boys and girls, who were from London, Toronto, and Hamilton. There were no organized sports, so we made up games as we went along and ran around in bare feet the whole summer. When it was time to go back to London for school, my mother asked me to get my shoes. I told her I didn't have any, and at first she didn't believe me. However, it was true, and Somerville, our chauffeur, was dispatched to drive me to a shoe store in St. Thomas. I was so embarrassed at having to walk on the sidewalk in my socks.

There are many good memories of life at Port Stanley: having *The Wizard of Oz* read to me over and over while I was in bed with the mumps; riding on the London and Port Stanley Railroad, which my father claimed was once the fastest electric railroad in all of North America; catching fish in a stream near the cottage; playing with my brother, Jack's, pet bunnies – one of which I lost.

Then there was the time Mary, who was about eighteen, had been grounded for some reason. In a fit of pique, she grabbed the car keys and jumped into her bright yellow Ford, which was parked in the garage. She gunned the engine and went roaring backwards. Unfortunately, the brewery's sales manager, who was visiting our cottage, had parked his car about ten feet from the door. There was a horrendous crash, and we all went running out. Mary wasn't hurt, but was mortified, and sat there sobbing in the front seat.

We used to drive to Port Stanley in a Packard limousine. I always wanted to ride in one of the Greyhound buses that we saw on the road, so one day, Mother bought two tickets from London to Talbotville, a small town near St. Thomas. The two of us rode on the bus, with the limousine following behind.

After the war, we had a chauffeur by the name of Allan. He had cooked in the army, so he also knew his way around the kitchen. Pressure cookers were the latest thing in those days, and Mother and I were in the kitchen with him once when he was stewing plums in a very large cooker. Unfortunately, he removed the lid prematurely. With a *boom*, scores of plums hit the ceiling. Allan took the Lord's name in vain, probably along with a few other choice words. I remember Mother scolding the poor man for using profanity.

I was eighteen when Father died and Mother sold the cottage. Those fifteen summers I spent at "Port" were an important part of my growing up and have left me with many fond memories.

Scenes from Childhood

My head is abuzz with dozens of somewhat odd memories from my early years.

I once took my bicycle apart when I was trying to fix something and went a bit too far, so I had to gather all of the parts in a cardboard box and take them to a shop to be put back together again.

While convalescing from my myriad illnesses and looking out at Victoria Park across the street, I used to watch fellows casually sweeping up trash in the sunlight. It seemed the perfect job to me. I also remember Mary trying so hard to arrange a birthday party for me when she was only about twelve.

And I can hear my namesake, Uncle Arthur, who was a surgeon with the Canadian Pacific Railway, interrupting my mother when she was answering my question about how their sister, Eileen, who was a nun, had died. Mother said Aunt Eileen (whom I'd never met) had died from eating a rotten egg, but Uncle Arthur bluntly stated, "Oh, for God's sake, Bessie, she died from galloping consumption." In those days, there was a stigma attached to tuberculosis, to use the technical term; it just wasn't discussed.

And then there was my one and only brush with the law. I was probably about ten years old at the time and was playing with three of the neighbourhood kids. We had my Daisy BB gun, a very popular toy at the time. Many kids owned one in spite of the fact that they could be quite dangerous. We were hiding under the front porch of a house about two blocks from our home on Central Ave. The three of us were peeking through latticework and shooting BBs at the rear end of a man who was cutting the grass across the street. Every time a BB struck him, he slapped his backside and we giggled. The man then went into his house for a while as we giggled some more and waited for his return.

The next thing we knew, a hand attached to the biggest policeman I had ever seen lifted each of us out from under the porch. He put us in the rear of his cruiser and drove us all home. He dropped the other boys off first, and then proceeded to our house. He left me in the police car while he ambled up to our front door and rang the bell. My mother was home. After a long conversation, the policeman let me out of the car. I was told to go into the house and wait for Mother while they finished their discussion. I went into the downstairs bathroom and cried my eyes out. Mother later told me that she was truly worried that I would have a criminal record because of this incident. The policeman assured her that this would not be the case and that he was certain this would never happen again.

During the early part of the Second World War, Father bought a twelve-cylinder Lincoln Zephyr and had two large propane cylinders installed in the trunk. It was probably the only car in London that had been converted from gasoline to propane because of rationing. I was with Pop on one of the few occasions when he drove the car himself. One time he ran out of propane in one tank and had to change tanks. We were right in the middle of the intersection of Dundas and Richmond Streets, and the whole of London seemed to be there, trying to help.

Chauffeurs played a significant role in my growing up. I learned that being a chauffeur requires a lot of patience. Many of our drivers were smokers, and some imbibed a bit too much alcohol on occasion. One story involved my aunt Jean, one of Father's sisters. She lived in Ireland, and was Lady Lister-Kaye, married to Sir Kennam Lister-Kaye. She was visiting Aunt Angie, the wife of my uncle Hugh. On this visit to London, they had enjoyed a leisurely lunch at the Hotel London, while Wilson, Aunt Angie's chauffeur, waited … and waited. By the time the ladies arrived at the car, he was thoroughly soused. The two elegant matrons eventually manoeuvred him into the back seat of the Cadillac limousine. Neither of the women had a driver's licence, but Aunt Jean vaguely remembered how to drive a car. Happily, they managed to make it back to Endiang, Uncle Hugh's home on the outskirts of London.

Our chauffeur, Somerville, taught me how to drive. When I took the test for my driver's licence on my fifteenth birthday, the only driving examiner in London was a Mr. Hueston, the father of one of Mary's best friends. Somerville sat in the back seat and chatted with Mr. Hueston while I drove around a few blocks and then parked in front of our house. And that was it.

Before obtaining my licence, I used to love riding my bike around town and watching the mileage recorder tick off the distance travelled. Then, at sixteen, I visited a motorcycle dealer to inquire about the Whizzer motorbikes I had seen advertised in comic books and other magazines geared to kids. Whizzers had a small gasoline motor that could be affixed to a large standard bicycle.

I was able to buy something like this on my own because I had a bank account into which I had deposited my war savings certificates. Father was amazed that I had saved nearly $500 and opened a new account with the Dominion Bank when I was about twelve. This was not the bank that he and Mother used, and he was impressed with my show of independence.

The motorcycle salesman quickly talked me out of the Whizzer, saying I should consider a real motorcycle. He ended up selling me a British model – a green BSA 125cc. I was overjoyed.

I quickly learned how to ride this new machine. I found I could zip around London and Port Stanley with ease. Since I couldn't take a passenger on my BSA, I soon traded it in for another British product – a single-cylinder Matchless 500cc. Helmets were not required in those days, and it's a wonder I didn't kill myself. I used to ride on gravel roads and on main highways in driving rainstorms, often at pretty high speeds. I had some close calls. On one occasion, a car pulled out of a driveway into

At age seventeen, with my best Marlon Brando look.

my path; when I slammed on the brakes, the bike slid on its side under the car – with me still on it. I had kept my leg inside the crash bar and miraculously came out of it unscathed.

At first my parents were not concerned about my motorbikes. However, once their friends cautioned them about their dangers, they had second thoughts. Father then proposed a deal that I was delighted to accept: If I would sell my motorcycle, he would buy me a second-hand car.

Father then asked one of the mechanics at the brewery if he could find a good second-hand car for his son. I sold the bike and in short order became the proud owner of a '46 Ford. In tinkering with the car, I found a set of burglar tools carefully hidden in one of the doors.

Sometime later, I heard that my old Matchless had been in a rather serious accident and the driver was badly hurt. Thank goodness for Father's advice. I must have had a guardian angel looking after me.

One of the reasons that growing up in London as a Labatt wasn't easy was that the legal drinking age was twenty-one, and this law was strictly enforced. As a teenager, I had visions of being caught drinking in a beverage room and finding my picture plastered all over the front page of the *London Free Press* the next day. For this reason alone, I couldn't wait to get out of London.

A vivid picture from childhood that has always lingered with me is of the Labatt Streamliner. It blazed many trails in its day. In 1935, Prohibition had ended but restrictions on advertising beer, wine, and spirits remained. At that time, beer was shipped mainly by rail, but trucks were increasingly being used. The big question facing Labatt's was whether trucks could be used as billboards without the Liquor Control Board of Ontario (LCBO) interfering.

Hugh Mackenzie, the new sales manager at Labatt's, and my father explored the idea of doing more shipping by truck with the Labatt name prominently displayed. Until then, Labatt's had been using a subsidiary company, Superior Transport, to distribute the product, rather than risk antagonizing the LCBO.

Hugh's wife, Alice, came across an article in *Fortune* magazine that suggested a skilfully designed truck could be used as a moving billboard. The Mackenzies discovered that the technical editor of *Esquire* magazine, Count Alexis de Sakhnoffsky, had designed sports cars in Europe,

PHOTO: RICHARD SPIEGELMAN

The Streamliner.

as well as the Nash automobile in North America. They commissioned the Russian Count, along with the White Motor Company, to design a tractor-trailer with a sleek, modern look. The result was the Streamliner, a fluid design in red and gold with curved corners and horizontal lines. I remember one being driven down to our cottage in Port Stanley for the whole family to see, and Father proudly explaining in great detail the new features, including air brakes (a first for Canada) and a cab that hinged forward for ease of repairs. The Streamliner even won a Best Design award at the 1939 World's Fair, in New York.

By 1939, there were eighteen of these vehicles on Ontario roads, and they attracted a great deal of attention. There were four series of trucks; the last version, and the most attractive of the Streamliners, was ordered in 1941, but delivery was delayed until 1947 because of the war. Of the fourth generation, ten were built for Labatt's and one was delivered to Princess Juliana of the Netherlands. The princess, who later became queen, had spent the war years in Ottawa and wished to transport her show ponies in a Streamliner.

Labatt drivers wore tailored uniforms and, after they were hired, were required to pass tests confirming their mechanical abilities. My mother was instrumental in the Streamliner project by introducing the St. John Ambulance first aid course to all Labatt drivers. By 1938, the course was being offered to all employees, with those who qualified given bonus.

Once a driver was fully qualified, he was then told to offer "courtesy service" to motorists who were experiencing an emergency, or who simply had a flat tire. The drivers were paid a bonus for each courtesy stop, as long as the motorist acknowledged the service by mailing in a postcard. The Streamliner and the services it rendered became a motorized goodwill ambassador for Labatt's as well as an integral part of its advertising strategy. The public was delighted with the service; both Mother and Father were proud of this initiative.

Father used to tell amusing stories about members of the public who were staunchly opposed to drinking, but who nevertheless gratefully accepted the beer company's assistance on the highway. There were numerous stories written in U.S. magazines commending the service rendered by Labatt drivers. The following is taken from Professor Albert Tucker's manuscript *A History of Labatt's*.

> *A member of the Kiwanis Club wrote the following in Kin magazine after a visit to Canada. "There is a very famous brewery in Ontario province. They have the most magnificent fleet of trucks that I have ever seen – long, streamlined red affairs that just purr as they flow along the highways … The service is given free and willingly, and no one says you have to drink their ale."*

CAMP

IN 1944, when I was ten, it was my turn to be sent off to camp. I went to Camp Ahmek, a boys' camp on Canoe Lake in Algonquin Park. It was run by Taylor Statten Camps, as was Wapomeo, the girls' camp about a mile away on the same lake.

Ahmek had been founded in the late 1920s by Taylor Statten, whom we called "Chief." It was highly rated in North America as a canoe-tripping camp. Pierre Trudeau and many other well-known North Americans learned their canoeing skills there. My brother and sister, as well as our own kids – Sheila, John, and Jacquie – all went to Ahmek or "Wap."

The camp train left Union Station in Toronto in the morning and took at least ten hours to reach Joe Lake station in the Park. The train arrived in the dark. Being only ten, I was allowed to sit on camp trunks loaded onto a big open boat called the *Bath Tub*, which meandered to the camp while the older kids walked about a mile from the train to the camp. At the station, I met my brother, who was a C.I.T. (counsellor-in-training), and helped unload the *Bath Tub* and its sister ship, the *Wash Tub*.

I was put in the Junior Section (now known as the Bantam Section). The younger boys' section (ages five to nine) was always referred to by the name "Inky," derived from "incubator." All campers were required to wear red bandanas until they had passed their twenty-five-yard swimming test, which was one length of an enclosure in the lake created by floating docks. Before campers could go "on trip," they had to pass their three-hundred-yard swimming test and be able to tread water for ten minutes. I was assigned to a cabin with boys from all over North America – San Francisco, Milwaukee, Cleveland, Kitchener, and Buffalo.

I will never forget my first canoe trip, a five-day excursion to Otterslide Lake. The portages were long, and we encountered our fair share of muck, leeches, rain, heavy winds, and rough water. The pack seemed unbelievably heavy to a sixty-five-pounder like me. That first year at camp did not make me a canoe-trip enthusiast. However, in later years, I came to love tripping and led long trips myself.

Chief was an impressive orator. After breakfast, he delivered an inspiring talk to staff and campers, holding everyone's attention with ease. He explained that rainy days were really silver days and that there were lots of great things to do on silver days. Golden days (sunny days) would be back soon. Following his remarks was a period of meditation while a musician performed.

The camp searched for extraordinarily gifted young musicians from the Royal Conservatory of Music at the University of Toronto. It offered them a month's stay at camp in exchange for entertaining campers with their instrument or voice. As a result, we were exposed to the talents of gifted operatic singers and string quartets. For me, the cello was the most inspiring instrument during meditation. These musicians and singers staged musicales at least twice a week and always entertained us after lunch on Sundays.

As a ten-year-old, I loved the Council Ring, which was held twice a month. As dusk fell during one of these events, we wrapped ourselves in Hudson's Bay blankets and walked back into the woods to the Ring. I have to admit that this part was a bit scary. Taylor Statten dressed up as an Indian chief, and he really looked like my vision of an Indian. The only problem for me was that he was still wearing his rimless glasses.

The lighting of the big campfire completely fooled me. Chief pointed his peace pipe at the base of the woodpile and said a few words, commanding the fire to light. With a big whoosh, it leapt into flames. For the longest time I had no idea how this happened. As I later found out, a steel wire had been attached to a stake at the base of the firewood that extended to the top of a rock face about a thousand feet away. A ball soaked in naphtha gas was sent hurtling down the wire at just the right moment.

As the drums were beating, Chief danced around the big campfire, chanting, "Wakonda day doo nee toe paw ah tone hay," which, he explained, meant, "Great Father, a needy one stands before you. I who speak am he."

Chief told us that, in the olden days, for a boy to become a man – a brave – he had to spend three days and three nights alone in the woods. He had to know how to make a fire and how to feed himself. If the brave couldn't take it, he could return to the tribe and the other braves would say, "Waa, waa, go back to the women and children." Chief then asked the campers if anyone wanted to become a brave. An older boy or young staff member with a classically trained singing voice "volunteered," and, with only a blanket, he set off into the woods singing a mournful tune.

This closing of the Council Ring ceremony, marked by the young man singing as he left our circle, was called Hiawatha's Departure. One singer was John Dempster, of the family that ran the Toronto bread company. As he got farther and farther away, John's excellent voice became fainter. There were interruptions to his singing as he tripped over branches, which caused us all to giggle.

During my first years at camp, we were encouraged to learn how to box. A regulation-size boxing ring was set up in the log "theatre" building. The ring was surrounded by seats on three sides, rising like stairs. The boxing ring was at the bottom – a bit like a hockey arena. These fights were amusing to watch. The boxing gloves were huge, and I doubt that many blows were actually landed. Knockdowns did occur, usually because the kid backing up tripped over his own feet.

All of this was intimidating to any kid, and it certainly frightened me. My "second," as they call your assistant in the boxing world, was my friend John Frankel. John's job was to give me water and encouragement between the rounds of my three-round fight. After carefully studying my opponent, John told me not to worry because he was only an Inky. It turns out he was right. The referee declared me the winner as he lifted me above his head and deposited me outside the ring.

One lasting memory of camp was the day we celebrated the end of the war with Japan, in August 1945. At dusk, we all gathered at the waterfront and threw a burning effigy of General Tojo off the twenty-foot diving board into the lake.

As I got older, I used to smoke the odd cigarette. In order to buy cigarettes, you had to walk to the Joe Lake store. One day, when I was walking alone on the way back from the store, I was confronted by a black bear. I had seen many bears in the Park and was not afraid of them. This bear saw me and ambled off the dirt road into the woods. For some reason, I threw a rock at him. He stopped, stood on his hind feet, and growled. In those days there was a comic book character named Alvin, whose hair used to stand straight up from his scalp. I was Alvin that day, as I slowly backed away to safety.

I had been a camper for six years, and at age sixteen, I wanted to be on staff, even though by the rules I was too young and should have been a senior camper. However, I did talk my way into being one of two office boys. We worked for the camp's general manager, George Chubb. One of my jobs working for Chubby was to phone food orders to the nearby town of Huntsville. One day, I called the Huntsville Dairy to order ice cream. Something went horribly wrong, with the dairy delivering twenty times more than the ordered amount. I got hell from Chubby, but the campers loved me because they had ice cream every night for two weeks.

Often, after dinner, many of the younger staff (or a few of the older campers) paddled canoes to Senior Island at Wapomeo, where the girls came down to the dock to chat. Once the sun began to set, the boys returned to Ahmek. One evening, my friend Gordon Derzon and I paddled to Wap, puffing on big Cuban cigars. Gordie was a canoe-tripping Wap guide, I was an Ahmek counsellor, and we thought we were big shots. Without warning, Gordie, who was in the stern of the canoe, threw up all over the dock. That ended our cigar smoking and our evening with the senior girls.

As an eighteen-year-old Mountaineer counsellor (I was in charge of fourteen-year-olds), I was the leader of a month-long canoe trip to

Pembroke, on the Ottawa River. The second-in-command of this ambitious venture was a New Yorker named Gerry Murphy. In addition to the two of us, there were four campers, two canoes, and a two-week supply of food. Much of this trip took us down the Petawawa River, with its many dangerous rapids. We portaged around most of the rapids, but I vividly remember nearly going over a fifteen-foot waterfall as we neared the Ottawa River.

Someone had told me that by stopping a freight train and taking it for fifteen miles, we could avoid some of the worst rapids. Where the river turned north, we placed our canoes and packs neatly by the tracks and waited patiently for the train to arrive.

We heard the whistle, and suddenly a giant train with two locomotives and about a hundred cars was bearing down on us. We began to wave T-shirts at the engineers, who paid no attention whatsoever.

Then the crew started to apply the brakes, causing dust and stones to fly everywhere. By this time, the locomotives were around two bends in the track and the caboose ended up right at our little band.

The two crew members in the caboose gruffly asked us what the problem was, and we asked politely if we could hitch a ride along this stretch of track. We were given a very stern lecture concerning the stopping of a train. They pointed out that this was a federal offence and that we could be jailed. After this harsh reprimand, they suddenly lightened up and told us to quickly put the canoes and packs on board and hop on. They told us to hang on tight as the locomotives started up because of the strong jerk at the end of such a long train. The crew could not have been nicer to us as we rode along in the caboose. As they let us off, they told us to tell the camp and the world that this antic was never to be tried again.

Once we arrived in Pembroke, there wasn't a campsite to be found. After much paddling, we finally found a beautiful grassy lawn on the grounds of what appeared on our map to be a convent. We two Catholics, Gerry Murphy and I, were sure we could sweet talk the sisters into letting us pitch our tents there, just for one night. In spite of our religious upbringing, we did not prevail, and we all ended up sleeping in a bandshell in the middle of town.

John Frankel recently reminded me of a similarly unsuccessful adventure, our visit to Bigwin Inn on Lake of Bays. Camp staff occasionally drove the thirty miles to get there to listen to the big bands. During this period, it was owned by Frank Leslie, a rather eccentric stockbroker. In John's words:

One night, although we were all under the drinking age, we visited Bigwin Inn with beer in our pockets. The moment we landed on the island, the Bigwin police, tipped off by someone on the mainland, shuffled us into their office. The cops asked our names which we all – very scared – dutifully gave. But when they asked you, you gave your name as something like Michelangelo Dambroski from Sudbury, Ontario (the name on the fake birth certificate you carried in case anyone asked your age). Upon hearing that, everybody in the room burst into hysterical laughter – except the cops. Fortunately, all they did was throw us off the island. I'm not sure we learned any lesson from it all. But maybe that's why we ended up at McGill in Montreal, where the bartenders had no idea how old you had to be to drink.

I have stayed in touch with many of my camp friends. The Taylor Statten organization occasionally holds a reunion in Toronto, which former campers from all over the world attend. It has been fifty-eight years since I last went to camp, and several of my friends have passed on. However, many of us are still going strong. In November 2009, Sonia and I invited three camp friends and their wives to visit us for a week at our home in Tucson. We had a wonderful time hiking, playing tennis, and swimming, as well as seeing the sights around the city.

At two o'clock one afternoon, Sonia and I had arranged a jeep ride in the desert for our guests – Judge Jim Felstiner and his wife, Barbara, John Frankel and his wife, Beverly Simonsen, from Toronto, and Gordon and Gail Derzon from Madison, Wisconsin. With considerable difficulty, the tour operator was able to locate a canoe in this desert environment. He erected an Indian teepee with a Camp Ahmek plaque and set up a Council Ring around a big fire. He also installed archery equipment as well as a horseshoe pitch.

The big event of the late afternoon was the water-boiling contest. Four small firepits had been dug. Each of us was given a small log, a pail with water in it, a sharp knife, a hatchet, and one match. In theory, the winner was the person who got his water boiling first. With the distractions of the

Top: Reliving Camp Ahmek in the Arizona desert, 2009.
Bottom: Gordon Derzon (left), John Frankel, me, and Jim Felstiner.

Water-boiling contest.

desert holding more appeal for some of our guests than this contest, only two teams participated instead of four. There was some disagreement as to whose water boiled first. Nevertheless, the BBQ dinner in the wild with tablecloths in the camp colours of orange and black went over well.

The eight of us reunited for dinner in Toronto in February 2010 at Jim and Barbara's home. Camp days never seem to end!

UNIVERSITY

MY years at university were fun-filled – with much more emphasis on fun than on scholastic endeavour. I had been accepted at McGill University in Montreal for the fall of 1952, but when Father died that summer, the family decided that I should stay in London for at least a year, because, with Mary in Montreal and Jack in Toronto, Mother would be living alone.

I therefore enrolled at the University of Western Ontario's Business School and thoroughly enjoyed my year. I made many new friends who later joined the Toronto business community and with whom I am still in contact.

My closest friend at Western was John Hanna, a personable and athletic young man from the small town of Wingham, a two-hour drive north of London. John's father was a member of the Ontario Legislature who owned two substantial retail businesses in Wingham. The following summer, John and his good friend Stewart Nimmo were driving up to see me at Taylor Statten Camp in Algonquin Park, and both were killed in a tragic automobile accident on Highway 11 where it crosses the Severn River. This was a great blow to me.

The spirit of camaraderie at Western was unique and continues to this day. As chancellor of Western from 2004 to 2008, I became increasingly aware of the special feeling of togetherness that seems to permeate this institution. Western's football team, the Mustangs, were a very important part of both the school and the community when I was growing up in the 1940s, and as a boy, I attended all of the games with my parents.

During my year at Western, Physical Education was compulsory and for some strange reason, wrestling became one of my favourite sports. On the academic side, Business 101, Spanish, and Public Speaking were all courses that I not only enjoyed but also found to be helpful later on.

For some years, I had longed to live far from London, because being a Labatt in London was somewhat stressful. Not only was it a relatively small town, with a substantial brewery founded in 1847 by my great-grandfather, but it also contained Labatt Park (which, according to Google, opened in April 1877 and is the world's oldest continuously used baseball park).

In 1953, I transferred into second-year Commerce at McGill. During my first year there, I lived at in residence at Wilson Hall and was elected to some lofty position on the hall's student council. The reason I won the election had nothing to do with public speaking or getting to know a number of the students. It boiled down to the fact that a friend who was studying architecture created an interesting mobile for my campaign and hung it in the main lobby. The name Labatt was prominently displayed and was easy to remember because of the beer. It was as simple as that.

I joined the Kappa Alpha Society (KA) on University Avenue and became quite active in fraternity life; in my second year, I was elected president of the McGill Chapter. We wore tuxedos to our monthly meetings and, after the meetings (and lots of singing), gathered for cocktails at the Berkeley Hotel (The B) on Sherbrooke Street.

Much has been written about initiations into fraternities, but their rituals are seldom recounted. I will not divulge the KA rituals, other than to say that they can be mentally stressful but are never physically challenging.

One episode during my initiation that stays with me was my preparation of a speech I had been asked to make to senior Kaps who had returned to the Kap House for a celebration. Coaching me for this presentation was Art "Moose" Pennington, a good friend from my days at the Taylor Statten Camps. He gave me a title for a speech, and we discussed an outline. I was to work on my dissertation in a small closet, for which purpose I was given a flashlight and a chair.

Just as I thought I had grasped the subject matter, Moose appeared, saying that he was so sorry to have to inform me that the topic had changed. This was followed by three or four further changes, and by the time I got in front of the esteemed group, not only was I confused and flustered, but they were in far too boisterous a mood to listen to anything. Nevertheless, I loved my years at the Kap House.

When I arrived at McGill, Montreal was undoubtedly the financial capital of Canada; the head offices of most of the leading banks and insurance companies were there, as were those of the two major railways, Air Canada, Bell Canada, Dominion Textile, Seagram's, and many other large firms. Montreal also had a broad manufacturing base. From almost any point of view, Montreal left Toronto, Vancouver, and Calgary far behind. No one in the early 1950s could foresee the rise of separatism in the 1960s and the damage it would do to the city. The Quiet Revolution under Premier Jean Lesage started in 1960, and its effects continue to this day.

Montreal was a wide-open town. After the Second World War, it became the gambling capital of Canada. This major industry was allowed to flourish and became one of the driving forces in the economy. The city was loaded with establishments offering all kinds of gambling – sports betting, blackjack, craps, etc. The province of Quebec was never "dry" during the Prohibition years, so Montreal boasted hundreds of quality restaurants and bars.

As young university students, we couldn't afford the finer clubs. However, my friend and fellow Kap John Frankel has reminded me that we did hang out at Café André (The Shrine), The B (Berkeley), The Ritz,

Mocambo, El Morocco, Rockhead's, and a number of clubs along St. Lawrence Main.

Montreal produced the wildest and most extravagant nightclubs in North America. Lili St. Cyr, the queen of striptease, played to sellout crowds at the Gayety Theatre and became Montreal's most famous woman. She was born in Minneapolis and also danced in New York, Miami, and Los Angeles. Her autobiography was written in French, and French Canadians thought of her as one of them, although Lili didn't speak the language.

On March 17, 1955, I found myself in a rather precarious situation as I drove along Ste-Catherine Street, oblivious to an event that was unfolding. Four days before, during a hockey game in Boston, the Montreal Canadiens' outstanding player, Maurice "The Rocket" Richard, had been suspended for the remainder of the season and the playoffs by NHL president Clarence Campbell, with whom he had a running feud. A native of Montreal, Richard had played with the Canadiens for eighteen seasons. He was an exciting player to watch and the first to score five hundred goals.

In those days, in the eyes of French Canadians, the city and their arena, the Forum, were controlled by the wealthy English elite. Campbell was seen as an arrogant Anglo who looked down on his French-speaking cohabitants. The suspension of Richard is said to have cost Richard the scoring title, and the Canadiens the Stanley Cup.

Four days after Richard's suspension, Campbell was pelted with food at a game in the Forum, and a tear-gas bomb was thrown in his direction. The Forum was evacuated and the angry fans poured out onto Ste-Catherine Street. The mob started walking east, and there I was, caught in the middle of the rioters, driving a car with Ontario licence plates. It would have taken just one person to say, "Let's get that Ontario car and turn it over." At the time, I had no idea what had caused the vandalism and looting that was happening in front of my eyes. I was very fortunate to escape unharmed. There are those who say that the riot was the symbolic beginning of the separatist movement.

During my two years at McGill, I learned to ski in the Laurentians and came to appreciate how cold Mont Tremblant can be when it's minus-forty with a wind blowing. On my first trip to Gray Rocks, a resort near

Tremblant, I rode up the chairlift with an attractive young woman from Detroit. We discussed the fact that we were both absolute beginners, but I learned a few minutes later that I was the only one telling the truth. My new friend took off from the top of the hill and I followed. Miraculously, I was able to execute the first couple of turns without falling. She then arrived at a relatively flat portion just before a steep downhill run, where she swished to a beautifully executed stop. Totally out of control, I slammed into her and we both rolled over the edge, down the slope, head over heels. Fortunately, neither of us was hurt, but I learned to always be wary of people, especially women, who speak modestly about their athletic abilities.

Not only did I learn to ski, but in my second year, I also spent quite a bit of time flying a rented aircraft out of the Cartierville Airport, to the detriment of my studies. In my first year at McGill, I had been able to slide by academically, but the second year seemed different for a number of reasons. Although I made many new friends, both male and female, I seemed to be somewhat depressed and lonely and could not motivate myself to tackle my studies. It seemed that I needed encouragement or simply a push. Finally, a professor suggested that I take a year off and come back after I had sorted out where I was going.

This turn of events was a huge blow to me, but I accepted it. I joined the accounting firm Clarkson, Gordon & Company in Toronto, where I succeeded in passing my final exams and became a chartered accountant. I fully intended to return to McGill, but my brother, Jack, talked me out of it. I have always regretted this decision, and it has bothered me all of my life. I believe in finishing what you start and have tried to instill this in my own kids. All of them completed their undergraduate and graduate degrees.

Had I gone back and graduated from McGill, I am quite sure I would not have continued in the accounting profession and my life might have taken a completely different path. Still, once I was at Clarkson's, I very much enjoyed working there. The CA designation gave me the credibility I needed later to succeed in the investment business. In hindsight, Jack's advice was sound. He could see I was enjoying what I was doing and was succeeding. Indeed, everything worked out for the best.

A European Summer

DURING my McGill days, I spent the summer of 1955 travelling in Europe with my good friend John Frankel. John and I still talk about that summer. We stayed at some grand five-star hotels and also in some really grotty ones – when we were about to run out of money and had to make do until we could reach the next American Express office to wire our parents for more.

We sailed from Montreal on the *Empress of Scotland*. This ship, operated by Canadian Pacific Steamships, was one of the last of the great ocean liners. Also on board was one of my mother's sisters, Aunt Florence. She was the widow of Dalton Colman, who had been president of the Canadian Pacific Railway Co., the parent company of CP Steamships. She was travelling first class and had advised me to make sure that John and I had our dinner jackets with us, since she intended to invite us to dinner. We were twenty-one, and even though we had our white dinner jackets packed away in our suitcases, we weren't nearly as worldly as we thought we were.

John and I were travelling third class and had probably one of the least desirable inner cabins on the ship. It was located well below the waterline and right over the propeller shaft. The vibration and noise were incredible. Our cabin mates were Hugh and Louie, two Scottish construction workers. They were delightful guys and were somewhat annoyed when Aunt Florence invited us up to first class and off we went in our dinner jackets. Hughie and Shoey (as we called them) thought it remarkably unfair that third-class passengers were not normally allowed go up into the first-class area, while first-class passengers had the run of the boat. If they couldn't go up to first class, then "to hell with 'em; those guys up there shouldn't be allowed down here," went their thinking. A steward from the first-class area escorted us to dinner. With the exception of this wonderful black-tie meal with Aunt Florence, the voyage was uneventful, although still quite an adventure for both of us. Upon landing in Liverpool, we took a train to London, where it was so cold – even in early June – that we went directly to our room at the Buckingham Hotel, turned on the gas heater, and climbed under the bedcovers.

The manager of the Toronto-Dominion Bank in London arranged

dates for us with Canadian girls travelling in Europe. One of these intro-ductions was to a girl from Vancouver named Mary Underhill, who was travelling with her grandmother. Mary ultimately married John Frankel's roommate at McGill, Oliver Warburton Nicholls. "Warbie" got his PhD in Mining Engineering from McGill and settled down in Royal Tunbridge Wells, near London. We had a great time in London as well as in Brighton on the south coast. We also met lots of English girls. As you might imagine, we met most of them in pubs – and not through formal introductions by bankers.

John Strathy and Bill Cox, who were working at the Lombard Bank at the time, introduced us to a couple of English girls (Mary Organ and Mary Smith) and an Australian girl by the name of Beverly. Of course, we never thought we would see any of them again, and probably behaved accordingly. Yet we ultimately learned how small the world really is. We saw the two Marys again when they came to live in Toronto for a while. In fact, somewhat to our dismay, we discovered that they had immigrated to Canada with us in mind.

We began the continental portion of our trip in Paris, where we bought a Panhard Dyna, a small underpowered French car with a very modern design. The idea was to sell it in Paris at the end of the trip. This arrange-ment worked out amazingly well; however, the special red licence plates given to tourists identified us as potential American suckers the minute we drove into any small town.

We got along quite well with our imperfect knowledge of the French language. However, one night in Pigalle, we were taken to the cleaners by two French girls, who charged many bottles of extremely expensive champagne to our account. We didn't have anywhere near enough money to pay the bill. I thought we could escape out of the bathroom window, but management had anticipated this type of situation and had put bars on the windows over the toilet. That left me no choice but to leave poor John as a hostage while I went back to our hotel to get more money. This was all very embarrassing.

After some great times in Paris, we headed for Spain, with no partic-ular itinerary in mind. As we travelled through the Bordeaux region, we decided to spend some time in Saint Jean de Luz and Biarritz. We then crossed the border into Spain and drove through the Pyrenees. This

In London on my summer trip to Europe.

Basque region is where some of my ancestors, the Labats (with one "t") lived before eventually migrating to Ireland.

On our first night in Spain, we stayed in a small town where nobody spoke English. We spoke no Spanish so all parties had to use broken French to communicate.

The roads in the Pyrenees were extremely rugged and somewhat dangerous, but the countryside was beautiful. It was a huge challenge for our little car, but somehow we made it to Madrid.

Prices during this part of our trip were extremely reasonable. The Ritz Hotel in Madrid, where we stayed, was quite within our budget. My memories of our visit to Spain include a bizarre moment. One day in Madrid, we went to a movie and were escorted to our seats by a rather large woman who stood over us until we gave her a tip. I can't remember the name of the movie, but it was preceded by a Grantland Rice short film on canoeing. It featured camping in Canada, and I was astounded to see myself on the screen, face to the camera, paddling a canoe on Canoe Lake in Algonquin Park. I felt like running onto the stage and crying out, "Look! That's me!"

We spent a great deal of our time in Spain with off-duty American sailors, ending up, on one occasion, in the torpedo room of a U.S. submarine, something that would never happen today with heightened security around all matters military.

We made our way to the Côte d'Azur in southern France. One night, John got all dressed up and visited the casino in Cannes. He did pretty well at the tables until a conniving girl spiked his drink and took all of his chips. John had to explain to his mother that he needed more money because the food in France was very expensive.

We left the French Riviera and headed for Rome. Our first stop in Italy was to the Leaning Tower of Pisa. Since we were almost broke, we were forced to stay in the worst hotel of the whole trip. The toilet was at the end of a long dark hall and consisted of just a couple of holes in the floor. We continued on to Rome, where we picked up our money from the American Express office.

It was here that we met Father Bates, an American priest who was a friend of my mother's. He was attached to the Vatican and specialized in canon law. Because he had spent many years in Rome, he was a knowledgeable guide. We visited parts of the catacombs that were not open to the public; he made Christian and Jewish history come alive. Father Bates explained to us that there were so many communists in Catholic Italy because faith is difficult on an empty stomach. He also arranged a private audience for us with the Pope – "private" in this case meaning we were with fewer than two hundred people. Nevertheless, this relatively small gathering with Pius XII was quite moving.

Father Bates gave us a farewell bottle of cognac, which we opened in

Venice as we travelled from the train station to the hotel in a gondola. We even shared it with the gondolier, who, filled with goodwill, tried to charge us twice the going price for the trip.

In Venice, we met up with Ann Westaway, a friend of John's from Camp Wapomeo. Ann must have been very well connected in Venice, because she invited us to a black-tie ball at the Lido. Here is John's recollection of the evening:

> *Until then, we had not had the chances we expected to crash European society. When we arrived at our hotel in Venice, there was a note saying that we were invited to a black-tie party by Ann, who lived in an elegant palazzo. Our chance had arrived, and we were totally unprepared. Our tuxes had not been out of the suitcase for weeks, and were as rumpled as old newspaper. We tried to get rid of the creases by steaming the coats in the shower, which worked only to a degree. We were far from the best dressed at the ball, which was held right on the Lido beach.*
>
> *We met two American guys, Freddy and Dave, who joined us before we moved on to Austria and Germany. They told us they were airline pilots, but I'm quite sure that this was not the case. Our little Panhard Dyna, loaded down with luggage on the roof and the four of us on board, barely had enough power to drive through the Alps. We could only make the steep grades if we kept moving. If, for any reason, we had to stop, my three passengers would get out and I would then put the car in its lowest gear. As the engine raced, the passengers would push as I let out the clutch. Then, as we slowly gained some speed, they would jump in. We successfully made it through the Grossglockner Pass into Austria, but it was certainly an adventure.*

Freddy and Dave used to get quite cross with us because when we were well behaved and polite, we let it be known that we were from Canada, whereas on the odd occasion when we were all a bit boisterous, we kept mum about our native land and were assumed to be Americans.

One evening in Vienna, John and I inadvertently drove through a checkpoint and ended up in the Russian zone, where we stopped to take a picture of a Russian military installation. The guards didn't seem to like that. When they approached us, John turned the car around and beat a hasty retreat. Had it not been for John's alertness, we might have ended up in some Gulag. We were eventually stopped by more friendly border guards and fortunately allowed to depart to the safety of the British zone.

The next leg of our journey took us to Germany. We visited Munich and stayed briefly in Freiburg. This is a university town, where the men wore lederhosen, played the accordion, and drank lots of beer. John left us in Germany because he had to get back to McGill to write an exam. I headed off to Denmark and Sweden with my two American friends. We arrived in Sweden literally the day after the country had changed from driving on the left, as in England, to driving on the right, to get its road system in line with the rest of Europe. The roads were chaotic and I remember once driving the wrong way around a traffic circle because they had forgotten to change the signage.

After our brief visit to Scandinavia, we found our way back to Paris. I sailed home first class, aboard the S.S. *Homeric*. This was a considerably newer and more modern vessel than the *Empress of Scotland*, which was built in 1906. On board, I met a lovely girl from California called Patra Mitchell, and we continued our relationship for at least a year. I visited her in California and stayed at her father's avocado ranch halfway between Los Angeles and San Diego. She and her mother drove across the continent to London and met my mother.

Things were getting pretty serious, although I had three strikes against me as far as Patra's father was concerned. He did not like the British, Catholics, or anyone connected to the liquor business. However, it was not her father's attitude that broke up our relationship. We were just too young and disorganized to get married.

IV MY SIBLINGS

JACK

IT was rarely discussed, but my parents' firstborn son, John Lynch Labatt, survived only one day. A year later, on June 8, 1928, my brother, Jack (christened John Pridham Labatt), was born. Jack was outgoing and good-looking, and more of an extrovert than I. Although he was only six years my senior, I had little contact with him growing up. It seemed to me that most of his friends were two or three years older than he, so I was very much regarded as the baby brother. Still, I remember him as a wonderful big brother who acted in a fatherly capacity toward me.

After attending an elementary school in London, Jack was sent to Grey Gables, in Welland, Ontario, a small but exclusive Catholic boarding school for boys, where he had his own horse, Dolly. As both Jack and my sister, Mary, were away at boarding school during my school years in London, I hardly saw them.

Jack returned from Grey Gables and finished high school at De La Salle College School in London. While there, he had a girlfriend, Sazz Wells (now Crosbie), who was a good friend of Mary's. Sazz remembers going to a dance at De La Salle and holding hands with Jack as they crossed Richmond Street. With great trepidation, she recounted this story to her mother and asked, "Do you think I'm going to get pregnant?"

Jack attended the University of Western Ontario and graduated with a bachelor of arts degree. While there, Jack was a founding member of the Western chapter of the Kappa Alpha Society. During the last year of the Second World War, he lied about his age and transferred from the UNTD

My brother, Jack.

(University Naval Training Division) to the regular navy, becoming an able-bodied seaman and sailing on a frigate. His ship was stationed in Halifax and had just sailed through the Panama Canal, heading to the Far East, when the war with Japan ended. The ship was redirected to Victoria, where Jack was discharged and returned home to London. He used to say he had fought in the war with Japan for one week.

Jack had always liked boats, including fishing boats, on which he worked as a teenager in Port Stanley. He was never seasick, even in the worst storms on Lake Erie. He also liked to recount many gripping stories of severe weather in the North Atlantic when he served in the navy. In his late teens, he took up flying with a vengeance, taking lessons at the London Flying Club at Crumlin, just outside London. He obtained not only a private pilot's licence but also a commercial one.

In the summers, he worked for a group out of Point Pelee, flying hunters and fishermen to northern Ontario as well as taking people for rides at local airports. The cost of these rides, an activity that was called barnstorming, was $5 per person. During his flying years, he owned three aircraft. Two of those planes, in my opinion, were quite dangerous.

One was a Sea Bee, a small flying boat with a pusher propeller mounted behind the engine. With its wheels down, this plane could not land in a stiff crosswind. Once, when he was landing at the London Airport in just such a wind, he had to fly the Sea Bee straight into the wind and, with permission from the tower, cut across paved runways. It was the only way to land with a degree of safety. If this craft lost power, it glided like a rock.

His Cornell was slightly less dangerous. Just after the war, you could buy this plywood trainer for practically nothing. It was a two-seater with a laminated wooden propeller and was capable of acrobatics. After one flight, Jack returned home with his clothing in shreds. Battery acid had leaked all over him when he was flying upside down.

His third plane was a Cessna 140 on floats. This one was at least airworthy. In 1946, he flew me in it up to Camp Ahmek. We took off from London and headed for Canoe Lake in Algonquin Park. It was a hot day and I was extremely airsick. Jack had no airsickness bags on board, so he had to lean across and hold the passenger door open while I threw up over the floats.

Jack didn't want to land at the camp dock on Canoe Lake with a brother who was as white as a ghost. Instead, we landed on Smoke Lake, where we stopped briefly at the Ranger Station until I was feeling better, before flying to the camp.

In 1949, Jack joined the accounting firm of Clarkson, Gordon (now Ernst & Young). At that time, the company was the pre-eminent accounting firm in Canada. Our father greatly admired chartered accountants and had pushed Jack to get his CA. Jack's outgoing personality, however, didn't blend well with the somewhat dull profession of accounting and auditing. After about a year in Clarkson's Toronto office, he returned to London to join Labatt's.

In the Family Business

Jack's fourteen-year career with the family firm was a very interesting time in his life, but it also caused him considerable distress and unhappiness. At the time he joined the family firm, in 1950, it was a public company. A family trust called the Voting Trust controlled a majority of the shares. My father was president of Labatt's and my uncle Hugh Labatt was vice president, positions they had held since the death of their father in 1915. While none of the seven Labatt sisters was involved in managing the business, Jack had two first cousins working at the firm – Alex Graydon and John Cronyn.

When Jack joined Labatt's, it was run by the aforementioned Hugh Mackenzie, general manager. Mackenzie was a good businessman, and John and Hugh relied on him. But with Jack and two Labatt cousins now at least *near* the helm, Mackenzie felt his power threatened.

Between 1952 and 1955, Mackenzie underwent two operations for throat cancer. During the second operation, doctors removed his voice box. His illness provided the occasion to arrange for his retirement.

The company's chairman, Dick Ivey, on behalf of the board, gave him a polite ultimatum, by letter, indicating that he should step down at the end of January 1956. Mackenzie was only fifty-four, and although the financial settlement was generous, he felt that he was being forced to retire, and not on his terms. After being informed of the board's decision, he returned to his office in a fury, grabbed the drapes, and tore them off the wall.

Jack was put through a training program, spending time in various departments of the brewery. He was then sent off to the Brewers Academy in New York City, returning to London as an accredited brewmaster, following in Father's footsteps.

Family control effectively ceased in 1964, when the Joseph Schlitz Brewing Company, of Milwaukee, Wisconsin, made a bid for thirty-five percent of the company. Although it was not a surprise to me, this takeover attempt was nevertheless a great blow and remained a grave disappointment to me for decades.

There are a number of reasons why a majority of my relatives were willing to sell control of the family business. From my perspective, there were three principal players involved in bringing the Schlitz offer to the board: Jake Moore, Dick Ivey, and Jack.

John H. "Jake" Moore had grown up in London and was socially acceptable to the local gentry and the business community. He had graduated from the Royal Military College in Kingston and had six years of wartime experience. He was an exceptionally gifted chartered accountant and was used to being in command, thanks to his military background. He had a strong drive to succeed, and many of his contemporaries were intimidated by his need to dominate. According to one observer, "All that he needed in pursuing his ambitions was visible material success."

Jake was a partner at Clarkson Gordon's London office, where he was in charge of the Labatt audit. He then joined Labatt's in 1953, three years after Jack arrived on the scene. In the early days, Jack was extremely impressed with Jake, as was Dick Ivey. After joining the company, Jake was immediately invited to sit with the executive group at board meetings. At meetings of the Voting Trust, Jack extolled Jake's virtues as an accountant, businessman, and devoted father of five. Jake was soon instrumental in preparing a report stating that if Labatt's simply maintained its present capacity, at the end of ten years it would remain a regional brewery while the competition would have become national.

My father had died in 1952, and his brother, Hugh, who had succeeded him as president, died in 1956. Jack was the obvious heir, if the presidency were to remain in the family. But he was considered too young, at age twenty-eight, and without sufficient experience. So my uncle Reg Jarvis, who was married to one of Father's sisters, Kitty, and therefore considered family, became president.

Unfortunately, Uncle Reg died just two years later, in 1958. Jack was regarded as still lacking in experience for the presidency. With the concurrence of Dick Ivey, Jack, and numerous family members, the board recommended that Jake Moore be appointed president and chief executive officer, the first non-family president of the company.

In preparation for a possible presidential position in the future, Jack was transferred to Toronto to manage the Copland Brewery, Labatt's first major acquisition. He was then moved to Winnipeg as vice president and general manager of three recently acquired breweries in Manitoba.

Although Jack did an excellent job of marketing Labatt products in Winnipeg, he was not particularly happy living so far from his friends in eastern Canada. He used to tell amusing stories about his years in Winnipeg, such as how he went to the airport when holidays were approaching and asked the sales agent to sell him a ticket to *anywhere*.

His one big achievement was turning Labatt's Pilsener Lager into "Blue," a great success as a national brand. The name came from the Winnipeg Blue Bombers Football Club. Even today, Labatt Blue is the company's top-selling Canadian brand.

It was during Jack's years in Winnipeg that his relationship with Jake Moore began to sour. Although he was not at all arrogant, Jack's confidence and exuberance were sometimes taken as such. As some have said, he inherited his impulsive warmth and humour from our mother. However, he did lack a certain business discipline, and this clashed with Jake's focused and controlled drive.

I once received a phone call from Jake asking me to speak to my brother about his attention to dress.

"He doesn't shine his shoes, and his suits are never pressed," Jake sternly informed me.

And I was also to talk to Jack about being on time for meetings. Somewhat threateningly, Jake stressed that it was very important that Jack change his carefree ways.

When I spoke to my brother, I discovered that, in the most recent instance, he had just returned from a hunting trip and showed up late for a management meeting that had been scheduled months before, with no time to change his clothes. I realized that Jake had a point.

From 1965 to 1975, Labatt's expanded the brewing operations with the goal of becoming a national organization. The company built a major brewery in Montreal and, through acquisitions, expanded into western Canada and then into the Atlantic provinces.

To raise equity capital, it sold shares through a series of "rights" offerings that gave the owner the right to buy Labatt stock at a discount to its market value. Family members did not exercise their rights; they were pleased to sell them because the income received was not taxable. There were a number of these issues. The ensuing reduction of the family's holdings, as a percentage of the company's shares outstanding, was dramatic. In fact, the family had reduced its holdings from about sixty percent of the company to slightly less than forty percent. Management became uncertain where control of the company would ultimately rest.

In May 1963, aware that control of Labatt's was no longer secure, my cousin John Cronyn and Jake Moore were introduced to Robert Uihlein, the president and controlling shareholder of the Joseph Schlitz Brewing Company. At that time, Schlitz was the second-largest brewing company in the United States.

The Labatt family was spread across Canada with some major shareholders living in the United States and others in England and Ireland. My aunts were quite elderly and were being counselled to diversify their portfolios. There were only four family members on the sixteen-member Labatt board.

My aunt Angela, who was the widow of Hugh Labatt, was quite influential with the elderly Labatt sisters, who controlled a major percentage of the Labatt stock. She also relied heavily on the advice of Dick Ivey, who for many years had advised both John and Hugh Labatt. In consultation with Dick, who felt that diversification was a wise move for the Labatt sisters, Jack suggested to them that a sale of half of the family's remaining holdings should be considered if a firm offer from Schlitz were to materialize.

At first, Jake appeared to be in favour of entertaining an offer from Schlitz, but his attitude changed after he and his wife, Woody, met the Uihlein family. Woody, in particular, was uncomfortable with that family's self-assurance and their total control of the Schlitz board – they owned ninety-three percent of Schlitz stock.

Jack, on the other hand, was impressed with Bob Uihlein and his flair for promotion. He was personally interested in selling shares and felt it wise for family members to diversify. After all, over the previous seven years, he had observed the total domination of board–management relations by Jake Moore. In my opinion, the major family shareholders would have retained control of the company if relations between Jack and Jake had still been on a friendly footing and Jack had advised them to do so.

Jack and Dick Ivey assured the Uihlein group that if they were to make a bid for thirty-five percent of the Labatt stock, the family would offer enough support to justify an offer. Only a small number of family members were against tendering their shares. My cousin Alex Graydon argued that if some members of the family needed money, other means could have been found that wouldn't involve selling effective control. According to Albert Tucker's *A History of Labatt's*:

> *The majority of the board took very seriously reports of a projected decrease in sales as a result of public disillusion and resentment that a historic Canadian company could so easily come under American control.*
>
> *Allyn Taylor, president of Canada Trust, and a recent appointment to the board, made an eloquent plea to seek a counter-offer. Having come to London from Winnipeg twenty years before, he was impressed with Labatt's steady expansion across Canada. The quality of its management was excellent, but it would certainly be threatened by the proposed change of ownership, which would also have an adverse effect on the value of the shares in the hands of the remaining shareholders.*
>
> *These statements, representing the majority opinion, strengthened the position of Jake Moore as he faced the first real test of his leadership. He had not been consulted and had learned of the offer only two days before its release to the family.*

Jake was angry but resigned himself to the situation when Schlitz's offer was announced. He sent a telegram to all managers stating that "control of the company will pass to new hands but the present management and methods will continue." To secure the support of senior executives, he guaranteed their salaries for three years.

He then solicited the help of Walter Gordon, his old boss at Clarkson Gordon. Gordon was a Liberal Member of Parliament and Minister of Finance from 1963 to 1965 in the government of Prime Minister Lester B. Pearson. When Jake turned to him, Gordon was chairing the Royal Commission on Canada's Economic Prospects. The Commission's reports expressed concern about growing foreign ownership in the Canadian economy. Gordon was noted for his economic nationalism and his support for new social programs.

With the help of Gordon, an investigation led by U.S. Attorney Robert F. Kennedy alleged that Schlitz wanted to control the California market through a Labatt subsidiary, Lucky Lager Brewing Company of San Francisco.

During the long court case concerning the Schlitz affair, with the board divided on the sale, Jack found it very difficult to function in a management capacity at the brewery. He resigned as a vice president, but he and one of my cousins, Dal Russel, remained on the board of directors. Dal was the son of another of my father's sisters, Aunt Mary. He was a hero of the Battle of Britain and was awarded a DSO, DFC and Bar, as well as the Croix de Guerre and Silver Star from France.

Court proceedings in the United States continued for more than two years. During this period, Jake Moore searched for an acceptable and friendly Canadian buyer for the thirty-five-percent block of Labatt stock now held by Schlitz. Using his Clarkson Gordon connections, he persuaded Brascan to buy one million of the 1.7 million shares available from Labatt's, with 300,000 of those shares being purchased by Investors Group in Winnipeg and 400,000 by Jonlab Investments Ltd., a holding company created for senior Labatt executives, including Moore. This transaction took place in April 1967.

Schlitz lost the court case and was forced to sell its thirty-five-percent interest in Labatt's to a consortium of three Canadian investment groups put together by Jake Moore. Both Dal and Jack resigned from the board. Jack felt he had received little support from the family and friends, which hurt him immensely.

Jake joined the Brascan board and, in 1969, was appointed its president. He retained his Labatt connection by staying on as the brewery's chairman. Brascan subsequently purchased the Jonlab block from Labatt's management.

In 1979, Brascan was taken over by Edper investments, the principal holding company of Peter and Edward Bronfman. This ended Jake's overpowering influence in Labatt's affairs. He retired in 1980 to London and died in 1993. That same year, Brascan sold its stake in Labatt's, leaving the company open to a hostile takeover. Management rejected an offer from Toronto-based conglomerate Onex Corp. as being too low, and, in

June 1995, the company was purchased by Interbrew S.A., a privately held Belgian brewer.

Life After Labatt's

After the imbroglio with Jake and Schlitz, Jack turned his attention to the design and construction of a ninety-three-foot three-masted steel schooner built at the Kingston Shipyard. This ship was designed to sail the world, and its construction was a joy for Jack compared with his extremely unhappy years at the brewery. He named her *Endiang*, which is a Huron Indian name meaning "our home." Endiang was the name of my grandfather's house, as well as Uncle Hugh's house, both in London.

After resigning from Labatt's, Jack moved to Toronto and bought a number of businesses in the photography and graphic arts field: Ashley and Crippen (photography), Ganes Productions (graphic arts), and Pantechnicon Productions (commercials). In 1965, he met his future wife, Lori Letnicke, at an Ashley and Crippen party hosted by his good friend, Dan Gibson. Jack's life then took an entirely new and positive turn. With partners Ian and Irene Taylor, he went into business on the island of Tortola, British Virgin Islands. Together, they incorporated Island Services (BVI) Limited. Through the Cockle Shoppe, Pasea Plantation, and the Tropic Aisle, they sold souvenirs, fabrics, office supplies, books, furniture, and business machines. He was also involved in Tortola's first commercial plaza.

In 1968, at the age of forty, Jack suffered his first heart attack. This was the beginning of a long downhill slide in his health. The attack occurred a few days after a strenuous winter walk over the ice to his cabin on Smoke Lake in Algonquin Park. The man sharing his hospital room at Mount Sinai was the owner of La Chaumière restaurant, the chef of which appeared daily with a gourmet meal, complete with wine, for both patients.

On one of my visits to see Jack in the hospital, it appeared he had just hidden a magazine under the covers. I asked him if he had been reading a men's magazine. He replied that it was, in fact, a nurse's manual on how to care for heart patients. He told me that of the nine things that predispose a person to heart disease, he had seven or eight of them.

Jack, the perennial bachelor, surprised many by marrying Lori. The

Jack and Lori's wedding, officiated by Father Murray Bannon,
who was related to my father's kidnapper.

wedding, on March 4, 1970, was celebrated at Holy Rosary Church in Toronto. The priest was Father Murray Bannon, who was related to one of Father's kidnappers. Jack was aware of this, but said, "Why not?" The couple honeymooned in Bermuda at the Palmetto Bay Club. It was a nostalgic trip for Jack because this was the house that our family had rented after our father's kidnapping. Jack was nearly eight years old at that time and remembered riding his bike from it to school.

Jack and Lori's dream was to sail *Endiang* around the world. That fall, they were bringing the schooner from the Caribbean to the Great Lakes for a refit when Jack had a second major heart attack, two hundred miles at sea, off Halifax. He spent a month in hospital where it was discovered that he had a tumour in his left lung. He went through radiation treatments and, in 1971, had one lobe of his lung removed. The pneumonectomy was performed by his friend from camp days, Dr. Griff Pearson, at Toronto General Hospital. Radiation treatments left him feeling miserable, and his angina remained severe.

After this setback, Jack and Lori abandoned their vision of circum-navigating the globe and sold the *Endiang*. In 1974, they bought an old farm in Maple Valley, about fifty miles north of Toronto. Jack became a gentleman farmer, impressing the locals with his knowledge and enjoying his red tractor.

In 1975, Jack finally fulfilled his dream of sailing around the world. He booked passage for the two of them on the *Queen Elizabeth II*. This was the ship's maiden voyage, which was entitled Around the World in 80 Days. Our mother died while Jack was in Bali; sadly, he was unable to attend her funeral.

During the 1970s, Lori was busy making films. In March 1980, she was out west researching a film on heli-skiing. Jack was in Tortola working with Ian and Irene on their various business ventures. Ian and Irene noticed that Jack was in bad shape almost from the moment he arrived in Tortola. He had recurring angina attacks, and his condition wors-ened daily. Jack had rejected the idea of open-heart surgery because he thought it was too dangerous, considering his lung problems. He decided, however, that something had to be done and hired a helicopter to take him to St. Croix, where he boarded a plane for Toronto. Lori returned from British Columbia, and they flew together to Milwaukee.

Jack had done considerable research and had great confidence in a heart surgeon at Milwaukee General Hospital. On April 13, 1980, the day before a scheduled angiogram, he died. He was fifty-two. Subsequent tests revealed that his arteries were so clogged, surgery would not have been feasible. I was in India when he died and was able to fly home in time for the funeral at Holy Rosary Church. There was not enough room in the church for everyone who came to pay their respects. I particularly recall that all of the senior managers from Labatt's were there, including Jake Moore.

In the latter years of his life, Jack had returned to religion and firmly believed in the existence of God. In the late 1970s, he began writing a book that he described as being short, concise, and "made necessary by my approaching death."

I wish we'd had a closer relationship, but it seemed that we always lived our lives in different locations. When I was growing up in London, Jack was at boarding school. When he was in London, I lived in Toronto. When he moved to Toronto, we lived in Montreal or Paris. At least when we moved back to Toronto from Paris in 1971, Sonia and I saw more of him and Lori at their house in Maple Valley.

I miss Jack very much. He was a wonderful brother, and I wish we had been closer in age. Perhaps, if I had been involved with him at the brewery, I could have made his career at Labatt's a happier one.

Jack died far too young.

MARY

MARY was born on September 8, 1930, which Mother told us was the Virgin Mary's birthday, hence her name. Four years older than I, she was a pretty and lively little girl.

My first memory of Mary goes back to when I was five. I had been playing with some marbles in a closet on the second floor of our home on Central Ave. in London. I accidentally swallowed one and, with tears in my eyes, ran to Mary and asked if she thought I was going to die. Her response was simply, "You might." Fortunately, she was concerned enough to call our mother at the Hunt Club to ask her.

One of my friends, who lived three houses away and shall remain nameless, was a bit older than I was, and bigger and stronger. Mary felt he was being mean to me and beat him up on my behalf.

Mary attended Saint Angela's School for girls in London until, at age fourteen, she was sent off to boarding school in Montreal. The school, Sault-au-Récollet, was run by the Sisters of the Sacred Heart and was located in Cartierville, a suburb of Montreal. The Sisters actually referred to themselves as the Ladies of the Sacred Heart.

To this day, Mary refers to the Sault (pronounced "so") as a prison, although she made a number of lifelong friends during her year at the school. When she first arrived, she was assigned a private room, which our mother furnished with heavy oak furniture. After a couple of months, Mary was charged by the sisters with organizing midnight feasts. She lost her private room and was reassigned to the dormitory. Father took me to the Canadian Pacific Railway station in London to pick up her furniture.

The next year, Mary convinced Mother that if she were sent back to the Sault, she would do something to get herself expelled.

Mother believed that Mary meant exactly what she had said and the next year sent her to Loretto Abbey, a Catholic girls' school in Toronto. Although this school was far less confining, Mary lasted only one year there and returned to Saint Angela's in London, to finish high school. She went on, at age seventeen, to Brescia Hall, a Catholic women's college affiliated with the University of Western Ontario.

Brescia Hall was quite a distance both from our home and the university

My sister, Mary.

campus, so Father bought her a bright yellow 1947 Ford that had been on display at the Canadian National Exhibition in Toronto. Once I had my driver's licence, Mary was always very careful to keep the keys to the car in her possession. My nameless friend from up the street, whom Mary had beaten up years before, showed me how to get into a locked car and hot-wire it. The two of us often took it for joy rides and were very careful to park it in exactly the same spot. When I mentioned this to Mary recently, she told me that she had no idea that we were doing this.

While at Western, Mary was chosen to be on a quiz show at CFPL Radio in London. The show was moderated by Paul Soles, who was a well-known personality who would go on to work for the CBC (Canadian Broadcasting Corporation). Father, Mother, and I huddled together beside an old wooden Marconi radio set, waiting for the broadcast to begin. The first question that Paul Soles posed, which he directed to Mary, was, "What is gorgonzola? Is it a cheese, is it a musical instrument, or a Spanish parlour game that somewhat resembles tiddlywinks?" Mary had no idea what gorgonzola was, nor did I. In a timid voice, she whispered, "A Spanish parlour game" – to which the moderator added incredulously, "… similar to tiddlywinks?" Poor Father groaned and nearly fell off his chair.

Mary graduated from Western with a three-year Arts degree, and then enrolled at the Katharine Gibbs School in Boston. At that time, the school offered a one-year course to college graduates who wished to become executive secretaries. Shortly after arriving in Boston, she was intro-duced to Harry French, who was doing his MBA at Harvard. After Mary graduated from "Katie" Gibbs, she obtained a green card and returned to Boston to work for the Red Cross campaign and also helped type some of Harry's assignments.

This became a serious romance, and it wasn't long before they were engaged. The date of July 5, 1952, was set for the wedding, but six weeks before tying the knot, they decided to call it off. Uncle Hugh and Aunt Angie had held a lavish engagement party, and beautiful gifts had already arrived from friends in London and from Harry's friends in the U.S.

Calling off the wedding on such short notice caused Mary a great deal of stress. She drove around London returning presents and helped care for our father, who by then was ailing, at our summer cottage at Port Stanley. Father died from a heart attack on July 8, only three days after the wedding would have taken place. Mary almost had a nervous breakdown and spent at least two weeks in her room following the funeral, before leaving to visit friends in Quebec. She eventually moved to Montreal, where she shared an apartment with three friends. She found a job in advertising and was paid a decent salary (quite a bit more than her roommates), although she admitted that she knew little about the industry.

Mary had many male friends when living at Sherbrooke and Guy Streets in Montreal. One of her beaus was David Morgan, whose family owned Morgan's department stores. The Morgan's in Montreal was by far the largest and best-known store in the city and was eventually sold to the Hudson's Bay Company. David and Mary were married in London in February 1954, and the reception was held at the London Hunt Club. The wedding of a Labatt and a Morgan garnered a considerable amount of press attention, which did not go unnoticed by some thieves. Upon arriving at the reception in the dead of winter, all of the ladies left their expensive fur coats in a room on the second floor of the club. When they went to retrieve them, they found that they had all been stolen. To my knowledge, the thieves were never apprehended.

Mary and David lived in Ottawa, where David was the manager of the Morgan's store there. They had a lovely baby girl, Jennifer. When Jennifer was two years old, Mary and David decided that the marriage was not working out, and divorced. Mary and Jennifer moved to New York and rented the fourth and fifth floor of a greystone on East 82nd Street.

It was not long before Mary became good friends with Bill and Lori Beacher, who owned the building and lived on the first three floors. Lori also ran a placement agency. After learning of her new tenant's background, she told her that she had an important client who needed someone to help him get organized, but that this was probably only a two-week assignment. The client was the famous writer John Steinbeck, author of numerous novels, among them *The Grapes of Wrath*, *East of Eden*, and *Of Mice and Men*, and winner of the Nobel Prize in Literature.

On a cold day in January, Mary walked to Steinbeck's brownstone on East 72nd Street, ten blocks away. Before meeting the author, she read a number of his books. However, just before being introduced, she caught a glimpse of him from a distance. He was sporting a beard. Mary felt that he didn't look like John Steinbeck, but did resemble Ernest Hemingway.

She suddenly thought that she had read all of the wrong books. However, everything turned out well, for it was indeed John Steinbeck. She was hired.

Steinbeck called his big cluttered office the Rat's Nest and the little office adjoining it the Mouse Nest. Mary's two-week assignment evolved into doing research for him for three years. He called her his little mouse, and her name appears in a number of his books. She became good friends with the Steinbeck family, and is still in touch with the novelist's son, John. She helped him recently in connection with a lawsuit over his father's estate.

In 1960, Mary decided to move back to Montreal. She didn't think it was fair for Jennifer to have to grow up in Manhattan, since she had no family in the area. Mary remained close to her ex-husband's parents, Henry and Gertrude Morgan, and felt very much at home in Montreal. She bought a house on Piquet Road in Westmount and began seeing her many friends there again.

At a dinner party hosted by her friend Brenda Norris (sister of former Prime Minister John Turner), who had also attended the Sault, she met Ruston B. Lamb, who was then dating a good friend of hers. At this first meeting, they didn't like each other; Mary especially didn't like the way he was treating his date. About three months later, they met again, and, only six weeks after this second meeting, on February 24, 1961, they were married. Our mother, the staunch Catholic, was quite upset with Mary's divorce and remarriage, but after being charmed by Rusty, she was able to rationalize everything by simply announcing that, "in God's eyes, Mary and David were never married."

Later that year, Mary and Rusty bought a beautiful farm property in Derby, Vermont. On February 9, 1962, their daughter, Brenda, was born. Mary now spends a good part of the year with Brenda and her son-in-law, Vitali Makarov, and her two grandchildren, in Vermont. The property is very close to Derby Line, which borders Quebec and Vermont. Houses on the north side of Derby Line are in Canada and houses on the south side are in the United States. Mary's eldest daughter, Jennifer, lives in Toronto with her husband, Keith Martin, and has three children of university age.

Rusty, was a *raconteur extraordinaire* and could hold everyone's attention as he recounted his early life in Quebec and his war stories. Rusty lost sight in one eye as a young boy after being hit by a javelin. Because of this serious impediment, he could not join the army at the start of the

Second World War. However, he somehow found a way to circumvent the rules and joined a famous Quebec regiment, the Black Watch, as a commissioned officer. Major Lamb was stationed in London, England, and worked with General Dwight Eisenhower's group that focused on planning the invasion of France. Being based in London in wartime was pretty exciting for a good-looking young man like Rusty.

Because of his office job in London, Rusty had no need for his army boots, and so they sat, stiff and polished, in his closet. After the allied invasion was well under way, Rusty organized an inspection tour of the field hospitals near the front lines. On this occasion, he wore his shiny boots, but since they had never been broken in, he developed some serious blisters. The driver of the Jeep, who was taking him to the front-line facilities, noticed that he was developing a pronounced limp and suggested he see a doctor at one of the hospital stops. Rusty kept stalling; however, when things got to the point that he could hardly walk, he allowed himself to be treated by a doctor and found himself in a field hospital full of soldiers suffering from extremely serious injuries. They sat him down on a high bench and carefully removed his boots.

The doctor took a look and said, "Oh, that's a nasty blister. But don't worry, Major, I will lance it, and you will feel much better."

Rusty fainted dead away and would have fallen off the bench if he had not been restrained. Rusty found all of this quite embarrassing but loved to tell this story on himself.

Sonia and I have taken a number of vacations over five decades with the Lambs, all of which were truly memorable. Travelling with them was always an experience. One of the earlier vacations was to John Gardiner's Tennis Camp in Scottsdale, Arizona, even though none of us was a competent tennis player. Rusty had the misfortune of having poor depth perception, because of his eye. He was always put in the least advanced grouping. However, this collection of "athletes" comprised some very interesting young women. One attractive young actress had zinc ointment all over her face, with a big blob right on the tip of her nose. Rusty always referred to her as "Becky, the bag of marbles."

After tennis camp, the four of us planned to fly on to Las Cruces near the tip of Baja California, Mexico. Rusty announced that he had forgotten his passport. We were leaving in two days, but he claimed to know someone very high up in the U.S. Air Force and was sure they would fly it down to him from Montreal. I found this story hard to believe, but, the day before our departure, the headwaiter announced to our table that a gentleman was at the desk with a package for Major Ruston B. Lamb. As Rusty was about to leave the table, a tall, distinguished Air Force general in full regalia marched up to the table and presented Rusty with his Canadian passport. I'm still not sure what shenanigans Rusty and Mary got up to in order to pull this off, but it was typical of the jokes we played on one another.

Leaving the Phoenix airport the next day for Mexico, Mary had a bag of moist laundry that she had prematurely yanked out of the dryer. Noticing this humid lump in a carry-on bag, Rusty asked the ticketing agent if he could hang these damp clothes on the leading edge of the wing in order to dry them. The playfulness continued when Rusty and I were at the front of the line checking our wives in, and Sonia and Mary were on the other side of the room – you could do this back then. Rusty was trying to fill out a customs form and shouted to Mary in a loud voice, "Mary, how old are you?" Being ignored, Rusty bellowed the question again, even louder. Mary came quickly across the room and whispered the answer in Rusty's ear.

On another occasion, while taking a two-week cruise around England and Scotland, Rusty sat down beside two elderly British ladies in Newcastle Upon Tyne and told them that we were American movie producers making a documentary about Britain. "Could we take your picture for the brochure we're putting together?" he asked. They primped and smiled for the camera as if they expected to become famous.

Newcastle is one of the roughest towns I have ever visited, and we had hired a taxi driver with more tattoos than Carter has pills. Even he warmed up to Rusty. As it got close to lunchtime, the driver poked me and whispered, "Rusty's gettin' grumpy – we'd better stop for lunch!"

On a three-week trip to Kenya and Tanzania, we stayed in some fabulous hotels as well as in tented "safari" accommodations. One elegant lodge was the Mount Kenya Safari Club. The four of us shared a spacious suite looking out onto a beautifully manicured lawn. Majestic large birds called Royal Ibis were strolling everywhere and could be enticed closer with pieces of bread.

In Kenya, 1984, on one of our many fun trips
with Mary and Rusty (in the middle).

Rusty and I thought it might be amusing to surprise Mary by luring one of these beautiful birds into her large bathroom. After a couple of martinis, we placed bits of bread every couple of feet from a large open sliding door to the bathroom "sanctuary." Then we hid like a couple of kids. My job was to let Rusty know when the bird was heading to the bathroom so he could shut the door. The code was "the bird is in." Fortunately for all of us, the birds were smarter than we were, entering the room only about one length before heading back out.

Rusty passed away in 2005, in his eighty-seventh year. Unlike our brother, who died too young, Mary and I still seem to be soldiering on. Mary continues to live in their house on Braeside Place in Westmount, Quebec.

V EARLY DAYS WITH SONIA

O VER the past fifty-plus years, many people have asked me a simple question, "How did you and Sonia meet?" My usual reply is that I picked her out of a catalogue. This statement is more or less true, but does require further explanation.

In the summer of 1957, I was working in Toronto for Clarkson Gordon and was sharing an apartment on Bathurst Street with two close friends, Don Greer and Bernie McManus. Both were fraternity brothers and have remained good friends to this day. It was a hot August day, and Don and I were trying to get a group together to spend the weekend at a cabin that my brother Jack and I had built on Smoke Lake, in Algonquin Park.

At that time, Don was dating Joan Branscombe, who had gone to Havergal College. We were both at Joan's house discussing the fact that I didn't have a date for the weekend. The Havergal yearbook was prominently displayed on the coffee table, so the three of us leafed through it, looking for someone who might be spending her summer in Toronto. On the first page was the games captain, Sonia Armstrong. After I'd expressed an interest, Joan called and explained the situation to her. Much to my surprise and delight, she accepted.

It was a great weekend, except for the fact that Sonia was not the least bit interested in me. She seemed to be fascinated by some guy who kept hanging upside down from the rafters at another cottage during cocktail hour. However, when we all returned to Toronto, I did persist in getting to know her better.

That fall, Sonia was also going out with another admirer, Ben Wright.

Sonia with her parents, John and Hélène Armstrong, and her older sister, Jacqueline.

By Christmas, I had become very ill with mononucleosis and spent three weeks in bed at my mother's house in London. After I recovered, I took a trip to the Caribbean, visiting Haiti and Cuba. This was in pre-Castro days and Havana was really swinging. During this "therapeutic trip," I learned that Sonia's friend Ben was suffering from the same disease that I had. What a coincidence. I also heard from Don Greer that, in my absence, another fraternity brother named Jim Stevenson was taking

Sonia out – and in my car, courtesy of Don lending him the keys! None of this stopped me from continuing to court her.

During the following winter and spring of 1958, I got to know Sonia's parents very well. Her father, John Armstrong, was one of five farm boys from the Barrie region. His parents were from Northern Ireland, and he was the only one in his family to have a university education. He was a lifelong employee of Bell Canada and was fortunate to have had a steady job during the Depression. In those days, his role at Bell was to help the company buy up dozens of small telephone companies and consolidate them into the Bell network. To achieve this goal, the family moved first to Lindsay and then to Welland, both small Ontario towns, before returning to Toronto.

Sonia's mother, Hélène, whom I called Madame Armstrong (and I addressed Sonia's father as Mr. Armstrong), was a petite Swiss lady from the small watch-making town of Chaux-de-Fonds, in the Canton de Neuchâtel. She was one of five sisters who immigrated to North America, all of them eventually ending up in Toronto. Madame Armstrong first taught school in Boston but moved to Toronto to be near her sisters, where she taught French at St. Mildred's, a private girls' school. She met Sonia's father when vacationing with her sisters on Lake Simcoe. The following summer, the sisters were introduced to the Lake of Bays when they rented the Pink Cottage, which was owned by the White House Hotel on Lake of Bays. White House is about a quarter of a mile from Clovelly Point, the site of the Armstrong cottage.

LAKE OF BAYS

IN the spring of 1958, the other suitors had given up, and my relationship with Sonia blossomed. We decided to marry and plotted how we would tell her parents. We were invited to the Armstrong cottage on Lake of Bays for the Victoria Day weekend in May. It was cold and blustery, and we were all gathered inside – the perfect time to broach the subject. I plied her parents with both Canadian rye and Scotch whisky, and we all had a wonderful evening. Suddenly, before I could bring up the subject, Sonia's father excused himself and went off to bed, leaving Mrs. Armstrong as my only target. By this time, Sonia had become frustrated with my procrastination, so she told her mother herself that we wanted to get married.

Mrs. Armstrong said, "You're kidding, aren't you?"

For whatever reason, I lightheartedly replied, "Yes, *I* am."

Sonia could have killed me at this point. I did eventually assure Mrs. Armstrong that we were serious, and we all went to bed wondering how Mr. Armstrong would take the news. The next morning, Sonia was determined that there would be no further waffling on the subject, so before we even sat down to breakfast, she said to me, "Arthur, don't you have something to say to my parents?"

I announced my intentions, and Mr. Armstrong's reaction to the news was simply that he wanted me to promise that Sonia, who was halfway through her four-year Honours Science degree in Food Chemistry, would finish university.

Although Mr. Armstrong's family were Orangemen from Northern Ireland, and my mother's family were Catholics from the south of the island, he and I got along famously. The reason was simple: We never discussed religion. Instead, we talked about cottage-related things like indoor toilets, docks, and lighting. The Armstrong cottage on Lake of

Our cottage at Lake of Bays.

Bays had only recently been electrified. My cottage in Algonquin Park didn't have power. In fact, it still doesn't.

Our current summer cottage is an expanded version of the same cottage that Sonia grew up in. In 1937, her father bought three hundred and fifty feet of shoreline near Clovelly Point. He had a construction shed moved over the frozen lake to a site overlooking a rocky point that is as beautiful today as it was then. Before we were married, I had been invited to visit on a number of occasions and was asked to sleep in the Ice House, a relatively small building, about fourteen feet from the kitchen door. Until very recently, it had been used to store ice cut from the lake in wintertime. Half of the building had a cot, and the other half had slowly melting ice encased in sawdust. The little building was home to dozens of mice, chipmunks, and god knows what else running around.

Going to the john was not a simple matter. I was shown the path to a two-holer deep in the woods, about a hundred and fifty feet from the cottage. I was used to these outhouses, having spent at least nine summers at camp. Armed with a flashlight, I found the place but had difficulty pushing the door open. When I finally succeeded, I was greeted by a large porcupine inside, which was eating the toilet seat. It was certainly a shock, but I escaped without any quill damage. Mr. Armstrong and I had to return to *la toilette* during the night to let this rather large critter out.

Once Sonia's parents were on board about the wedding, we announced our engagement, at the end of May, with the wedding planned for September 6, 1958. The early September date allowed Sonia to continue her studies and me to write my CA exams. In fact, our rationale for getting married at this stage of our lives was that we were both studying, so why not study together? What we failed to consider, in our state of bliss, was that my exams were in the fall and hers in the spring. Thus, our intense periods of study *never* coincided.

During that summer, we were busy preparing for the ceremony, to take place at Holy Rosary Church in Toronto. The reception was held in the dining room of the Benvenuto (now Scaramouche), with Sonia's sister Jacqueline as maid of honour and Don Greer the best man. We spent our honeymoon at the Ariel Sands hotel in Bermuda. Then it was back to work for me at Clarkson Gordon and back to the University of Toronto for my bride.

Our wedding on September 6, 1958, at Holy Rosary Church.

Smoke Lake

When I was sixteen, my brother took out a twenty-one-year lease on a bit of land at the far end of Smoke Lake in Algonquin Park. We talked our father into giving us an old bicycle shed from Port Stanley, measuring twelve by twenty-one feet. We had a carpenter at Port Stanley put some windows in it, then had it taken apart and shipped by truck to the Smoke Lake landing in Algonquin Park. In addition to this nondescript building, we also had a small bunkie, ordered from the Eaton's catalogue, delivered to the Canoe Lake railway station in the Park.

Even though I was only sixteen, and had no building experience, it became my job to put these structures in place. I had a young helper, who might have been fourteen, and the two of us somehow floated these two dismantled buildings down Smoke Lake to Jack's leased property. We were able to put the bunkie together, but there was no way we could rebuild the bicycle shed.

We worked long hours cutting hemlock posts for the foundation of the bicycle shed, digging the holes, and carefully placing the posts in exactly the right spots. At this point, I realized that we badly needed help. Fortunately, I found a carpenter, by the name of Felix Luckasavitch, who lived in Whitney, a small town just east of the Park. Felix quickly became my newest best friend.

When he saw what we had done, he and his brother immediately dug up our foundation posts and threw them into the woods. Hemlock posts will rot and are no good for a foundation, Felix told us. His crew quickly cut new cedar posts, dragged the building structure up from the water, and put the shed back together.

One lesson I learned from living in the bunkie with no amenities – no electricity, water, refrigeration, or stove – was that just keeping my young helper and me alive from day to day was a major undertaking. For example, we buried a metal garbage can in a nearby stream to keep our food fresh. There were no grocery stores within fifty miles.

After a couple of years of spending part of the summer on Smoke Lake, disaster struck. A large black bear broke through a wall of the shed and decided to spend the winter lying on our queen-size double-decker mattresses, causing them to collapse. The bear bit into many cans of pork

Top: Cooking in the bike shed at Smoke Lake.
Bottom: My sister, Mary, at the bike shed.

and beans, pulled down the stovepipes, and spread soot all over the place. The cabin was such a mess, we decided to take it down and build something substantial. It was at this time that Sonia appeared on the scene, so she helped plan a modern, glass-fronted cottage designed by our friend Gord Smeaton, who was studying architecture at the University of Toronto.

The Smoke Lake cottage had no road access, electricity, or telephone. It was situated on a secluded bay about two and a half miles from the parking area and was a bit of a challenge for us when coping with our three small children. We had to put chicken wire all around the front porch to keep everyone safe. We always kept an eye out for bears; on more than one occasion, we saw a black bear sniffing the laundry on the clothesline. The washing machine was in the boathouse and was powered by a gasoline Briggs and Stratton two-stroke engine. When pressed into service, it bounced across the floor; when it reached the other end of the boathouse, we knew the laundry was done.

Everything was powered by propane, including the lights, fridge, and stove. One day, Sonia returned in the outboard with a load of groceries and announced that she had just met a new neighbour, a United Church minister. She then proceeded to tell me that this nice man had told her you could now buy a *propane* television set. There must have been some miscommunication.

In those early days at Smoke Lake, we all did some rather foolish things, such as water skiing at night. Before we had any children, we often had three or four couples up for the weekend and partied into the wee hours. One weekend, Mary was visiting from her home in Montreal. She had recently been divorced from her first husband and had invited a very interesting Greek, Demitri Cerigo, who had a PhD from a British university. Although we were all casually dressed in north woods clothing, Demitri was the epitome of fashion, with his tailored shorts, knee socks, and Gucci loafers.

At that time, we had a twelve-foot Mahone Bay molded plywood boat, with a twenty-five-horsepower motor that was too large for a boat that size. (I had bought that motor when I was seventeen, with the proceeds from selling my Matchless motorcycle.) We decided to go water skiing, with John Frankel driving, Demitri sitting in the front cockpit, and Don

Greer, the intended skier, sitting on the edge of the dock. We tied the towrope to the right-hand rear carrying handle of the boat. Because Don was a fairly heavy fellow, we suggested that John take off at full throttle with about twenty feet of slack rope.

The next thing we knew, the rope snapped taut, launching the boat "into an orbital arc," as John described it, and flipping it over. Demitri, still nattily attired, right down to his Guccis, shot out of the boat like a rocket. Don had gone only ten feet from the dock, and John was swimming around in circles, but he still had the controls in his right hand, saying to everyone that at least he hadn't panicked. The boat was upside down with the Johnson outboard sticking straight up.

Fortunately, no one was hurt, and we got the motor going again within a couple of hours. As John put it later, he was "pretty sure that was the first attempt in the modern world to launch man into outer space and where NASA got the idea."

There were many interesting characters living in the Park in those days. One was Wam Stringer, a member of the famous Stringer family from Canoe Lake. When Wam dropped in, unannounced, we knew we were in for a long and booze-filled evening. One time, he ate dozens of live minnows and got so blasted that we practically had to carry him to his boat. I told Wam one day that someone had seen him portaging my square-end canoe along a section of railway track in the Park. I then pointed out to him that his friend Gibby had worked on this canoe for me. His reply was simply, "Oh, was that *your* canoe I snaffled?"

One of the Stringer men was a park ranger. Other members of their family enjoyed "borrowing" his uniform and pulling tourists over who were driving through the Park. Most of the cars they targeted had U.S. licence plates. They welcomed these drivers warmly to the Park and asked if there were any firearms in the vehicle. The answer was nearly always negative. The second question, however, caught many folks off guard: "Do you have any liquor in the vehicle?" If the answer was, "I've got a bottle of Scotch and some gin," the "park ranger" asked for the items to be handed over and promised to give them back when they exited at a Park gate. Of course, the liquor was long since consumed by the time the unsuspecting tourists left the Park.

When there was a report that leases in the Park might not be renewed, a number of locals asked the lessees if they had insurance on their cottage. If the reply was yes, they would say, "If you would like me to put a match to her, just let me know." Shortly after Sonia and I moved to Montreal in 1964, we sold the cottage to my brother, Jack. Although he died in 1981, the cottage is still there, owned by his widow, Lori.

Sonia was a competent canoeist and had participated in a number of regattas at the Bigwin Resort on Lake of Bays. However, she had never been on a canoe trip. As we set out on her first, I packed a very heavy pack for her and a somewhat lighter one for myself, since I had to carry the canoe as well.

As we were approaching our first portage leaving Joe Lake, we saw a bunch of neophyte Boy Scouts from Buffalo. I decided to show the boys how tripping was really done. I explained to Sonia that we would paddle the canoe onto a sandy beach and that she should jump out and pull the canoe up a bit onto the beach. I would then lift her pack from the canoe and put it on her back so she could get going across the portage. I was barely able to lift the pack from the canoe but eventually got it on her back. She put the tumpline on her forehead and moved about three steps forward. I then noticed her legs start to wobble, and the next thing I knew, she fell over backwards and was lying face upward on her pack, like an overturned turtle. Fortunately, I had brought an extra pack, so we repacked the heavy one into two as the scouts sauntered across the portage, casting scornful looks in our direction.

After the death of Sonia's father, in 1962, Madame Armstrong continued to spend most of the summers at her cottage on Lake of Bays. We visited Granny with our small children and were of some help in keeping the property in reasonable shape. The old icehouse next door was expanded into a small, self-sufficient cottage with its own kitchen, bathroom, and bedrooms. When our family moved to Montreal, in 1964, we found the drive from Montreal to Lake of Bays too long for the kids and preferred spending our summers in Quebec.

Although Granny knew all of the neighbours very well, she needed company close at hand, so she rented the "little cottage" to a family from the Cleveland area, the Landmans. When we were living in Paris, Granny told us that she had severed one-third of the property and sold it, including the little cottage, to these tenants.

Although we were happy that she had the Landmans close at hand, the fact was that only fourteen feet separated the two cottages. Shortly after we returned to Canada in 1971, we were able to repurchase the cottage from this family, who bought another one close by.

Critters, whether porcupines or bears or something else, were always a problem. I had been clearing some brush on the property and fell backwards onto a wasps' nest that was attached to a rotting log on the ground. Thousands of yellow jackets started to chase me, and I ran around frantically trying to get out of my blue jeans, because they were thick with the ferocious beasts.

Sonia and her mother were chatting in the little cottage, and I didn't want to run in on them covered with wasps. I kept shouting, "Where's the wasp spray can? Where is the bomb?" All Madame Armstrong heard was "bomb."

"Mon dieu, une bombe, une bombe!" she shrieked.

I finally was able to get my jeans off, and Sonia found the spray. I had lots of stings, having failed to outrun those truly vicious creatures.

VI EARLY DAYS IN BUSINESS

CLARKSON, GORDON & COMPANY

IN 1956, after my years at McGill, I joined the Canadian accounting firm Clarkson, Gordon & Company (or, as we always called it, The Firm). At the time, it was an elite finishing school for accountants, as well as Canadian business people in general. There were very few graduates of business schools in those days, and a CA (chartered accountant) designation was highly regarded.

Because my father died when I was leaving high school, I had very little guidance at this important time of my life. Growing up, I had always assumed that I would join the family business one day and sit in my father's and grandfather's corner office. However, with the death of my father and my uncle Hugh, Jack advised me that it was unlikely that the company would remain in family hands. In fact, by the time I was in my twenties, the brewery had been sold. This was a huge disappointment for me. As time passed, however, I realized that it was the best thing that could have happened to me. It forced me to map my own future, which meant so much more because I proved to myself that I could achieve success on my own. My time at Clarkson Gordon marked the start of my own true road, wherever it might lead.

THE FIRM AND ITS PARTNERS

Clarkson, Gordon & Company was founded by Thomas Clarkson in 1864. He had emigrated from England in 1802, settling in York, a small town of eight thousand people, which in 1834 was incorporated as a city and renamed Toronto. Clarkson was a leading member of the local business community. Three years before Confederation, he formed a trustee and accounting venture that is seen as the origin of the modern firm.

When I joined the firm, there was an unwritten dress code that required junior auditors to wear a dark suit, white shirt, and conservative tie, as well as a fedora. My father always wore a fedora, but, as a twenty-year-old, I felt quite strange with one perched on my head. Thankfully, that requirement went out the window about a year later, as did my fedora.

In those days, the workweek for all employees, students-in-accounts, and partners included Saturday mornings.

Skipping ahead a bit, when I left in 1962 to join the investment banking firm McLeod Young Weir & Co., Clarkson Gordon was approaching its one-hundredth anniversary. There are few major firms in Canada with the longevity and quality of Clarkson Gordon. Writing in the *Financial Post* magazine in 1983, Peter C. Newman described the company as one "whose imprimatur at the bottom of balance sheets has become recognized as the Canadian equivalent of a royal seal." He went on to say, "Partners tend to speak in hushed tones about 'the Firm' as if they were discussing a religious experience or, at least their membership in a very private club."

In 1965, soon after Clarkson's centennial, journalist Barbara Moon wrote a marvellous article on the firm in *The Globe* magazine. She said that the wife of one of the partners announced that "there was a difference between being a chartered accountant and being a Clarkson man." Ms. Moon went on to say, "Clarkson, Gordon and Co. was the unofficial but effective finishing school – the only one in Canada … for young men of the Upper Class."

The article described the process of "acculturation," whereby new recruits gradually became acculturated in matters of style and dress, as well as professional conduct: "A Clarkson man never opens his mouth about a client's affairs; a Clarkson man is quietly self-confident; and a Clarkson man works nights, holidays and weekends, if a client needs him." In those years, accounting and legal firms were careful never to advertise their services. The Moon article caused some of Clarkson's competitors to chastise partners in the firm, claiming it was advertising.

In 1989, David MacKenzie of Clarkson Gordon published a book entitled *The Clarkson Gordon Story*, in celebration of the firm's 125th anniversary. I have used this book for some historical background on the company, as well as for references to what others say about it. The book quotes Colonel Lockhart Gordon's response, when he was asked by the U.S. Securities Commission for information on accounting principles in Canada: "Accounting principles in Canada are what Clarkson, Gordon does."

Although Clarkson's Montreal office had opened in 1922, its staff was almost exclusively English speaking, as were its clients. When Marcel Caron joined the firm in 1943, he was the sole French-speaking articling student. The senior partners saw great potential in him and, in 1949, invited him to become a partner. Once the Quiet Revolution arrived in the 1960s, Marcel was key to making the Quebec practice fully bilingual.

Walter Gordon, who was the senior partner, became well known across the country and was seldom in the office because of so many other demands on his time. From 1955 to 1957, he chaired the Royal Commission on Canada's Economic Prospects. He was an ardent Canadian nationalist and, in 1962, was elected to the House of Commons as a Liberal member. He was Minister of Finance in Lester B. Pearson's cabinet and later helped found the Committee for an Independent Canada. Throughout his career, he became increasingly determined that control of Canadian companies should remain in Canada.

Although I never met him, I did receive encouragement and good advice from his brother, Duncan. He was a great "people person" and was very good at counselling partners and staff. A strong proponent of being visible, he believed in "management by walking around," a practice that I tried to follow later in my career at Trimark, the company that I co-founded. While he never became active in politics, he did share his brother's belief in a strong and independent Canada. The firm and the Hospital for Sick Children were his life. He worked hard for the hospital during his business career, serving as chairman of its board for more than a dozen years.

My Years at the Firm

I remember Father, who had died four years earlier, telling me that accountants don't necessarily get rich but they seldom starve, because people will always need them. He had a bachelor of science degree and never really understood financial statements. He often said, "Balance sheets and profit and loss statements are Greek to me." However, he truly admired accountants and had observed many of them rise to the top rungs in Canadian business. In the 1950s, more than sixty percent of all CA graduates left public practice to take on business roles. He strongly encouraged Jack and me to become CAs.

My first choice was to work in Clarkson's London, Ontario, office, since I knew a number of the partners in my hometown. However, they explained that they thought it would be far better for me to work at head office in Toronto, which had a larger, more diversified client base. They also confided that they were suggesting Toronto because Clarkson Gordon did the books of many prominent Londoners – although they knew I would be discreet, my presence on the scene might be of concern to some clients. I was more than happy to work in Toronto, because having the Labatt name in London was a bit of a burden.

The offices in Toronto, at 15 Wellington Street West, were in a prestigious old stone building with very high ceilings. At the start of my second week on the job, I was leaning against the desk of an attractive receptionist at nine-fifteen in the morning when the retired senior partner, Colonel Lockhart Gordon, walked in. In a very loud voice, he asked her to find Arthur Labatt.

"He is right here, Colonel Gordon," she replied.

I jumped to attention, and, at his command, followed the dignified gentleman, as he swung his cane and fedora, on into his private office.

I panicked, wondering what Colonel Gordon could possibly want to talk to me about. I hoped it wasn't an accounting question, because I didn't know a debit from a credit. All I had done in my first week on the job was run around town picking up bank statements for clients.

Once I was in his office, he asked me to do him a favour. He proceeded to explain that his office had very high windows that were difficult to open. Handing me a pole, he indicated how to pull the top window down.

Clarkson Gordon Toronto with its large windows.

I passed this first test with flying colours, and we had a very nice chat. He explained that he knew my mother well from their long involvement with St. John Ambulance, and that she had mentioned my name to him.

I was assigned to work with the audit staff of a young partner, Bill MacDonald. Bill was a wonderful gentleman who took a strong personal interest in my progress. I give him full credit for making sure my attention and drive did not wane. Sadly, Bill died of a massive heart attack in his early forties. The supervisor of the audit staff I was working with was Vern Howe, who was to become a good friend and, later, one of the principal investors in Trimark Investment Management. I still see Vern on a regular basis. Another of my supervisors was Ian Adam, who had just been transferred to Toronto from Clarkson's Vancouver office. Ian and his wife, Sonia, became good friends and spent many weekends with us at our cottage in Algonquin Park.

My close friend Bill Crawford was another business colleague in those early days. Upon graduating from Cambridge University, Bill was recruited in the U.K., arriving in Canada about a year after I had started. He used to jokingly say that I taught him everything he knew about accounting. Bill is a medieval Latin scholar and said the only thing he was suited for was reading inscriptions off tombstones in Germany. Bill retired from Ernst & Young as a senior tax partner but continues to work with me as my principal financial advisor. He has helped me immeasurably for more than fifty years.

The smartest person I have ever worked with is Rod Anderson. He and I started together, working for Bill MacDonald. He had a degree in Honours Physics from the University of Toronto and, within three years, graduated as a CA with the national Silver Medal in Accounting. For a year, I tried to compete with Rod, then finally realized that no matter how hard I tried, I would never be able match his abilities. This change in attitude made me a much happier person. Rod not only is an extraordinarily gifted and pleasant individual, but he also organized the *Canadian Encyclopedia of Music* and has written several books on accounting and auditing, as well as a libretto for an opera. In a letter to a professor at the University of British Columbia Business School, Ross Skinner, a senior partner, said Rod was "one of our most brilliant students in a generation."

New employees were given a numbered green leather manual that contained all of the required auditing and other rules of the firm. We were to use green pencils when checking accounting records and were instructed, when examining documents or cheques, to stamp them using a green "bopper" (a large rubber stamp) inscribed with our name. As trainees, we were often given pretty basic jobs such as examining cancelled cheques, counting securities in a subterranean vault, taking soundings of oil in large storage tanks, or measuring cement in silos. Usually, these latter tasks were done at midnight in the cold and dark, on December 31, the company's year-end. The last two tasks worried me a great deal because of my fear of heights. And, needless to say, they wreaked havoc with my New Year's Eve celebrations for a couple of years.

Another task assigned to juniors was that of a porter to carry the heavy comptometer. This machine, and some of the ladies who could add lengthy columns of figures on it in a flash, often accompanied staff on audits. One of the staff members was my friend Walt Stothers, who always barked at me, "Speed it up, Labatt!" as I struggled to lug this heavy contraption to a waiting train. Walt went on to head up a new group to help small business in the Toronto area, called the Toronto Business Advisory Group (better known as T-BAG), which was very successful. Its name was later changed to the more dignified sounding Entrepreneurial Service Group.

Counting securities can be a bit boring. Many bond and share certificates contain beautiful artwork of bare-breasted damsels. One of my colleagues, whose name I won't mention, decided to enhance the artwork on some of these certificates, much to the distress of the institution holding them and to the manager and partner in charge of the audit. However, the prank did get lots of laughs from our fellow juniors at the time.

Among the major audits I worked on over the years was Noranda Mines and its many subsidiaries. I spent numerous winter months in the city of Noranda, in northern Ontario, as well as in the Gaspé region of Quebec. I remember having to walk backwards against the wind from the Hotel Noranda to the mine site in a minus-forty-degree gale, enjoying the Back Alley Bar in nearby Rouyn, and generally having a good time with my auditing colleagues. Going deep underground as well as visiting the smelter created indelible memories. In the summer months, I spent a week driving to small northern Ontario towns to do the audit of many mines that are now defunct. Local lawyers hauled out musty old ledgers. After blowing the dust off them, I reviewed the few dozen accounting entries made during the past year.

I worked on a number of other major audits over the years, including Massey Ferguson, John Inglis, Dominion Securities, Falconbridge, St. Marys Cement, Canada Life, CIBC, and Ontario Hydro. I owe a lot to Clarkson's for the six great years I spent there learning the accounting profession. Obtaining my CA designation under the firm's auspices gave me credibility in the business community and was a turning point in my life. During my years in their Toronto office, I met dozens of individuals, both fellow workers and clients, who became lifelong friends.

In addition to the senior partners I have already mentioned, another partner who helped me was Ken Lemon, who moved from Toronto to the London (Ontario) office in 1948. He became managing partner in London, a post he held for twenty-five years. Equally influential was

Arthur John "Pete" Little, originally a Londoner, who was with the firm in the Toronto office for forty years until his retirement in 1974. Other friends who rose to senior levels in the firm include Ron Gage, David Lay, Henry Pankratz, Bob Lord, Steve Lowden, Ross Skinner, Bill Farlinger, Gerard Limoges, Jack Biddell, Don Scott, and Michael Mackenzie.

This period of my business career and the ten years with McLeod Young Weir & Co. that ensued were very important to my professional standing and people's perception of me. Although I was a Labatt and presumably wealthy, the fact that I always had a job seemed to resonate with many business people.

I was often asked, "What motivates you?" This was not an easy question to answer. I always looked forward to going to the office and especially enjoyed my relationships with colleagues and business clients. I didn't consider my nine-to-five activities "work" in the sense of a duty or something to be endured. It was part of my life and gave me a focus apart from my family responsibilities. I suppose I always wanted to be at or near the top of the organization I was associated with, but this was not what drove me.

Sonia and I always seemed to live a little beyond our financial means. We were not extravagant, but we did enjoy the luxury of having some additional funds beyond my salary as a result of income from my inheritance. Despite that backstop, it never entered my mind that those funds were sufficient to sustain a lifestyle that I had enjoyed from childhood. What was most important to me was that the capital left to me would act as a security blanket if my family ever really needed it. The last thing I wanted was to be seen as what was then called a remittance man – someone who was infamously shipped off to the colonies from Britain and didn't do a lick of work, relying solely on a regular allowance from their family.

Someone once told me that Jake Moore (president of Labatt's) was quite impressed that I kept plugging away. Moore, who was a driving force in the business community, unfortunately had an ongoing hostility toward the Labatt family; as described above, his relationship with my brother, Jack, was very strained. His attitude, however, exemplified the way some people viewed me and anyone else born with a silver spoon in their mouth.

McLeod Young Weir & Co.

Toronto

In September 1962, I planned to take a few weeks off from Clarkson Gordon to talk to people in the business community, hoping to figure out what to do with the rest of my life. Although Clarkson's had indicated that they would like me to remain with the firm, they understood my desire to explore the business scene. I will never forget Duncan Gordon's advice when I told him I was interested in looking for work in areas other than public accounting.

He said, "You mean that you don't wish to be a 'technician.'"

I had never thought of accounting this way. He suggested that I could remain a full-time employee of the firm but take some time off to look around the business world. He felt it was important that there be no gaps on my résumé. How dramatically times have changed, with career variety now being the norm. Recently, a retired long-term employee of Eastman Kodak told me that today too many years with one employer on one's résumé can be perceived as a negative.

Under the terms of my father's will, Royal Trust was the manager of all securities held in the John Labatt Estate. However, I had some stocks in my own name and dealt with Tony Corson, a sales representative at McLeod Young Weir & Co. I told Tony that I was looking around and that I was not particularly enamoured of auditing.

He left the room for a moment without any explanation and then came bounding back saying that he wanted to introduce me to John Dinnick. He neglected to inform me that Mr. Dinnick was the newly installed president of McLeod Young Weir. John was quite an engaging man and, as I was later to find out, the consummate salesman. He definitely was someone who could, as the saying goes, sell refrigerators to Eskimos.

John and I had a good chat about my background, and he seemed impressed that I had passed my CA exams. He asked if I had considered the securities business, and I told him that I had. I mentioned that I had spent three years on the audit of Dominion Securities, a larger competitor of McLeod, and that I knew most of its key people. I deliberately did not mention that it seemed to me that DS was not a happy place at that time.

I was a bit anxious that he might ask me why I had not applied for a job at that brokerage firm.

We talked for some time. John made an excellent case for a career in the securities business in general and at McLeod Young Weir specifically. The next day, I received a call from Tony telling me that John would like to see me again and wished to make me an offer.

When we met, John said he was embarrassed to be proposing such a low starting salary. He pointed out that I had no experience in the securities business and that he hoped I would understand his position. In fact, I was pleasantly surprised by his offer. The amount he had in mind was considerably higher than I had expected. I found out later that this was because John had called a good friend who was a senior partner at Woods Gordon, the consulting arm of Clarkson Gordon. His friend did not know me personally and thought I had at least two or more years' seniority than was actually the case. I was the happy beneficiary of the incorrect information he gave John about my salary at Clarkson Gordon.

Not knowing exactly what to do with me, they put me in the small and newly created research department. The head of the department, a Dutchman named Hank Bos, was a bit miffed that he had not been consulted in the hiring process, so he assigned me to a small desk with no telephone. With the help of my co-workers, I found a chair, a lamp, and a working telephone. Two of my research associates were David Rea and David Kerr. After nearly fifty years, I still lunch with them on a regular basis. The third associate was Bill Mills, an Ottawa native who arrived on the scene at McLeod with considerable writing experience. Bill was a charming man; unfortunately, he died about twenty years ago.

In the Research Department

In the early 1960s, oil and gas pipelines were being built across the country. Initial public offerings (IPOs) in this new sector of the economy were an important source of revenue for underwriting firms such as McLeod. I was assigned to learn as much as possible about oil and gas pipelines; it was hoped that, over time, I would become a specialist in all regulated utilities. Within six months of working in the research department, I was asked to put together an institutional report on TransCanada PipeLines. TransCanada was growing at a rapid pace and the company was a major underwriting account of the firm and an important contributor to McLeod's bottom line.

When I started this project, I knew little regarding gas throughput, where new lines might be built, the cost of these lines, and the profitability (or otherwise) of a major expansion of the system. In doing my research at TransCanada's head office on Eglinton Avenue in Toronto, I became friends with a number of individuals in the accounting department.

One day, someone gave me gas-throughput estimates for the next ten years, information that was not meant for outsiders such as I. Though not quite sure what to do with these projections, I studied them carefully and made a substantial number of changes to my analysis in order to make my conclusion considerably less optimistic. Among other things, I lowered the unit gas price numbers and upped the construction costs, both by a substantial amount.

When I presented a draft of the report to the directors of MYW, they were very skeptical. Unknown to me, one of McLeod's senior directors there gave a copy of the draft study to TransCanada management for their thoughts. Management told McLeod that they didn't agree with much of the report but admitted that the scenario presented was plausible. The next thing I knew, this junior analyst was on a plane to Vancouver to talk to some major institutional clients. For better or worse, I was on my way to being an analyst to be reckoned with.

The research reports were written to help the retail and institutional brokers recommend securities to their clients. The stockbrokerage business in those days was quite different from what it is today. Each retail broker was essentially a manager of his or her client's portfolio. The broker picked individual stocks, made decisions regarding diversification and asset mix, and was paid for these services through brokerage commissions. Today, most portfolios are essentially managed by professional money managers, with the client relationship handled by the broker for a fee that is not based on brokerage commissions.

At the time, in addition to research reports, a broker's knowledge of the securities recommended to clients came from a wide spectrum of sources – newspapers, analyst reports, and meetings with company management, industry associations, and fellow brokers. There is far more regulation today regarding insider information than was the case in the early '60s. My colleague, Bill Mills, used to paraphrase Oscar Wilde when he said, "Private information is the source of nearly all the world's great fortunes."* Indeed, in my opinion, there was a great deal of stock trading in those days that was based on insider information gleaned from conversations with management, directors, and others in the know. Today such information sharing, known as tipping, is illegal and can result in fines and jail terms.

Each individual in the research department focused on a few industries. David Rea, for example, was the mining guru. David took his responsibilities seriously, and the rest of us used to play tricks on him just to see his reaction. On one occasion, we knew that David had a personal investment in a penny mining stock of a flooded mine in Nevada. The mine was being pumped out, and I asked a friend on the trading desk to create a phony ticker tape giving progress in pumping out the mine and also presenting a rising stock price. We then asked the trader to personally hand this tape to David. Neither the trader nor I realized that this tape was transmitted to all of McLeod's branches in southern Ontario, except for Toronto. The phones from the branches started ringing off their hooks. Our joke had backfired badly. We were all given a reprimand for these antics and promised to behave ourselves.

Traders Finance Corp. was McLeod's largest underwriting client, and I was asked to do a report designed to reassure institutional clients about the creditworthiness of the various debt and equity issues of the corporation. Traders was similar to a better-known competitor by the name of Household Finance Corp., which loaned money to individuals purchasing household items such as furniture and appliances.

One of Canada's major lenders in this field was Atlantic Acceptance Corp. This company was on the verge of collapse, and McLeod felt that an in-depth study of the industry was in order. I had lots of help from Traders management in putting this report together and learned a great deal about an industry that doesn't exist any more. After the report was published, I spent almost two weeks presenting it to major institutions in the United States. It was the fall of 1964, and a small group of us drove through beautiful New England with Bob Wadds, the manager of McLeod's New York

---

* I looked this up recently and learned that Wilde's actual words were,
   "Private information is practically the source of every large modern fortune."

office. Bob was famous around the firm for his somewhat lavish lifestyle, his many marriages, and his engaging personality. Those were the days of the two-martini lunch, and I think we visited all of the top restaurants in New England as well as many in New York City. Atlantic Acceptance did collapse in 1965, while Traders carried on.

Part of my duties included looking after Colonel Gordon Weir, a retired director who was one of the founders of the firm. He maintained a small office right behind the trading desk and often invited me to join him for lunch in the ladies' dining room of the National Club on Bay Street (it had a nicer ambience than the main dining room there). Col. Weir was in his eighties and had a son, John, who was a partner at Wood Gundy, a larger competitor. McLeod had a strict rule against nepotism; children of living partners could not be employed by the firm.

The first time Colonel Weir and I returned from lunch at the National Club, he confided in me that, after lunch, he liked to have a little snooze on his couch. After he lay down, he asked me to cover him with newspapers. He said that when he woke up he had no problem knocking them onto the floor but when going to sleep it was virtually impossible for him to pile them on. I assured him I was more than happy to do this but suggested he buy a lightweight blanket. He would have none of this, saying that he wished to stick with the newspapers.

Colonel Weir was very generous to Sonia and me. Later, when we moved to Montreal, he hosted a special farewell party for us at the Hunt Club. At that time, club members had to supply their own liquor, and I remember the Colonel lugging in two briefcases full of booze. I must have looked like I needed exercise, because, as parting advice, he recommended that I keep fit, citing McLeod's president John Dinnick as an example of someone who took physical fitness very seriously.

CLEARWATER FIORD

Although airlines were not my area of research, I was asked to do some work on Nordair, a regional Quebec airline based in Montreal. In addition to a number of routes in the Province of Quebec, Nordair also had exclusive scheduled flights to the eastern Canadian High Arctic. After my analytical work on the company, I wrote a favourable report. Out of the blue, Nordair chairman Jim Tooley phoned me in Toronto and asked if I could meet him at the Montreal airport by ten the next morning for a very special trip. The purpose of this particular outing was a three-day visit to a small, remote fishing camp on Clearwater Fiord about sixty miles west of Pangnirtung, on Baffin Island. Among the previous guests was Pierre Trudeau.

We set off in a Grumman Goose, an eight-seater flying boat from the Second World War. Jim's other guests included Henry Marks, a charming and very wealthy New York City lawyer, Lorne Bouchard, a well-known Quebec artist, and Harry Teasdale, the president of Mitchell Holland, an upscale interior design firm in Montreal. The camp, run by a young Scottish couple, was situated in a very beautiful and almost inaccessible fjord.

Because of weather conditions, what was to be a weekend fishing trip turned into an eight-day marathon.

Our accommodations consisted of canvas tents, set on wooden frames, each one with a small gas heater. Although this trip took place in late June, all of us, except Henry, had brought a parka, long underwear, and warm socks, in case of cold weather. We were right to bring such attire. The weather was damp, the temperature barely above freezing. We all chipped in items to outfit Henry with warm clothes, but he refused our offerings, preferring to wear his T-shirt and suspenders. This despite the fact that he was in his sixties, not in robust health, smoked heavily, and liked his Scotch.

When the time came to leave, the plane that brought us in tried hard for several days in succession to pick us up, but on each occasion the ceiling was too low for a landing. The camp was situated on a rather narrow fjord, and Jim Tooley, our host, would go outside the dining cabin, mount a little hill, and talk by radio to the pilots. We passed the extra days happily, catching lots of Arctic char and giving them to the Eskimo (which is what the Inuit were called in those days) families who lived in a little settlement nearby.

In the land of the midnight sun, we had almost twenty-four hours of daylight. When we weren't fishing or eating, we played cards with the kids who were helping their elders with the guiding. Food was certainly not a problem. We ate char cooked in every imaginable way and had lots of booze and wine. We started to worry that perhaps Henry's cigarettes might run out. Worse, Henry's health was deteriorating and his round-the-clock card playing with the kids didn't help.

Finally, on the eighth day of what was supposed to be a three-day adventure, the plane was able to land, and we flew back to Montreal. Henry was hospitalized with severe pneumonia and, after about a month of care, fully recovered.

After we moved to Montreal, Sonia and I became good friends with the Tooleys and the Teasdales and were treated to a number of trips to the High Arctic – Resolute, Hall Beach, Pond Inlet, and Foxe Basin. Sonia and I have made numerous trips since then to both the Canadian Arctic and well as the European Arctic, and we hope to find the time to sail the Northwest Passage.

IN THE MONTREAL OFFICE

In 1964, after three years in research in the Toronto office, I heard that Martha O'Donnell, a key analyst in McLeod's Montreal office, was leaving the firm. She had been a one-person research link between the Toronto office and the Quebec sales force. I felt I needed a change, and after much discussion, Sonia agreed that we should move to Montreal. I lobbied the Toronto partners for this position and got it. I felt I would feel quite at home in Montreal. I had attended McGill University, and my sister, Mary, lived there, as did dozens of aunts, uncles, and cousins. Our three kids were just starting school, and the thought of a bilingual education for them appealed to us.

The head of the Montreal office was George MacDonald, who had led the New York office and later would become president of McLeod. I had a small, private office next to his and an excellent secretary, Edna MacPherson. Edna was not a young woman, but on weekends she tried things like water skiing and platform diving, sometimes hurting herself seriously.

The Montreal office was a fun place to work. It was on the thirty-fifth floor of the new CIBC building at the corner of Peel and Dorchester (now René-Lévesque Blvd.) and was well laid out to cater to both the retail and institutional businesses of the firm. The language of the office was English; about one-third of the office staff was French speaking.

Although I thought that my job was to work with the retail salespeople, things didn't turn out that way. The mid-1960s were a time when many smaller private companies were interested in going public and issuing shares in the market. Every week or so, George MacDonald had a meeting with a company that was looking to McLeod to take it public. I became George's assistant and put together a lengthy memorandum for the Toronto underwriting group extolling the virtues of each proposed issuer.

Among the deals I worked on were Coorsh Delicatessen, Bick's Pickles, and Peerless Carpets. I truly enjoyed doing this type of work, and the firm decided that maybe this was the area of the business, now called corporate finance, for which I was best suited. As a result, I ended up working on big bond deals for companies like Canada Iron Foundries and Bell Canada. However, after about two dozen rewrites of a prospectus with the firm's lawyers, I realized that this type of work was even more tedious than auditing. Nevertheless, I learned a great deal; this work helped me understand the business of an investment banker.

Sonia and I met many lifelong friends who worked in the Montreal office at that time, including Wilmer Crawford, David Moore, David Hackett, and Bill Marshall. Another good friend, Graham Weeks, was an institutional sales representative in the Montreal office when I arrived on the scene. He ran into our family the day after our arrival while we were having breakfast at the Queen Elizabeth Hotel. While still a bachelor at the time, he was great with the three kids. Although he was from British Columbia and not a native Montrealer, he helped both Sonia and me become familiar with life in Montreal and the ski country nearby.

When Sonia and I needed a bit of change, Graham suggested that the three of us take a brief holiday in Bermuda. He was a regular at the Horizons Hotel just across the road from the Coral Beach Club and even had his favourite room – number nine. Graham was very successful chatting up girls when we were spending the day at the beach. I recall an opera singer, named Bridget, who was very charming. Graham regularly placed her near us, then sauntered off, leaving us to look after her. Another delightful lady was a medical doctor by the name of Noelle Grace; originally from London, Ontario, she was a resident at the Montreal General Hospital. This relationship with the Doc, as we referred to her, went on for some time, since she and Graham were in the same city. When George MacDonald was hospitalized with heart problems, Noelle took a very special interest in him.

After we left Montreal for Paris, Graham continued to focus his attention on attractive ladies. He met his wife, Judy, skiing at Stowe, Vermont. Judy was a widow with three young children whose husband, Bill Hyland, had died of a heart attack. Graham turned out to be a loving father to their three kids.

Back to George MacDonald, for a moment. I was pulled into a situation involving his son that wasn't exactly part of my job description. It happened on St. Jean Baptiste Day, one of the most important holidays in Quebec. It takes place on June 24 and, in some fashion, has been celebrated in Quebec since the 1600s. In recent times, the annual parade in Montreal has been promoted by the sovereigntists to celebrate the nationalist movement in Quebec.

George and his family lived in one of the penthouses of the Château apartments on fashionable Sherbrooke Street in downtown Montreal. He and his wife, Betty, were away, so their son, Peter, and his friend, Quig Tingley (who worked at McLeod), gathered some friends on the flat roof of their apartment building to watch the parade. As the brass band passed on the street below, they threw some small stones, which were part of the roofing material, in an attempt to hit the tuba.

Suddenly, about a dozen armed policemen appeared on the roof, arrested everyone, and carted them all off to jail. It could be argued that their incarceration saved them from being attacked by an angry mob. I received a call from a frightened Peter, who said he was in jail with Quig and the others and needed to be bailed out.

I was thirty at the time – not even ten years older than Peter and Quig – and was about as flustered as the accused. Bail had to be in cash, and the banks were closed because of the holiday. There were no cash machines in the 1960s, and I needed to raise $1,000 to bail out the boss's son and an employee. In the end, I didn't have to come up with the money as I was eventually able to reach George, who made arrangements to have the young men released.

THE QUIET REVOLUTION

The Quiet Revolution was a period of extreme change in Quebec as well as in the rest of Canada. During this period, politics realigned into federalist and separatist factions. The government of Quebec had been controlled for many years by conservative Maurice Duplessis, leader of the Union Nationale party. Electoral fraud and corruption were commonplace in Quebec. Though the Catholic Church was not unanimously supportive of Duplessis, the bulk of the small-town and rural clergy supported him.

The Quiet Revolution began in 1960 with the election of the Liberal provincial government of Jean Lesage. It is generally thought to have ended with the October Crisis of 1970, but I believe it continues to this day.

As part of the changing environment, the provincial government took over health care and education, which had been in the hands of the Roman Catholic Church. It also took measures to increase Québécois control over the province's economy, including the creation of the Caisse de Dépôt to manage the money collected from citizens for Quebec's pension plan, the nationalization of the hydro companies, and education bills requiring newcomers to the province to study in French. These measures, as well as a number of other things undertaken by the government, convinced me that remaining in Montreal required mastering the French language.

In 1964, the Quiet Revolution was becoming noisy. I didn't realize it at the time, but this period of intense change in Quebec had a profound effect on our whole family. The ongoing English–French language war was constantly in the headlines, and I was upset at the sense of being increasingly disliked by French-speaking Quebecers. In Quebec at that time, it would have been better to have been an American than an anglophone Canadian.

I nevertheless look back on the four years living and working in Montreal as a great time. Montreal is a wonderful and vibrant city, and Sonia and I were very happy there. It is surrounded by beautiful countryside in all directions and has extraordinary summer and winter sporting facilities. But the problem with learning French in Montreal was that there were too many English speakers in the city – one million in a city of two and a half million; it was therefore just too easy to get by speaking English only. With these thoughts in mind, Sonia and I pondered where we would like to learn French. We first thought of Quebec City, even Chicoutimi, but didn't think we would exactly fit in.

We then decided that Paris, which is the centre of the French language and culture worldwide, might be the place. Sonia's mother is Swiss French, so Sonia was away ahead of me in the language department. Our three children were just starting school, so a move would not be too disruptive.

MOVING TO PARIS

We decided to remain in Montreal until Expo 67 closed in the fall. I told George MacDonald about our plans and my strong desire to master the French language. He said he fully understood the situation; however, I now feel that he thought we would change our minds. We sold our house on Daulac Road to John Lynch Staunton, who was then a Montreal city councillor and later would be appointed a senator by Brian Mulroney.

When we sold our home, George realized that we were serious. His first question was, "What are you going to do in Paris?" I replied that I was not sure, but I had a few options. My first wish was to spend four or five months studying French, without any outside business distractions. After that, I told him, it was possible I would actually return to accountancy, although this would not be my first choice. Canadian CAs are fully recognized in France and can practice without further exams.

Another possibility was to try to get a job with an American investment bank in Paris. All of the big New York brokerage houses had offices in Paris, and friends had told me that my background would be most welcome. I did mention to George that I had no intention of working for a Canadian competitor in Paris, because I was very happy at McLeod and wanted to keep my options open with the firm in the future. Dominion Securities, Wood Gundy, A.E. Ames, and Lévesque Beaubien all had branches in Paris.

Jim McLaughlin was the McLeod partner in the Montreal office in charge of the European business. A Montreal native, he had married a lovely French-Canadian lady, Clautile, and his French was excellent. Jim had been pushing the firm to open a European office.

About a week after I talked to George, I received a call from Jim, who explained that at its last meeting, the board of MYW had voted to open a representative office in Paris. Would I be interested in running it? It certainly was not what I had in mind; the challenge of operating in French on another continent was overwhelming. How would I find any free time to learn the language? My French was high-school level from Central

Collegiate in London, Ontario, where nearly all of my teachers had been former Scottish schoolmarms.

Still, the offer was both flattering and challenging. Given my position as an analyst, this was a major opportunity, one that was difficult to refuse if I had any intention of staying with the firm. So I accepted.

What I had not realized at that point was that the Paris office was to be a sales office set up to sell Canadian securities (bonds and stocks) to institutional investors. My training had been as an accountant and auditor, and more recently, as an analyst. Quite apart from linguistic difficulties, I was not trained in how to find clients, how to introduce myself, how to make presentations, and how to sell!

To make matters worse, not only had the French never heard of McLeod Young Weir & Co., they could not even pronounce it. Ultimately, I started introducing the firm using my own name. When I phoned someone, I simply said, "C'est Monsieur Labatt à l'appareil."

Once the decision had been made to open two offices in Europe, one in London and one in Paris, the McLeod directors wanted them both up and running immediately. Jim Stewart was to manage the London office, and I was to head up a representative office in Paris. The next question was how to divide the continental business. Although Jim McLaughlin was in charge of Europe, he reported to Frank Evans, a senior director who had a deep and gruff voice and, with his cauliflower ears, resembled a wrestler.

Frank took Jim Stewart and me aside and carefully crafted a statement that Jim was to be in charge of the U.K., Ireland, and most of the continent, except for France, Belgium, Luxembourg, and Switzerland, which were to be my domain. He then asked if we were both in agreement with this division of responsibilities. This had been discussed many times, and we both said that we agreed. However, after a brief pause, I asked Mr. Evans if I might also have Italy since I had travelled with Jim McLaughlin on two occasions from Switzerland to Milan and we had made some contacts there. He said he didn't see why this should be a problem.

Afterwards, Jim Stewart said, "You b*gger. When you asked for Italy, I thought I should specifically ask for all of the Scandinavian countries, but thought if I did that, everything might get completely out of hand."

This discussion over territory was a little like arguments in McLeod's offices in London, Ontario, and Windsor over who should cover Chatham. We young international types were just haggling on a bigger scale.

In the fall of 1967, all of our family belongings were shipped by sea from Montreal to Paris. We had rented a furnished apartment on Avenue de Breteuil just behind Les Invalides, in the seventh *arrondissement*. However, I kept my best business suits with me in case the shipment went astray.

Before going to Paris, Sonia and I had been invited to a black-tie business affair at the Plaza Hotel in New York, where we stayed in a small suite. As I still had a couple of days of business meetings following the party at the Plaza, Sonia returned to Montreal. I called the desk and asked to be transferred to a regular room. I was wearing a sports coat and left my tux and two business suits hanging in the bedroom closet. Leaving the door slightly ajar, I watched television in the living room while waiting for the porter to transfer my luggage and suits to a new room.

While I was waiting, someone entered the bedroom and made off with everything hanging in the closet. The major problem with this theft was that all of our worldly goods, including the rest of my business attire, were in transit on the high seas. When we arrived in France, I had two tasks. First, to get organized and find suitable office space. Second, to find a good tailor.

One strong recommendation for a first-class tailor was a Monsieur Creed on Rue Royale, close to Place de la Concorde. This Monsieur Creed was no relation to the Creeds in Toronto, who were well known in the clothing business. I made an appointment and arrived at the very elegant establishment and explained the urgency of the situation. I carefully picked the material for two made-to-measure business suits. As I was being measured by very professional Italian tailors, I glanced over at another gentleman who was standing on a nearby pedestal and immediately recognized him as the Prime Minister of France, Maurice Couve de Murville. We smiled politely at each other. These new suits were extremely expensive. Sonia tells me I have never looked so dapper and well turned out since.

Finding an office in Paris was quite a challenge. Nearly all of McLeod's competitors had elegant premises on Place Vendôme, right in the heart of Paris. Limited space was available in these prestigious old buildings, and I spent hours with realtors looking at possibilities. While searching for the perfect spot, Alex de Takacsy, who ran the Royal Bank of Canada's

Paris branch, lent me his office for a few weeks, after which I moved into shared space near the Opéra. After looking at renovating space on Place Vendôme (at huge expense), I received a call from a Monsieur Menial, who was the senior partner of Morgan Stanley in Paris. He indicated that he might have the perfect spot for me. It was in their building at 4 Place de la Concorde, right on the main floor. The space had been occupied by Drexel Harriman Ripley, a well-known New York investment firm that needed to expand and was moving up the Champs Elysées.

This was the perfect address. The office was the right size and overlooked the Place de la Concorde. It had fourteen-foot ceilings and was beautifully appointed, with panelling throughout. Before settling on this location, I submitted a number of cost estimates to Toronto regarding office rental, staffing, and travel. There was no way around it: Maintaining a Paris office was going to be very costly indeed.

The only spare telephone in our apartment on Avenue de Breteuil was located in what I would describe as a large broom closet. I took a call in that room one evening from a senior director in Toronto. He told me he had been studying the cost estimates I had submitted. Would it be possible to operate the Paris office from my home, rather than from an expensive downtown office? Little did he know that at least three brooms had fallen on my head during our brief conversation. I told him in no uncertain terms that this was not part of the deal and that there was no way I could do so.

I signed a nine-year lease on the office space at Place de la Concorde, and everybody seemed happy. That is, until our president, John Dinnick, visited Paris shortly after we had moved in. He walked around the premises, admired my large oval marble desk, opened an interior door near the desk, and shouted, "I don't even have one of these!" He was referring to my own washroom facilities. I pointed out that I had nothing to do with this installation – it was simply there! I don't know whether he was mollified or not, but he didn't order me to move out.

By the spring of 1968, I was finally settled into our new office and fortunately had hired an assistant, Giselle, whom I had met at a shared office near the Opéra. Giselle was perfect for my needs. A German who had worked for the British Army in Berlin after the Second World War, she had married a Frenchman and had been living in Paris for a number of years. She was outgoing, well organized, and trilingual – English, French, and German. She could get by in Spanish and Italian as well.

THE STUDENT RIOTS

The year 1968 was also the time of the student riots or, as the French called them, *Les Evénements de mai*. They actually started in early March, shortly after a student uprising at Columbia University in New York. What happened in Paris, and in many other French cities, was far more serious than the student protests in the 1960s in the United States. The events of May had a profound effect on France and the entire region. The protests began as a series of strikes at universities and then spread to *lycées* in Paris, the schools that prepare students for university. The de Gaulle administration's attempts to maintain order inflamed the situation and led to street battles with police in the Latin Quarter, in the sixth *arrondissement*, only twelve blocks from our apartment.

As things heated up, we could hear the riots from our apartment. There were usually two or three grey buses full of riot police parked on the boulevard in front of our apartment. The police played cards on the bus. When they took a break for some fresh air, they talked to our kids and held their skipping rope for them.

Once we were caught in a traffic jam in our Citroën (with tourist plates) while driving along Boulevard St. Germain, near Boulevard St. Michel. Hundreds of protestors were on one side of the street and a huge police presence on the other. Several canisters of tear gas had been fired. While we were stopped at a traffic light, the rioters started to rock our car, to the point that Sonia and I feared the car would be overturned. We were prepared to abandon it and run for our lives. In the nick of time, the light changed and we were able to make it home safely.

What made the student protests so lethal was the fact that the students were joined by eleven million French workers, roughly two-thirds of the country's workforce. The French economy started to close down. There was no mail, no banking, no transportation, no gas, and no garbage collection, and the supply of food was quickly diminishing. The government was close to collapsing. Charles de Gaulle, the president of France, had taken temporary refuge at an air force base in Germany.

Apart from the one terrifying incident, the situation had a pleasant side for us, at first. There was less traffic congestion. When the Metro and the buses stopped running, I could walk the mile and a half to the office in the beautiful spring weather. Giselle had not yet started, but my assistant, Mme Collet, couldn't get in to work. Our head office in Toronto saw pictures of the rioters on the cover of *Time* magazine and of the damage they caused. They then telexed me to not worry about the office but to save my family. At first I laughed this off, but when all transportation stopped and the supply of gasoline ran out, I began to take this advice very seriously.

I kept our Citroën DS 21 at a BP Station. I had been assured by the owner that he would always have gas for his good customers because he had non-unionized workers bringing in the fuel. When I asked him to fill it up one day, he said he had no more fuel because the fuel truck drivers were afraid of the strikers. That clinched it. I had a little more than half a tank of gasoline, enough to get to the Belgian border. To ensure the safety of my family, I decided to leave.

Within a couple of hours, the six of us, including our Swiss-German *au pair*, piled into the car and took off for Belgium and points beyond. All of the autoroute toll booths were closed, but there were strikers with cardboard boxes stopping cars and asking for donations. Needless to say, we were quite generous and then moved on. We made it to the border and stayed one night in Bruges. The next day, we drove to The Hague in the Netherlands and registered at a five-star hotel.

When I realized how expensive it would be for our family to stay there for an extended time, I explained our situation to the concierge and asked him if he could recommend a much less expensive place in the countryside. He suggested a resort on a small island in the Zuiderzee, a shallow inlet in the northwest of the Netherlands. From our rustic inn there, we looked out on the ocean and the beach. With the fog rolling in and the salt spray, I thought this was what Sable Island, off Nova Scotia, must be like.

After a few days in this remote place, I called the Canadian embassy in Paris. I had no idea who was on the other end of the line – it could have been the janitor or the first secretary. I introduced myself and asked his opinion on what was happening in France. He told me that he didn't know any more than what he could glean from the newspapers. I told him we were on a small island and could not find either a French or English newspaper anywhere. All of my information came from the bartender. The embassy official told me in a hushed voice that, in his opinion, civil war was about to break out. Upon hearing that bleak forecast, Sonia and I decided to pack up and head for England. I could just as easily work out of the London office until things settled down in France. We spent about five weeks in London, an enjoyable experience for all of us.

In mid-June, General de Gaulle made his triumphal return to Paris and marched up the Champs Elysées. It seemed that things were settling down and it was time for us to return to France. I remember well the date of our move because it was the day that Bobby Kennedy was assassinated: June 5, 1968.

Once we had returned to a normal Paris environment, it was time to get down to work. When we left Canada, Colonel Weir gave me a very old and badly typed list of European banks that he had called on in the 1930s. As I understand it, the Colonel used to travel alone in Europe for as long as three months at a time, doing what we termed "cold calling," arriving at a prospect's office without an appointment. He was a very gregarious man and developed a long-distance relationship with his contacts. His cryptic handwritten notes were beside some of the names on the list he had given me. These notations were sometimes quite amusing; at other times they were not at all flattering to the institution or the individual involved.

I started calling on the Colonel's special European clients. Most were small private banks in Belgium, Luxembourg, and Switzerland. Many of these banks had remained in family hands during the Colonel's forty-year absence, so I was dealing with the grandsons or great-grandsons of his clients. While this list was not that useful to me, I have to say that these bankers never forgot me because my list was so out of date.

After about a year and a half in France, I had compiled my own client list of about two hundred institutional names. Most of the names were from Colonel Weir's list, but the business was not rolling in. A friend from Canada, Paul Crosbie, dropped by to stay with us for a few days. He and his wife, Sazz, and their three daughters had just returned from a visit to Turkey and all were wearing Turkish pants where the crotch is as low as your knees. They were travelling in their minivan along with a dog, three goldfish, and a parrot.

I confided in Paul, who was the branch manager of a small Canadian investment bank in New York, that I was working as hard as I possibly could but without attracting much business. He gave me some critically important advice. He said I was suffering from what he described as "branch office syndrome." From his experience, he said, when you're sitting next to a telex machine in a small office, there is a tendency to become overly concerned about what the senior partners in Toronto are thinking about you. This is especially true when you're miles from head office and few stock or bond orders are being transmitted over the wire. He assured me that head office wasn't thinking about you at all; they were all out at the Toronto Golf Club trying to improve their game.

I showed him my client list, and he advised me to cut it down from two hundred to perhaps a dozen names. We both felt that I could keep in touch with the others by mail or by phone, but would concentrate on six or seven Swiss accounts with the balance made up of the largest banks in Paris and Brussels.

Visiting institutional clients wasn't too onerous once the initial contact had been arranged. I personally looked after the Swiss banks and the insurance companies headquartered in Switzerland. My associate, Claude Decoster, directed his attention to the banks in Paris and Brussels. Claude grew up in Lille, in the north of France and had worked for Dominion Securities before I hired him. He knew the Canadian market and had considerable nerve in approaching senior executives and establishing our presence in Paris. He was tall and blond and a bit of a ladies' man.

I also worked closely with my colleagues in our London office and often travelled with one of them in to Zurich, Basel, and Geneva. The salespeople working for Canadian brokers in Europe were a mixture of nationalities and were all characters.

One very amusing fellow was Bob Campbell. A Montrealer, Bob had been a money manager with Bolton Tremblay, an investment-counselling firm I worked for when I eventually returned to Canada. Bob and I must have seemed like a couple of incompetents, especially when travelling by train in Europe. We often got lost, couldn't find the right train, or were crammed into overcrowded compartments with suitcases falling on our heads. Bob reminded me a bit of Monsieur Hulot from the famous French film *Monsieur Hulot's Holiday*.

I could introduce Bob as a renowned oil specialist one day and as a metals specialist the next day, depending on the stock we were promoting. He was extremely knowledgeable and convincing. Many of our clients were gracious and gave us considerable time to allow us to describe the companies we were urging them to invest in. We tried to stick to the larger, better-known Canadian companies, because newer clients were not comfortable with names they had never heard of. For example, the top three names that everyone knew were Canadian Pacific, Alcan, and Imperial Oil.

In the 1960s, the Canadian stock market was far more important relative to world markets than it is today. A balanced international equity portfolio would have at least a five percent weighting in Canadian companies, usually resource stocks. Today, a one-percent exposure to Canadian stocks might be tops, given the number of Canadian companies that have left the country as well as the greater investment choices available in emerging markets.

Many of our clients were charming Old World characters. Dr. Wolfensberger, who managed money for Swiss Bank Corporation in Basel, always greeted us by saying, "Good afternoon, gentlemens." Bob and I talked about oil wells and mining sites as if we knew every inch of the Canadian Arctic and the Laurentian Shield. As we talked, we both observed that the good doctor was beginning to nod off. When this happened, we changed the locations of the mining properties or the oil wells to test whether *anyone* was paying attention.

In addition to being a travelling salesman in Europe, an important part of my role was hosting lunches or dinners for visiting provincial delegations from Canada or for large corporations.

On one occasion, I was asked to host a lunch for Michel T. Halbouty from Houston, Texas. Although Mr. Halbouty had a French *prénom*, he didn't speak a word of the language. He was born in Beaumont, Texas, in 1909, the son of a Lebanese immigrant who ran a grocery store. Halbouty was a geologist, petroleum engineer, and a "wildcatter" who had authored five books and hundreds of articles on the oil business. At the time of his visit to Paris, he was working with Premier Joey Smallwood of Newfoundland, trying to attract investment for offshore drilling in that province.

We were successful in attracting many European oil specialists to meet

Halbouty and had arranged a luncheon meeting at a prestigious club close to the Elysée Palace on Faubourg St. Honoré. I introduced Halbouty to the audience, who found him intriguing. He was credited with discovering more than fifty oil and gas fields, declaring bankruptcy twice, and coming back to regain his wealth.

As the guests were leaving after his presentation, he took me aside and told me he was so impressed with my command of the English language. I thanked him for his compliment and didn't explain further.

Day Job, Night Job

By 1970, business was booming and now six of us were operating out of our office. We had completed a very profitable $60-million (US) financing deal for Elf Erap, the large French government oil company. Even the day-to-day stock and bond business was breaking even. I was working under increasing stress and started to have problems sleeping. I had tried many times to quit smoking and thought I would feel better if I finally succeeded in doing so.

Sonia told me I should just cut down on the number of cigarettes because I wouldn't be able to really stop. Her words were something like, "You have tried many times, but let's face it, you can't do it." That did it. I quit cold turkey!

Quitting caused my stress levels to go through the roof. Often feeling faint when waiting for the Metro, I made myself stand well back against the wall so I wasn't in danger of falling into the path of a train.

My life was further complicated by the fact that I had both a day job and a night job. The day job was the traditional office role, and the night job was entertaining clients from Canada who were vacationing in Paris. Senior executives would be told to drop in and say hello when they were in town. It was very easy to find our office right at the corner of Place de le Concorde and Rue Royale, and they arrived unannounced. I enjoyed meeting them, but it often made for very long days. Sonia often joined me in accompanying these VIPs to the Lido, the Folies Bergère, and the Crazy Horse. I had seen these shows so many times I was quite aware when various "acts" were taking the night off.

I wasn't quite sure what was at the root of my stress, but I knew I had to seek professional advice. I was referred to a psychiatrist at the American

Hospital in Paris. He was a brilliant man who had been born in Russia but trained in France and the U.S. He taught a course in St. Louis, Missouri, each year, and his English was excellent, although we often conversed in French. He couldn't really understand what McLeod Young Weir's business entailed, and was curious why I was so keen to succeed at a firm whose name was so hard to pronounce.

He pointed out that my anxiety levels had been building up for a long time and that I was simply *un peu dépaysé*, or out of my comfort zone. A direct translation would be "out of your country," but he said that one could be *dépaysé* just moving from eastern to western France. He also told me he had many patients with similar symptoms, a revelation that made me feel a lot better. The doctor said that since my problem had been building up for some time, it would take time for my anxiety/depression to wind down. He gave me a prescription for Dogmatil and told me to drop by once a month as he gradually reduced the medication.

Although I am making light of this grim episode, my depression was deep. I will never forget my distress and pain. This experience is one of the reasons that I am so supportive of the Centre for Addiction and Mental Health (CAMH) in Toronto. Despite the fact that I was living in such a beautiful city, I wanted to escape to the Kootenays in British Colombia. I have never visited the Kootenays, but this mountain range sounded quiet, serene, and remote. Sonia gave me good advice, saying, "Never make a major decision when you're feeling really down." I also suspect that she did not want to move to the Kootenays.

I think part of my problem was that I wasn't convinced I wanted to remain in the brokerage business. The boom times following the Second World War had been good for the securities business, but I sensed that serious problems lay ahead.

THE 1970S OIL CRISIS

The stock market peaked in 1969 when we were in Paris, and the early years of the '70s were a disaster for investors. The cause was the oil crisis that started in 1967, when Israel launched the Six Day War and won a significant amount of land in the Middle East. In 1973, Arab forces retaliated, on Yom Kippur, the holiest of Jewish holidays. At the same time, Saudi Arabia's King Faisal convinced other oil-producing nations in the region to place an embargo on crude oil sales to Western countries. This was a political tactic designed to pressure the United States into demanding that Israel withdraw its troops from the Arab territories they had occupied since 1967.

With the embargo on the West, the Arabs realized the power they had over the world through oil. The immediate results of the oil crisis were dramatic. The Organization of the Petroleum Exporting Countries (OPEC) raised crude oil process from $3 (US) a barrel in 1972 to $12 (US) a barrel in 1974.

The U.S. Congress responded by ordering a speed limit of fifty-five miles per hour on highways. American automakers started building smaller, fuel-efficient cars as well as some diesel vehicles.

A severe recession hit much of the Western world, and the Dow Jones dropped forty-five percent over a two-year period ending in January 1975. Total consumption of oil dropped twenty percent in that period, due to the decline in economic activity as much as to any conservation measures.

By the mid-1970s, Middle Eastern nations were again shipping oil to Western nations, but at an inflated price. Inflation was running considerably higher than the traditional annual rate of one to two percent, while unemployment was also at a record high. The era of boundless economic growth, which had been in effect since the Second World War, was over.

BACK TO CANADA

Sonia and I contemplated a move away from Paris, and as far as I was concerned, perhaps even a switch to a new profession. I had spent a lot of time in Switzerland and knew many Swiss bankers. Sonia's mother was Swiss. We thought this factor and the senior legal help available to us would permit us to get a long-term visa to live and work in Geneva. However, this was about a year after Investors Overseas Services (IOS) had collapsed, and foreign-investment people, particularly Canadians, were looked on with suspicion. IOS had its offices in Geneva, but the 1969 public offering was done in Canada. Some investors around the world lost everything.

Moreover, Sonia's image of Switzerland was somewhat at odds with reality. She grew up in Ontario with a Swiss mother from the French part of the country and viewed Switzerland as basically French. Of course, she knew there were German-speaking Swiss, because her Uncle Emile was Swiss German, and that there were a few Italian speakers, as well as those who spoke Romansch, the fourth official language of the country. However, it was only after we had travelled to Switzerland a few times that she realized the country was about eighty percent German speaking and the French were a minority.

I had a ten-year French visa and could have lived in France and commuted daily to Geneva as a *frontalier*. Alternatively, we could have lived in the Canton de Vaud, next door to Geneva. However, we wanted to live right in the Canton de Genève, but the residency rules there were more rigorous. If Sonia's father had been Swiss, this would have made things easier. Because of the difficulties in obtaining the proper status, we started to think about moving home to Canada.

At the time, Canada was living through its own crisis. While we were in Paris, mailboxes were being blown up in Montreal; the FLQ kidnapped a British diplomat; the Quebec Minister of Labour, Pierre Laporte, was murdered; and Prime Minister Trudeau declared the *War Measures Act* and sent in the army. Although our French-language skills had improved greatly, the prospect of moving back to Montreal did not appeal to us.

In Paris, we felt a similar divide. Because there were relatively few Canadian residents in Paris, we were certainly on the guest list of the Canadian embassy, and had been invited to a number of functions there. However, as former Quebecers, we had never received an invitation to Quebec House, an institution that, in some respects, was competing for recognition with the embassy. We observed a lack of camaraderie between francophone Quebecers living in Paris – the federalists versus the sovereigntists. When the Liberal leader, Robert Bourassa, was elected premier of Quebec in 1970, Sonia and I finally received an invitation to Quebec House and met him.

We considered a move to Vancouver, Calgary, or Toronto and finally settled on Toronto. Just as we were about to leave Paris, John Dinnick called. He told me he had an idea that might interest me. He said the firm was going to move my good friend Jim Stewart, the manager of the London office, to New York, and would I like to move my family to London and run all of the European operations from that site? I told John that our furniture was already on the high seas en route to Canada.

He said this was not a problem; they would simply turn the container around and send it back to London.

We did give this opportunity some serious consideration. We both liked London, and I felt I would be more comfortable working in an English-speaking environment. However, we decided to continue with our plans to return to Canada. In hindsight, this was very fortunate, indeed, for otherwise I would not have met my future business partner Bob Krembil and would not have started Trimark Investment Management.

Having decided to return to Toronto, we boarded a transatlantic liner, the *Leonardo da Vinci*, in Genoa, and after a couple of stops in the Mediterranean and a visit to Lisbon, we sailed on to Halifax and New York. The ten-day trip to New York was a very a special one for all of us. We were travelling first class and were bringing our little French Peugot 504 home with us. The first few days on the Mediterranean were calm and beautiful, but once we passed Gibraltar, the seas became rough.

Dinner on board the Leonardo da Vinci *on our return to Canada from Paris in 1971.*

The Captain's Dinner was a formal affair. I remember working hard to get the twins, Jacquie and John, dressed, and was wondering why this work fell on my shoulders. The fact was that Sonia and the twins were not feeling a hundred percent. This became evident after John had left the cabin but came running back and said that he had "throwed up" on the deck. I corrected him by saying, "You threw up," to which he replied, "That's just what I said – I threwed up." That evening, Sonia and the twins ate apples and crackers calmly on the back deck, and Sheila and I dined with the captain. The children took Italian lessons on the way home and managed to pick up a lot of the language.

When we arrived in New York, we were not sure whether Jacquie's still roiling stomach could stand the long car ride from New York to Toronto, so we put her on a plane to Montreal, where she was picked up her aunt Mary and her daughter, Brenda.

Mary and Brenda are ardent animal lovers – and this is an understatement. Driving to Mary's house along the Decarie Expressway, the threesome spotted a stray dog huddled under an overpass bridge. Mary pulled onto the shoulder of the road, got out with Brenda, and proceeded to climb the embankment to rescue the poor animal. Jacquie was quite impressed. The new stray was added to the menagerie of cats and dogs already living in Rusty and Mary's home.

When we spoke to Jacquie on the phone later that day, we asked her about her trip and her stay with the Lambs. She simply said, "Everything is great but it's a little like *Dr. Doolittle* here."

VII   A CHANGE OF PLANS

WHILE we were in Paris, I had been named a director and a vice president of MYW. When we returned to Toronto, it seemed they didn't know what to do with me. I was given the title of Director of Research; my job was to significantly expand the research and analytical expertise of the firm. This was a great challenge, which I enjoyed very much; that pleasure, however, did not make it any more likely that I would stay in the stockbrokerage business for the rest of my working life.

Indeed, in the fall of 1972, I decided to leave McLeod Young Weir, although I had thoroughly enjoyed my ten years with the firm, especially the camaraderie with my colleagues, who remain friends to this day. They put on a very nice goodbye party for me, and most of my good friends attended.

I had no clear idea what new direction to take. The only industry I knew reasonably well was finance, but I was interested in taking a different career path. I had many friends in the accounting and law professions and intended to contact some of them to try to narrow my choices. The oil boom had already started in Alberta; this was one area I planned to pursue. I knew Don Getty from my days in London, where he played quarterback for the Western Mustangs. Don, who later became premier of Alberta, advised me to look into the real estate sector, especially in the Fort McMurray area.

One rather bold move I made was to talk to a senior executive of the British American Oil Company. I had taken a pleasure trip with the Edmonton Chamber of Commerce covering the western part of the Northwest Territories. I had an interest in the Arctic but didn't know the

Western Arctic well. So when I saw an ad in the paper for this trip, I jumped at the opportunity.

I asked my contact at BA Oil, who was a fellow member of the Canadian Opera Company board, why Imperial Oil was the only oil company supplying fuel to this vast region. He explained that Imperial Oil had a refinery at Fort Albany on the Mackenzie River, which gave them quite a price advantage. However, he said this was a good question and that they were looking into it.

He then asked me what I knew about the distribution of oil products. I told him I was a neophyte, but I could put together the smartest team in the business. He asked if my wife would be willing to live in this harsh environment. I said we would make our home in Edmonton and I would commute. I planned to pursue this further but was not yet convinced that this was the right move.

Before I could explore any of these avenues further, I received a telephone call from Lorne Webster in Montreal, who was a good friend of Mary's. Lorne said he had heard that I was no longer with McLeod, and that he would like to meet me to discuss his new financial services company, Prenor Group Ltd.

Lorne and a number of Webster family members had acquired two insurance companies, one a life company and the other offering general insurance. Both of these companies, Les Prévoyants du Canada and Les Prévoyants du Canada – Assurance Générale, were Quebec-based and entirely French speaking. He had also purchased a small trust company, North America Trust, and named the holding company Prenor Group Ltd., the name being derived from Prévoyants and North America. The well-known investment management firm Montreal-based Bolton Tremblay was also owned by Prenor.

Lorne said he wanted to expand Prenor across the country and make it less dependent on the Quebec market. He asked me to join him and said I would be in charge of everything west of the Ottawa River. Of course, there was nothing in Prenor west of the river except the three-person office of Bolton Tremblay in Toronto. Although I would still be working in the financial-services business, the challenge was appealing; I joined Lorne in his new venture without hesitation.

The Webster family was well known in Quebec as industrialists and financiers. The patriarch, Senator Lorne Webster, who was Lorne's grandfather, had amassed a considerable fortune. He was a major importer of coal from Wales and later became involved in the steel business, fuel-oil distribution, retail, and major contracting. For example, the Beauharnois Canal, built in 1929–32 near Montreal, was one of his ventures. He left his fortune to his five boys and one daughter. Lorne's father, Colin, and his uncle, Howard, continued to grow the assets. Most of the senator's sons and his daughter pooled their inheritance under Colin's direction, but Howard went his own way. Lorne's brother, Ben Webster, was a successful venture capitalist who lived in Toronto.

Lorne felt strongly that his family, having settled in Quebec City in the early nineteenth century, were as much Quebecers as his French-speaking neighbours. A very likable and charming man with a good sense of humour, he got along famously with the francophone community. His commitment to remaining in Quebec during the difficult period of the 1970s, after René Lévesque came to power and separatism was rampant, rather than joining the English exodus to Ontario along with Sun Life and other corporate head offices, went over well.

Board meetings of the Prenor insurance companies were held in French. Lorne was the chairman of each company and I was a director along with about a dozen of the francophone elite of Montreal. Added to our challenges of keeping up, in these meetings, with spoken French, Lorne had a tendency to fall asleep. I tried to sit next to him or across from him so I could gently kick him under the table whenever I saw his eyes begin to close behind his half glasses.

THE INSURANCE GROUP

MARCELLIN Tremblay was the president of both the life company and the general insurance company. He is a marvellous man, and I am still in touch with him. Marcellin has written many articles on the history of insurance in Quebec and was a great friend of Claude Castonguay, former CEO of the Laurentian Group, also a Quebec-based insurance company. It was Castonguay who was credited with bringing government-run health care to Quebec, when he was Minister of Health in the provincial government.

Marcellin was a great orator and a committed federalist, in spite of the fact that he came from the Saguenay area, a strongly sovereigntist region. Sonia and I attended many conventions of the insurance companies, and I heard Marcellin speak out bravely against separatism. On one occasion, in Mexico, he likened the peso (worth about twelve cents at the time) to the value of a hypothetical Quebec dollar if the province were to separate.

Marcellin was highly regarded in the insurance industry across Canada but was especially well known in Quebec. His wife, Laurette, was charming, and their daughter, Danièle, a judge on the Federal Court, was married to Canada's chief justice, Antonio Lamer.

After board meetings, Marcellin invited us all to lunch at the Club St. Denis, the most elite club for French-speaking business people. Over the years, he introduced me to many of the top people at the Caisse de Dépôt, and to senior executives of major francophone institutions. The chief operating officer of Prévie (the life company) was Roger Decary, and the COO of Prévale was Raymond Viger, both competent executives and excellent leaders.

Before I joined Lorne, Serge Rocheleau, a young and very bright French Canadian, was his right-hand man at Prenor. We got along very well. Serge introduced me to the younger French crowd, and I got to know many people I would never have met in Westmount, the mainly English bastion where we lived. Serge married Lise Watier, the founder of the cosmetic firm bearing her name.

One major acquisition in which I was deeply involved was Prenor's purchase of the Northern Life Assurance Company, headquartered in London, Ontario. Northern Life was controlled by Dick Ivey, a good friend of mine. I had heard rumours that he was uncertain what to do with the company. It seemed to me that it would be a perfect fit for Prenor. Although he and Lorne were directors of the Bank of Montreal, they didn't know each other very well. After much consideration, Northern Life was acquired by Prenor in a stock deal that put Dick Ivey in the position of being a substantial shareholder of Prenor Group Ltd.

Another Prenor venture in which I was closely involved was the creation of a new general insurance company in Toronto. Hans Johne, a businessman who moved to Canada from Germany just after the war, approached Marcellin with a novel idea: the creation of a general insurance company that would specialize in offering automobile and home insurance to employee groups. Group insurance in the life insurance business was very common, but the notion of offering general insurance coverage by way of payroll deductions was quite new. Marcellin and the other senior executives embraced the idea.

We named this company The Personal and established its headquarters at the intersection of the Queen Elizabeth Way and Highway 427 in Etobicoke, in Toronto's west end. We had a large and brightly lit sign on the building – THE PERSONAL – that could readily be seen from both expressways. Selling the idea of this company to employers was not easy, but The Personal eventually succeeded and grew into a mid-sized and financially stable insurance underwriter. Two of its clients were the Canadian army and Ontario Teachers. Both groups were difficult for different reasons. The army group caused problems because military policyholders got drunk in the mess hall on Friday evenings and, when the bar closed, drove their cars into trees. The teachers were smart and better drivers, but they were good bargainers and quite demanding.

Bolton Tremblay

BOLTON Tremblay's Toronto office was my primary responsibility. The firm was well known in the field of pension management because of Hamilton Bolton, who had founded the institutional publication *The Bank Credit Analyst*. Although Bolton had only a small presence in Toronto, I argued that we needed some established and experienced portfolio managers based in the Toronto office. I canvassed all of the institutional brokers I knew from my days at McLeod Young Weir. Two individuals at the top of the list were Russell Morrison and Bob Krembil. When I first approached them, in 1975, they told me they were quite happy working for themselves at their new investment-counselling firm, Morrison, Krembil Ltd.

Two years later, however, I received a call from Russell while Sonia and I were on a Butterfield & Robinson bicycle tour in France. He explained that Commercial Union Assurance, which owned Planned Investments Ltd., the distributor of four mutual funds that Russell and Bob were managing, wanted to get out of the fund business. The life insurance sales force at Commercial Union was not interested in selling mutual funds, and Planned Investments was losing money. Russell explained that he and Bob didn't want to be "business people" hiring and firing staff; they wanted to be investment managers only. Would Prenor be interested in talking to Commercial Union?

At first, Lorne and Serge were very much against getting back into the mutual fund business. They had been in this business before I joined them and explained to me that if the performance results of the mutual funds were not good, finding and retaining pension and private clients would be very difficult. In the end, they came around because they thought so highly of Bob and Russell. Bolton bought Planned Investments and the management contracts for the four mutual funds being managed by Morrison, Krembil Ltd. Russell wanted the title of Adviser at Bolton. One of his idiosyncrasies was that his title had to be spelled with an "e" – the American way. Bob joined as a vice president and was seen as the lead manager of the four funds –Taurus Fund, Canada Cumulative Fund, Planned Resources, and Canada Growth, which, despite its name, was an international fund.

Bob Krembil was a native of Saskatchewan who had worked for General Electric in Montreal. That is where he met his wife, Linda. The two moved to Toronto, where he worked with various companies before setting up Morrison, Krembil Ltd. with Russell. He obtained his MBA from York University in 1971, as well as a CFA from the Institute of Chartered Analysts. He received a Doctor of Laws (*honoris causa*) from York University in 2000, and in 2005 was made a Member of the Order of Canada. He remains actively engaged in philanthropy and investment management on behalf of the Chiefswood Companies and the Krembil Foundation. He is also involved in breeding and racing thoroughbred horses.

A great deal has been written about Bob's investment approach. In looking at the Internet recently, I came upon a number of interesting statements. In a globefund.manulife release, Bob is described as "a living legend in investing." The release goes on to describe "Mr. Krembil's value-oriented approach of looking for undervalued businesses and holding them until the market recognizes their potential."

By this time, I was president of Bolton and can attest to the fact that we knew little about the mutual fund business. The real reason Bolton Tremblay bought the fund management company was to obtain Bob and

Russell's investment expertise for Bolton's pension and private client business. I explained the situation to Bob McRae, a former Trans Canada Airlines (now Air Canada) captain and president of Universal Funds, which later became CI Funds. He said that, in his opinion, we would go broke in the mutual fund business because we didn't know what we were doing. After trying to convince me to sell the newly acquired funds to CI Funds, he told me there was a fellow in Halifax, Michael Axford, who really knew the business and who wanted to move to Toronto.

Mike had been a career officer in the British army; his last posting was in Malaysia for nearly ten years. He joined the army at a very young age and used to jokingly refer to himself as a child soldier. He attained the rank of Major in the Ordinance corps. He retired from the army in the early 1960s, and with his wife and two young daughters, set sail for Halifax, Nova Scotia. He had been offered a job in Halifax but discovered, when he arrived, that there had been a misunderstanding. There he was in a new land, without any employment. He had acted in a management capacity during his army years and had much to offer a potential business operator. However, he ended up as a mutual fund salesman for United Funds and later held a senior management position with a company promoting scholarship funds in the Maritimes.

The purchase of the fund contracts cost Bolton a nominal amount. As buyers, we were able to utilize a multi-million-dollar tax loss carried on the books of Planned Investments. Moreover, the timing of the purchase was perfect because the Toronto Stock Exchange had performed poorly in 1976 but would show solid growth for the next three years. As a result, the funds we had just purchased enjoyed excellent returns. Michael Axford, who later became my partner when we founded Trimark, joined Bolton and was put in charge of fund sales and fund administration. Unfortunately for Commercial Union, they sold their fund business at absolutely the wrong time.

Before Bob and Russell joined the firm, Bolton Tremblay had an office on the twenty-fifth floor of the Bank of Nova Scotia building at the corner of King and Bay streets. The elevators in the building stopped at the twenty-fourth floor, where a wide marble circular staircase went up to our floor. Ray Lawson, a former lieutenant governor of Ontario, was a major investor in Taurus Fund and always attended its annual meetings. He was ninety-one and had to be helped up the marble staircase by his driver. After the meeting, a number of us were walking with "the Honourable Ray" as we approached the staircase. He missed the first step, but I was able to put my arms around him and grab the banister at the same time he was about to fall forward. Happily, he was not hurt; had he fallen, it would have been disastrous. I phoned Lorne and said we had to move immediately. We went across Bay Street to First Canadian Place and set up additional space for Bob and Russell.

In the process of expanding our Toronto presence, we hired a number of new people. Stephen Thibedeau was our newly appointed stock trader and had recently moved to Toronto from Bolton's head office in Montreal. Stephen was from the Maritimes and didn't speak a word of French. He told me that with his surname he was okay in Montreal until he opened his mouth.

Bob and Russell's secretary, Sharon Gignac, joined us at our new premises and asked me if I would consider hiring her half-sister, April. April was a very attractive young woman and sported a tattoo. Sharon further explained that April had grown up in New Orleans and had led a very rough life. She had no office experience, so I asked Stephen to take her under his wing and teach her everything he knew about the business.

A year later, at Christmas, April asked if she could have a chat with me, and would it be all right if she shut my office door. She then explained that she wanted to thank me for having hired her, that this was by far the best job she could ever have imagined, and that Stephen had been so nice to her. She then said that she had a Christmas present for me and handed me a little bag with a bow on it. I looked in the bag and asked her what it was. She smiled and told me it was the very best Colombian Gold, and that the papers for rolling "joints" were also in the bag. She couldn't figure out what to get me for Christmas, she said, and thought this was a great idea because, since I was so square, I probably wouldn't know where to buy the stuff. Sonia and I tried one and threw the rest away.

My eight years with Bolton Tremblay and the other Prenor subsidiaries were happy ones. In those days, the four pillars of the financial world in Canada were the chartered banks, the insurance industry, the trust companies, and the investment dealers. I was involved with all of the pillars except banking. The portfolio managers in Montreal, Toronto, and

Calgary were an impressive group, and the firm grew steadily during my time with the organization.

Mitch Bourke was the senior portfolio manager and had been with Bolton Tremblay for many years. He was well regarded in the Montreal financial community. Although the 1970s were difficult years in Montreal, the relationships between our francophone and anglophone managers remained congenial.

North America Trust

At the time that we were expanding Bolton Tremblay's office in Toronto, we took adjacent space and set up a branch office for Prenor's trust subsidiary, North America Trust. During the 1970s and 1980s, the growth of the trust companies was impressive. These small- to medium-sized trust companies were really mortgage-lending operations and were draining business away from the banks and the large, established trust companies, such as Royal Trust, Montreal Trust, and Trust Général.

North America Trust had almost the same name as a much larger competitor, North *American* Trust. This caused a bit of confusion, mostly to our benefit. Our trust company was well financed and run by experienced professionals. My current executive assistant, Odette Goodall, joined North America Trust in the fall of 1980, then left and would later join Trimark, in 1991. Odette has been of great assistance to me and our entire family since that time, and she has helped immensely in putting these stories together.

Lorne Webster and Serge Rocheleau's belief in the potential for growth in this area of business led to the purchase of a larger Ontario-based trust company, Sterling Trust. Shortly after the acquisition, Prenor sold Sterling Trust to Trust Général in Montreal in return for shares in the latter. Prenor had been quietly buying into Trust Général. The combination of the exchange and purchased shares made Prenor the largest shareholder in Trust Général. Shortly after closing the deal with Sterling Trust, Lorne was elected chairman of Trust Général.

Royal Trust was the pre-eminent trust company for wealthy anglophone Canadians, and Trust Général was its counterpart for the French-Canadian establishment. I was appointed to the board of the latter and had numerous conversations with Lorne about his plan for Prenor to become Trust General's controlling shareholder. Although Lorne was well liked by management and had deep roots in the province, he was, nevertheless, an English-speaking Quebecer. I felt that this major investment in the Trust was going to give him problems. My views had little impact on Lorne or Serge. Many Montreal business people had confided in me about their concerns for Prenor as the controlling shareholder of Trust Général, but they didn't want to confront Lorne.

Without consulting Prenor, the management of Trust Général proposed issuing more stock in the company that would be purchased by francophone institutions. The board was divided on the strategy but finally agreed to it by a substantial margin. This confirmed the reality that the francophone business community wanted control of Trust Général to remain in the hands of francophone Quebecers. The cost to Prenor of maintaining its stake was prohibitive. Lorne lost his controlling interest.

No-fault Insurance in Quebec

IN 1978, no-fault automobile insurance was introduced in Quebec. The goal of this type of insurance is to lower premium costs by avoiding expensive litigation over the causes of accidents while providing quick payments for injuries. No-fault insurance has since come to Ontario and is in force in about a third of the United States.

But in 1978, few people in the insurance industry in Canada truly understood the economics of this new approach and how to price the policies. In hindsight, it appears that Prenor's insurance subsidiary, Les Prévoyants du Canada – Assurance Générale, put too low a price on its new policies and, in so doing, obtained a huge increase in revenues as consumer flocked to the "best buy." However, when the claims came rolling in the following year, the costs nearly bankrupted the company. The large loss that Les Prévoyants suffered was a terrible blow to the insurance group at Prenor, and to Lorne. The only way out was to sell Prenor's five insurance companies – the two life companies as well as those in the general insurance business – as a group. The whole package was purchased by the Desjardins Financial Group.

Everybody knew about Prenor's difficult situation. Early in 1980,

Bob Krembil asked me to see if selling the Prenor mutual fund business would be helpful. The story of our approach to Lorne is outlined in the chapter on Trimark.

The BNP Board

IN 1974, I was invited to join the board of BNP (Banque Nationale de Paris) Canada and remained on that board for fourteen years. At that time, BNP was the largest of the French banks – the others being Banque de Paris et des Pays-Bas, Société Générale, and Crédit Lyonnais. While my French was reasonably good, I was by no means fluent. I continued to study the language and quietly worried about the quarterly board meetings and the socializing afterwards. I spent a month at the Alcan School in Chicoutimi, attempting to become comfortable with Québécois French.

There were several high-profile Quebecers on the BNP Board. Among them were Robert Parizeau, the brother of Jacques Parizeau, who would later became premier of the province, and Pierre Laurin, whose brother, Camille, was the author of Bill 101, the famous Quebec language bill. I came to understand from these charming individuals the fervent desire of most francophone Quebecers to have their own country, although by this point I thought they had already become *maîtres chez nous* (masters of our own house). In 1976, when the separatist Parti Québécois won the provincial election, there was jubilation in the BNP boardroom, though several staunch federalists were present, including me. It was awkward for me to witness their joy; I was genuinely concerned about the breakup of Canada.

It is estimated that after the PQ victory, more than a quarter of a million English-speaking Quebecers left the province, with the majority of them settling in Toronto. Also, a number of large financial institutions, such as banks and insurance companies, moved their head offices to Toronto.

Sonia's French is far better than mine, and she was a great asset on the social side, since a number of board meetings were held in Paris and elsewhere. At BNP's suggestion, several of its board members, as well as some Prenor managers, attended a children's charity fundraiser, Le Bal des Petits Lits Blancs (Ball of the Little White Beds), at the Louisiana Superdome in New Orleans. It was the first time Le Bal had been held outside France.

The president of France, Valéry Giscard d'Estaing, attended, and there was a considerable Montreal presence. After the festivities, we all wandered around the jazz quarter on Bourbon Street, listening to Dixieland music, spilling booze, and sprinkling powdered sugar from *beignets* on our black dinner jackets until the wee hours of the morning.

On another occasion, the chairman of the bank, Gérard Llewellyn, and his wife were doing a cross-Canada tour and visiting Toronto for the first time on an official visit. Sonia and I were asked to hold a dinner party for them at our home on Old Forest Hill Road. The guest list included BNP's top clients and read like a Who's Who. This was probably the most elaborate party we have ever organized. It was catered and supervised by John Arena, who ran Winston's on Adelaide Street.

Llewellyn is a Welsh name and is pronounced "Leveleen" in French. Gérard and his wife were charming and spoke excellent English. Sonia and I were sitting with them, and Sonia was telling a story in French, gesticulating dramatically with her hands. The table was laden with crystal glasses full of wine. With a whoosh and a clatter, she knocked over her glass, spilling wine across the table directly toward the chairman. The waiters cleaned this up in a flash, and dinner continued. Unfortunately, later in the meal, Sonia did a repeat performance, this time directing the spillage to the other side of Mr. Llewellyn.

The next week, we were travelling with the Llewellyns in Alberta and British Colombia, visiting BNP offices in Edmonton and Vancouver. Sonia apologized to the chairman, saying she was mortified by the two occurrences. Mr. Llewellyn replied simply that it had not been a problem and, "Vous avez bien visé" (You aimed well).

I did quite a bit of travelling with Lorne, attending insurance conventions. He was full of fun and liked to play childish tricks on his colleagues. Once, in Vancouver, we had been eating Chinese food, which included, of all things, chicken feet. When I retired for the night, I felt a bump under my pillow – and there was a chicken foot. It was unfortunate that Lorne did not join us at Trimark, to which story we now turn. We tried hard, over many months, to come to some kind of a partnership deal with him, to no avail.

VIII TRIMARK

IN my entire career, the most surprising, gratifying, and financially rewarding venture was the co-founding of Trimark Investment Management Inc. (TIMI) with Bob Krembil and Michael Axford.

The idea of starting a mutual fund management company first arose in the spring of 1980, when I was president of Bolton Tremblay. Bob, a senior portfolio manager in charge of managing four mutual funds for Bolton Tremblay, asked me if I thought Lorne would consider selling the firm.

At the time, Prenor still owned, in addition to Bolton Tremblay, three general insurance companies, two life insurance companies, and a small trust company. Since Prenor was in bad financial shape because of huge losses in the automobile insurance business, Bob thought selling Bolton Tremblay might help Prenor's financial situation.

I told Bob that Lorne was a collector of companies and was an unlikely seller of any of Prenor's subsidiaries. Nevertheless, I agreed to speak to him. I told Lorne the only way to retain top-quality investment managers such as Bob was to sell them a significant piece of the company.

I also had decided it was time for a change in role. I told Lorne I would be joining Bob; we would be making a bid for the mutual fund side of Bolton or, if he preferred, for the total company, which included pension fund management and the private client business. A third employee of Bolton, Michael Axford, soon joined us. The three of us were, in Lorne's mind, hostile bidders. We hired the law firm of Tory, Tory, Deslauriers and Binnington and the accounting firm of Clarkson Gordon to help us construct our bid.

We put a high valuation on Bolton Tremblay's fund business and asked Lorne or Prenor to remain as a partner in the ownership of this new venture. We negotiated for nearly eight months, making a number of offers. We would have been content to buy fifty-one percent of the fund business or even fifty percent and be equal partners. We outlined our plans to enter the U.S. market as well as to set up some international funds. We had done extremely well in the fund business in Canada since getting into this field three years earlier, and the funds division was by far the most profitable part of Bolton Tremblay's business.

Lorne always listened carefully and then sent us back to the drawing board, but the answer was effectively no. Bob and I decided to make one final trip to Montreal to ask him if any deal was possible. Lorne and the president of Prenor, Serge Rocheleau, had become tired of our persistence and told us that none of our offers was acceptable. Bob, Michael, and I tendered our resignations and decided to start a new company from scratch.

My secretary at Bolton Tremblay, Adrienne Bradley, joined us. Adrienne and I initially worked from an office in the Royal Trust Tower lent to us by my old employer, Clarkson Gordon. We then moved to office space at First Canadian Place. A fund accountant, Steve Thibedeau, and a young receptionist, Halina, completed the group.

Sailing into a Recession

By now it was 1981, and interest rates had soared to nineteen percent. Inflation was rampant and we were heading into a very serious recession. The stock market was falling. It was absolutely the worst time to start a mutual fund management company that invested other people's money in the stock market. It was my job to raise money for the two mutual funds we wished to launch, and also to find financing for the management company. September 1, 1981, was to be the launch date for our two funds, but as August rolled around, we still had no name for our new venture and lacked the resources to hire professional help.

One day, Mike Axford announced that he had come up with the perfect name: Almark Management, and the funds would be called Almark Funds. I asked him what was so special about that name, and he explained that because it started with an "A," investors would look up the price in the newspaper for our mutual funds and ours would be near the top of the listings along with the well-known AGF Funds. Also the name was not too long, it was easy to remember, and worked well in both official languages. Best of all, it had all our initials in it – **Arthur Labatt**, **Michael Axford**, and **Robert Krembil**. Mike Axford, who was the consummate sales manager, said this is how we would explain the name to the independent financial planners who would be our "sales force."

Unfortunately, it turned out there was already an Almark Financial Corp. in Alberta; however, Mike then came up with the name Trimark,

Flanked by my two Trimark partners,
Bob Krembil (left) and Michael Axford.

based on the fact there were three of us. So we settled for Trimark. I, being the "AL," was left on the cutting room floor.

Bob thought the stock market might remain weak for an extended period and that we should raise enough money to weather a three-year bear market. The three founding partners invested $300,000 in total and six outside investors another $300,000. They were Sonia, Vern Howe, Don Greer, Art Binnington, Butterfield & Robinson, and Bill Graham. We also had the ability to call on an additional $200,000 from our outside investors if we needed it. In the end, we didn't.

In addition to raising money for the management company, it was my job to find investors willing to invest in our two equity funds, Trimark Fund, an international fund, and Trimark Canadian Fund. Our goal was to start each fund with $500,000, which was quite a bit of money, considering the negative atmosphere of the time. An even more difficult task was to find 150 individual investors for the Trimark Canadian Fund, the minimum number required to make it eligible for registered retirement savings plans (RRSPs). Even though the minimum individual dollar investment in an RRSP was only $500, it wasn't easy to find that many people willing to invest in our new fund.

Searching for Investors

WHAT did the trick was the decision to phone the presidents of the investment banking firms that I knew from my days at McLeod Young Weir & Co. I called ten firms and explained our need for a significant number of individual investors for our RRSP fund. I asked each president to find ten of his partners who would be willing to invest $500. Within days, we had a hundred new investors. I have always been grateful to them; most of these individuals kept their money in the fund for the next twenty years.

With the help of our lawyers, Stikeman, Elliot, the three of us wrote much of the new fund prospectuses – the lengthy regulatory document that was required for each one – ourselves. We knew our way around a fund prospectus; it was literally a job of cutting and pasting to come up with one for our Trimark funds.

We were starting up a mutual fund management company at an extraordinarily difficult time – right at the bottom of a bear market.

At first, our growth was very slow, but this was actually a blessing in disguise. Russell Morrison, who had been Bob's business partner before they joined Bolton Tremblay in 1977, gave us lots of sound advice. Russell had been in the mutual fund business in the 1960s and had sold a fund management company to Bernie Cornfeld, who was famous – or rather, infamous – as the founder of Investors Overseas Services (IOS). Russell never got along with Bernie and used to jokingly refer to him as "old cornflakes."

Russell told us not to do our own back-office work. He had experienced first-hand the turmoil that can occur when business volumes heat up. We did not heed his advice, believing that we had the necessary expertise to look after accounting matters and order processing. However, as our business started to grow, once the stock market improved, the back office became a nightmare.

Here's how the business worked. An application to buy units in either of our two mutual funds, Trimark Fund or Trimark Canadian Fund, arrived by mail from independent mutual fund dealers and brokers across Canada. If there were a number of orders, our dealers were advised to pin the settlement cheque for the full cost to the appropriate orders. Michael Axford, who was our administrative guru, advised everyone in our small organization to make sure we did this or we were lost. To make matters worse, payments for the orders were often delayed. We still had to set up the orders and then wait for the cheques to arrive, at which point we could reconcile the orders.

At this time, we had our first in-house computer, a Pixell, with eight processing terminals, which we thought was a big deal. However, the machine was very temperamental and broke down frequently. Our computer operator, Stan Sluce, was overwhelmed with this monster and told us he thought dust was causing many of its problems. He advised us to build a plastic tent around this rather large machine, and, additionally, not to allow anyone into the computer room.

Because of computer breakdowns, lack of staff, and a growing number of orders, we were falling behind in our processing. I often thought of Russ Morrison's warnings. As the orders piled up, some with cheques dutifully pinned onto them, others without, we put the unsettled orders into neat little containers, which we jokingly referred to as shoeboxes. The order date was carefully written on the boxes with a marker pencil. This date was critical in order to be able to put the right purchase price on the order, since the funds were priced daily.

I arrived for work one morning and asked our receptionist, who also opened the mail, if there were many orders that day.

"Oh yes, Mr. Labatt," she said, "there are about two feet of them." She indicated the size of the pile with her hands.

I was overwhelmed, because I knew that we were already a few days behind in processing. Visions of all those shoeboxes that we had stashed away in every nook and cranny danced in my head.

To solve our problems, we finally hired experienced senior management, got rid of the old computer, bought a big IBM machine, and expanded into larger premises. We gave the old machine to the Scarborough School Board; it was absolutely unsaleable. Even before this computer episode, I remember buying an Apple IIe computer in Montreal and unpacking it with the help of my friend Chuck Kennedy. This was the first personal computer I had ever touched. The year was 1983.

Our first office on the ninth floor of First Canadian Place was quite small, but presentable, when visited by dealers and occasionally by investors in our funds. We didn't want the office to appear lavish, nor did we want to give the impression that Trimark might not be in business for the long run.

Mike Axford was the perfect person to introduce our mutual funds to financial advisors. The 1970s were a terrible time for mutual funds because IOS had given them a bad name. The word "mutual" was so distrusted at that time that the Canadian Mutual Funds Association changed its name to the Canadian Investment Funds Association. Mike knew the independent mutual fund dealers right across the country and had sales experience as a dealer himself. Together, we made a cross-country tour to explain our new company and win the support of these independent salespeople. By this time, after nearly three years in the fund business with Bolton, I also knew many of the dealers, as did Bob. His ten-year track record in managing Taurus Fund as well as Canada Cumulative Fund was well known to the dealers. This is what convinced many of them to put new money from their clients into our funds.

The Rise of the Financial Planner

THE fund dealers, now known as financial planners, were the sales force for the mutual fund industry in the early 1980s. Mike Axford was adamant that stockbrokers would never sell funds, so we virtually ignored them, putting all of our efforts into establishing solid manager/client relationships with the dealer community. For many years, Mike was right about the brokers. However, in the 1990s, many of them began to act as financial advisors. Instead of selling individual stocks, they started to recommend managed products, which gave mutual funds a major boost.

Over the years, I enjoyed working with the financial planners and saw this group grow into a sizeable sector within the financial community. Names such as Regal Capital Planners, Great Pacific, and Ted Thompson Investments no longer exist. Most of these firms were consolidated into larger entities. I made many good, long-term friends with financial advisors, including brokers, and remember these days fondly.

In early 1987, Mike decided to retire. He was fourteen years older than Bob and seven years older than I. His decision was made before the October market crash, at a point when our assets under management were approaching $900 million. Mike had been in the fund business in the 1960s, and had experienced the stock market meltdowns of that decade and again in 1981, when we started Trimark. He made his shares available to some key employees at a fair valuation and realized many millions in capital gains. He and his wife, Madge, moved to Bermuda for a number of years but ultimately settled in Florida. Mike obtained his green card so he could work in the U.S. He dabbled in real estate and probably did well in this growing sector. He became a serious boater and fisherman and has enjoyed his retirement years.

Bob and I tried to talk him out of retiring by saying it was just too early to cash in. Little did any of us know how large Trimark was to become. As the years progressed, our head count started to soar. We were very fortunate to be able to rent space right next door to our original office on the ninth floor at First Canadian Place. The tenants in this office were a group of energetic young men who were operating some kind of a fund. When business was slow, they played football; we heard lots of noisy thumps and bangs coming through the walls. When I was introduced to them, they were lined up like a football team and were about to throw a Hail Mary pass.

Even this additional office space soon became insufficient, as Trimark continued to grow. Space was available, however, on the fourth floor of the building, but it was about twice the square footage we thought we needed at the time. Bob was reluctant to sign up for this large area; he believed in the theory that when additional square footage is available, people will expand into it. Somehow, we convinced him that we could build a wall so the extra space would not be apparent. We called this Bob's wall, and the subterfuge lasted about a month. This area filled up rapidly, and we started looking at office availability in Scotia Plaza, on the other side of Bay Street.

Even so, everyone knew each other and we would celebrate each person's birthday with cake and candles at the office. However, because we were a small, hands-on organization, we made our share of mistakes. One example pertained to a data entry clerk who made two hundred and thirty consecutive errors in setting up purchases for the funds. In those days, a dealer could charge a nine percent commission on smaller orders, but this clerk put these orders through at 0.9 percent. Needless to say, we heard about our errors quickly.

Momentum

We wanted to keep things small, but this was hard to do with so many good people adding real value and expecting to work in a growth environment. It was a bit like a long freight train slowly gathering speed; once the thing gets going, it's tough to slow it down. We were lucky in being able to maintain a small-company atmosphere while turning into a medium-size organization.

Once we had five-year performance numbers for our funds, investor confidence followed, and our growth began to accelerate. Managing this growth was a challenge. We tried hard to run a relatively flat and efficient organization, with as few hierarchical levels as possible, and at the same time remain organized. In the early years, I knew everyone's name, but as we grew, I remembered every face but couldn't always put a name to it. I utilized what was called "management by walking around," which I don't think would be taught at most business schools. People knew who I was and felt comfortable raising issues with me. We were successful in maintaining a team culture with an open-door policy, attracting many of the best people in the industry.

Another factor in keeping a congenial atmosphere was not to take ourselves too seriously. We had always enjoyed Christmas parties, but as our numbers grew, we had to rent hotel ballrooms that could accommodate the thousand or more guests. We had begun to advertise nationally and had many talented marketing people in our organization. One creative individual suggested that we make a humorous video to be shown at our Christmas party. Many of us got dressed up in outlandish costumes and did song and dance acts for all of the partygoers. We certainly did poke fun at ourselves. These videos went over in a big way and over the years became increasingly outlandish. Our chief financial officer once got his tie caught in the cheque-signing machine, a calamity we were only too pleased to re-enact for the crowd.

As the company grew, we formed a social committee that focused on a number of employee functions at the Toronto office. These included an RRSP party held in March after the end of this very busy season, a boat cruise around the Toronto Islands, a golf day as well as the annual children's Christmas party.

Going Public – Almost

In 1987, we had reached such a size that we decided to go public. We hired Gordon Capital to do an underwriting. Everything was proceeding as planned until the market crash of October 19, 1987. Before the crash, our assets under management were approaching $1.4 billion. After the market meltdown, they stood at $800 million. Close to $500 million of the decrease was caused by the drop in market value of our two equity funds, and the other $100 million by redemptions.

In response to the dramatic drop in global markets, we withdrew our request for a box at the new SkyDome, cancelled a planned holiday in Bermuda for Krembil, Labatt, and wives, and deferred our move to Scotia Plaza. Later that fall, we also decided not to proceed with our public stock issue, because market conditions were so poor. As it turned out, however, the market correction of 1987 was short-lived; as the stock market recovered, we were soon back above $1 billion in assets under management.

For a few years we resisted a trend in the industry in which some of our major competitors introduced elaborate sales conferences to reward top producers. However, we finally did succumb to this type of marketing and for a couple of years held some very successful "conferences." For our tenth anniversary, in September 1991, we held a very enjoyable sales convention for our top financial planners at Minaki Lodge in the Lake of the Woods area. This hotel had recently been completely renovated by the Ontario government and was a spectacular setting. The weather was beautiful. For entertainment, we brought in the extremely popular singer/impressionist André-Philippe Gagnon.

Another memorable extravaganza took place in Tucson, Arizona, in April 1990, at the Westin La Paloma Hotel. On the final evening, we hired seventy-five Jeeps to take the two hundred and fifty financial planners and their spouses on a tour of the desert called Dining in the Desert. Toward the end of the tour, we all stopped for pistol shooting and a few cocktails. Just when everybody thought this was the climax, a couple of cowboys on horseback rode in and told everyone to move along quickly because a cattle drive was about to come thundering through the area where we stood. The announcement was just a ruse to move the guests around a rocky hill to an elegant, white tent with a wooden dance floor. There were waiters in black tie, a string quartet and harpist, and silver bowls for hand washing. High-quality "johnnies on the spot" were not far away.

However, just as we were about to dine, we were deluged by a downpour. The large tent kept us dry, though the orchestra had to reposition itself quickly. Such storms are rare in the desert at that time of year. Nobody has forgotten this very successful finale to one of the last of these big sales conventions. They were effectively prohibited by the Ontario Securities Commission in the early '90s, even though the advisors told us that the conferences were, in fact, truly educational and beneficial to their practice.

A Wealth of Suitors

AFTER our aborted initial public offering (IPO) in the fall of 1987, our business continued to thrive. Bob and I were approached by a number of institutions interested in buying a major stake in the company. The most persistent and best organized was the Royal Bank of Canada. From time to time, Bob and I were invited to a private luncheon in the bank's panelled dining room and were introduced to a number of senior executives. We discussed the mutual fund business in Canada and Trimark's progress in gaining market share across the country.

No specific proposals were ever made at these lunches, but it was obvious to us that the bank was interested in forming some kind of relationship. Later on, it made more specific verbal overtures. The stumbling block was who would wield control. The bank was quite firm that they required at least fifty-one percent of the enterprise.

Another interested party was the Ontario Municipal Employees Retirement System (OMERS). OMERS is one of Canada's largest pension plans and would have been content with a minority position. Negotiations were moving along well with senior management, but OMERS decided not to proceed.

Early in 1988, I received a call from Maggie, executive assistant to Austin Taylor, President of McLeod Young Weir & Co. I knew both of them well from my days at McLeod. Maggie asked if I was free to have lunch with Austin. She explained that Austin seldom left his office for lunch because, being claustrophobic, he hated to have to use the elevator. Would I be available to have a sandwich lunch with him today in his office?

An enormous man with a commanding voice, Austin was a wonderful character. When I arrived, he was eating chocolates, and, after offering me one, he came right to the point.

"Arthur, do you want to sell it?'

"Sell what?"

"Trimark."

I didn't quite know what to make of the conversation, so I just said, "The whole thing?"

"Yes, the whole thing," he answered in a very low voice.

I then went on to explain that Trimark was not for sale and that the company was recovering nicely from the October '87 market meltdown. Austin didn't take no for an answer. He said the problem was that we were asking too much. I pointed out that since Trimark was not for sale, how could we be asking too much? Austin was obviously putting a valuation on Trimark based on the prospectus prepared by Gordon Capital a few months earlier. He then said that he admired us for what we were doing.

At that point Maggie knocked on the door and said in a breathless voice, "Austin, they're here!"

"Who's here?"

"The boardroom is full of lawyers."

McLeod Young Weir was the first of the Canadian investment dealers to sell to a chartered bank. McLeod had been purchased by the Bank of Nova Scotia, and the day of my lunch with Austin was the official closing of the deal. Both Austin and Maggie had forgotten this critical date. Austin left hurriedly, but before he did, he mentioned to me that he had the support of the CEO of the bank, Ced Ritchie, in making an offer for Trimark.

Going Public – Again

FOR the next few years, we maintained our independence. In April 1992, Trimark proceeded with an IPO through a group of investment dealers led by Dominion Securities that also included Wood Gundy, Scotia McLeod, and Burns Fry. We sold $30 million in shares, or slightly less than half of the company, to individual and institutional shareholders.

If there was a single defining moment in the evolution of Trimark, it was this IPO, Trimark's transformation from a private company to a public one listed on the Toronto and Montreal stock exchanges. The management of Trimark tried hard to keep the same *esprit de corps* among all employees, and, to a great extent, we were successful.

Being a public company helped our sales of mutual funds considerably. Our annual meetings were well attended and received considerable coverage in the press. We brought in a number of new senior executives to help us broaden our range of products. Many of the senior portfolio managers, as well as senior executives, benefitted handsomely through stock ownership and options. However, our dealings with certain senior portfolio managers took on a tone that, in some ways, was similar to negotiating with star athletes in a professional sports franchise.

The early 1990s in the Canadian market was the best time for an IPO in the mutual fund sector. Trimark had excellent ten-year fund performance numbers relative to our competitors. Over the ten-year period since we began operations, our assets under management grew exponentially – to over $2.5 billion by January 31, 1992 – and the number of unitholder accounts exceeded 235,000.

Another very important factor was how well the mutual industry in general was doing. Based on data from the *Financial Times of Canada*, mutual fund assets under management had grown forty-four percent to $62 billion in the year ending January 31, 1992. A report by Ernst & Young forecast a continuation of rapid growth, with assets under management expected to reach $293 billion by the year 2000.

The increasing popularity of mutual funds was due to a number of factors. The demographic profile of the country was producing a shift from consumption to saving as the baby boomers got closer to retirement. The recent decline in inflation, accompanied by lower interest rates, caused people to move their money from savings accounts and guaranteed investment certificates (GICs) to equities, in the hopes of getting better returns. Moreover, the annual contribution that an individual could put into an RRSP had been increased from $7,500 to $15,000.

These factors, plus the fact that more and more brokers were becoming financial advisors, all helped to put the fund industry in a very positive light. Rather than recommending trades of individual securities, stock-brokers were now becoming "asset mix specialists" and advisors. And rather than recommending individual stocks and bonds, they now advocated mutual funds managed by professional money managers.

Trimark was always able to attract high-calibre executives to its board. These included Brad Badeau, Art Binnington, Ruth Corbin, John Evans, Jim Fisher, Bill Harker, Vern Howe, and Ed Waitzer. I sat on it as well, with Bob Krembil as chair.

Strategic Challenges

THE Trimark board faced a number of strategic issues.

The first was how to finance commissions on the sale of mutual funds. Trimark had been funding commissions on the sale of its back-end load funds, the Select Funds, from cash flow and bank borrowings. Approximately $18.5 million of the $30 million issue was used to repay the company's indebtedness to a Canadian chartered bank, and the remaining proceeds were used as working capital.

The major Canadian chartered banks, which were getting into the mutual funds business themselves, had made it quite difficult for fund companies such as Trimark to borrow in order to fund commissions to dealers. Eventually, one of the banks broke ranks and came up with a methodology that allowed Trimark to fund commissions. When I mentioned this to a senior person with another bank, he assured me that I must be mistaken. He stated unequivocally that no bank would agree to do this. It is my guess that an "understanding" among the banks had evidently been broken.

The second issue was how to provide the quality administrative service that the advisors needed. During Trimark's early years, we had problems with floods of orders coming in as we started to grow. These problems continued to be an important concern that threatened not only Trimark's growth but also the reputation of the entire industry. Trimark played a major part in helping pay for the new technologies that enabled advisors to sell funds without creating an avalanche of paper. This initiative included the formation of FundSERV, which initially helped Trimark distinguish itself from its competitors but eventually became a common order and settlement system for the entire industry. Mutual fund dealers could now compete with the banks and brokerage firms.

Our good fund performance, coupled with the company's excellent customer service, pushed Trimark even farther into the limelight and caused our growth to accelerate. During the years 1991 to 1996, Trimark also opened sizeable sales offices in Vancouver, Montreal, and Calgary.

The third issue the board wrestled with was how to broaden the range of products. Trimark was also was successful in this. Our array of fund offerings was continually expanding, and we held large meetings across the country when we were introducing new funds. In addition to the annual meeting for Trimark Financial Corporation, we organized yearly presentations for brokers and dealers outlining the performance of our family of funds. These gatherings were well attended – a far cry from the very early days, when Bob Krembil and I drove through a snow storm to an investor meeting in Peterborough, where we had about a dozen people in attendance.

These carefully scripted presentations required management personnel as well as fund managers to improve their public speaking skills. I personally found being centre stage a challenge, but I persisted and became a reasonably proficient speaker. You never know precisely when or whether you are going to win over an audience. When I was speaking to about four hundred investors in Kelowna, British Colombia, I made a few comments about our family's wonderful golden retriever. After the meeting, about a dozen women approached me and we discussed our pets. Business picked up in that region. Some of the dealers told me later that the consensus was that anybody who loved dogs, and particularly golden retrievers, couldn't be all bad.

The Boom Years

THE boom years of the mid-1990s caused our fund sales to skyrocket; monthly sales were as high as $500 million, equal to the combined sales of all of our competitors in that month. There is no question that the Trimark name became a powerful brand right across the country. There are many reasons for this. One of them is that we were able to attract and retain many talented and loyal individuals. I would love to name them, but the list is so long, I fear I would inadvertently leave someone out.

Most of the bright and capable people we hired over the years worked out extremely well. Of course, there is always some turnover, which is unfortunate. But Trimark staff did an excellent job of maintaining an easily understood investment and business philosophy for the company, all while maintaining the company's integrity.

In the late '90s, Trimark stayed out of tech stocks, as did many other value investors. We were concerned that the run-up in their prices had no lasting foundation. When the tech boom was heading for its peak, investors redeemed $6.6 billion from the Trimark funds over a thirty-month period. Net assets under management by Trimark declined to $23.5 billion as at December 31, 1999, from $29.1 billion a year earlier.

Nortel Networks Corp., formerly known as Northern Telecom Ltd., was Canada's leading high-tech company, which, together with its parent company, Bell Canada, came to dominate the Toronto Stock Exchange (TSE) Index. At one time, these two companies represented two-thirds of the TSE's value. Nortel hit a high of $124.50 and carried Bell Canada stock to record highs. From a market capitalization of $400 billion when the tech bubble burst, Nortel's market cap fell to less than $5 billion. Nortel filed for bankruptcy protection in 2009, and the stock is now worthless.

While Nortel, Bell, and the other tech stocks were pushing the TSE into the stratosphere, the relative performance of many of our funds suffered. Trimark, which for many years had been the epitome of prudent professional money management, was now being questioned as to whether it had lost its way in a new high-tech world. Although most of the large firms distributing Trimark funds did not come out publicly in favour of recommending that clients bail out of Trimark funds, they made it clear to their sales force that they would not discourage a trading opportunity.

Even the journalists and financial planners who had been loyal supporters over many years were beginning to question our wisdom during what would turn out to be a high-tech bubble. During this difficult period, Trimark slipped from its position, less than two years prior, as the second-largest fund company in Canada, falling behind Royal Mutual Funds, Mackenzie Financial, Fidelity, and TD Asset Management. This phase of relative underperformance caused the share price of Trimark Financial Corp. to slide from a high of $42 to around $15.

This was also a period of consolidation within the mutual fund industry, as both small and large fund companies were acquired or merged. Mackenzie Financial agreed to be acquired by Investors Group; AGF Mutual Funds acquired Global Strategy; and C.I. Mutual Funds and BPI merged, as did TD Asset Management and CT Investment Management.

Merger and Sale

TRIMARK also participated in the consolidation by merging with AMVESCAP Plc, one of the world's largest independent investment management companies, with more than US$400 billion under management.

The U.K.-based AMVESCAP, now called Invesco, was busy elsewhere buying GT Global Funds in Canada, AIM Funds in the U.S., and Perpetual Funds in the U.K. AMVESCAP in Canada was, at best, a midsize company, with $10 billion under management; it would have been forced to grow or sell, because it provided neither top performance nor the best products or service. Since the pool of Canadian fund investors was not growing at a brisk pace, AMVESCAP desired to grow much larger in Canada in order to stay competitive. They felt that merging with Trimark would enable them to combine two different investment styles, offering Trimark investors more options than had previously been available.

A merger of AMVESCAP and Trimark would create the second-largest mutual fund company in Canada, with more than $35 billion in assets under management. The only mutual fund company that would be larger was Winnipeg-based Investors Group, with $44 billion under management.

Numerous other parties were also interested in Trimark: Onex, Templeton, A.G.F., Mackenzie, Amex, Putnam, American Capital, and C.I. Funds. Sometimes, arrangements for secret meetings got mixed up and we found ourselves meeting two interested parties at the same hotel. This happened when Bob and I met with AMVESCAP executive chairman Charles Brady, and AIM's U.S. CEO Robert Graham, at the Intercontinental Hotel in Toronto. A meeting with the Mackenzie people, scheduled to take place at the York Club, was inadvertently switched to the Intercontinental. It turned out that they were waiting in another room down the hall.

On February 24, 2000, the board of directors of Trimark decided to pursue a number of informal expressions of interest, together with help from our financial advisor, RBC Dominion Securities. By April, we were focused on one candidate. Trimark issued a press release announcing that it was in discussions concerning a possible merger. Events then moved quickly. Four days later, Trimark entered into retention agreements with eleven senior executives of the company, entitling them to substantial severance packages. At our request, these golden parachutes did not apply to Bob or me.

On May 9, we made it official: AMVESCAP and Trimark announced a merger agreement, entitling Trimark shareholders to a combination of cash and shares worth C$27 per share, up from C$17 at the beginning of the year.

The response of both the Canadian and international press was generally favourable. Analysts said more deals in the sector would surely follow, and they did. Maitland Lammert, an analyst at Edward Jones, described it as "a generous offer ... at a nice premium to where Trimark was trading before the deal rumours emerged." "They had to pay a high price to seal the deal," said a Toronto-based analyst, who wished to remain anonymous.

Dan Richards, of Marketing Solutions, said, "Many shareholders are getting a good deal, considering how low Trimark shares have plunged recently." He added, "Trimark is also dealing with a company with a solid track record of successful acquisitions. In return, AMVESCAP is getting a very deep Canadian equity team, probably the deepest among the Canadian mutual fund industry."

It was a difficult time for me. We had just come through an incredible decade for equities, but looking to the next ten years, Bob and I were worried. We could see that the mutual funds industry was changing. With the increasing involvement of banks, it was becoming more competitive. While I had mixed feelings, I knew we had to be fair to our shareholders. The board agreed that the AMVESCAP offer was a good one and that this was the right thing to do, for all concerned. I still think it was the right decision.

Bob and I resigned, but I was asked to return as non-executive chairman of what was then called AIM Trimark. I was happy to do so. I was able to help management with the progressive integration of the AIM and Trimark people. I also made a number of cross-Canada trips introducing senior AIM executives to financial planners and brokers. These advisors had been important supporters of Trimark over many years. On these trips, the company chartered a Challenger jet. As a result, we covered the entire country in a very efficient and comfortable manner.

On the morning of September 11, 2001 (now more commonly known as 9/11), our group was in Saskatoon preparing to speak to a large gathering of advisors. Just before leaving my hotel room, sometime before seven-thirty a.m., Saskatchewan time, I turned on the television to see a large passenger jet slam into the first tower of the World Trade Center. By the time it was my turn to speak, the meeting had already started, and the audience and the presenters had no idea what was happening in New York. As I went into the meeting someone told me that the second tower had been hit.

I did my best to explain to the audience what I knew of the situation, and when I finished, I got a standing ovation. I'm not exactly sure why this occurred, but it may have had something to do with my glowing comments about Saskatoon in particular, and Canada in general, and the peacefulness we were all so lucky to enjoy.

Because of the horrendous events in New York, Washington, D.C., and Pennsylvania, all flights in Canada and the U.S. were grounded, so we spent three days in Saskatoon. Unlike some who were stranded far from home, we enjoyed beautiful weather; we rented bikes and travelled for miles along the Saskatchewan River, played golf, and saw all of the sights. I had never visited Saskatoon and was very taken with the city.

I spent three years as chairman of AIM Trimark (now known as Invesco Canada Ltd.). I also continued as chair of Trimark Trust and thoroughly enjoyed remaining close to many long-time colleagues. Although the Invesco people wanted me to stay on for another year or two, I decided it was better to retire before someone asked the question, "Is he never going to leave?" So I did retire, on July 31, 2005.

Today, I can proudly look at the thirty-year results for the Trimark Fund: A $10,000 initial investment in 1981 would be worth $232,400 today – an annualized return of over eleven percent.

But, just as important, I took away wonderful memories from the whole experience. When Bob, Michael, and I started Trimark, we had no idea of the incredible success that would ensue over the next two decades. We felt we understood the fund business and had an investment philosophy that we believed in and could articulate. Our plan was to run a small, focused operation that would produce good returns for the investors in our funds. We didn't have grandiose plans regarding future growth.

Starting an investment company at the bottom of a deep bear market was difficult, but we knew intuitively that it was an incredible investing opportunity and would only help us in the long run.

The people who joined us were remarkable and the camaraderie and esprit within the organization were infectious. Although there have been some remarkable corporate achievements in the digital world, the success and growth of Trimark were impressive.

I will always have fond memories of the employees, distributors, investors, and friends who helped make Trimark the success it is today, and wish to thank everyone who believed in us for their loyal support since our inception in September 1981. Trimark was certainly the highlight of my business career.

IX BUSINESS ADVENTURES

OVER the past fifty years – before, during, and since my time with Trimark – I have been involved in many small business ventures. I once read that only one in ten venture capital investments is a winner – and my record can attest to this bit of wisdom. In the early 1960s, I made some modest investments in several new enterprises started by close friends. Having known them for years, I was really betting on their drive, talent, and integrity. In most cases, I got quite involved with these companies in their early years and learned a great deal about industries that were foreign to me. I quickly learned that start-ups take considerably longer to mature and require more capital than originally envisioned before they become profitable – *if* they become profitable. My experience with these undertakings was usually positive and provided an interesting diversion from my day job.

My first such venture took place in the late 1950s, when I was articling with Clarkson Gordon. I made a small investment to help a friend, Tom Lowes, from Buffalo, who was a talented graphic artist and photographer. We bought a small brownstone house in downtown Buffalo, and, with my modest financial backing, Thomas Lowes Associates was born. It did well in its first four years because Tom had two excellent clients – Fisher-Price Toys in Buffalo and the Hammermill Paper Company, based in the state of Washington. His company had a handful of employees, but, needing an experienced sales manager to generate new business, Tom eventually brought in his son, Kevin. The company continues to enjoy success and now operates out of New York City.

In 1962, when I was working in McLeod Young Weir's research

department, a fraternity brother, Don Greer, started Duracon Precast Industries Ltd. to make manholes and catch basins. Manholes are basically concrete pipe with steps; they are installed vertically and taper to the size of the manhole cover. Don's father had been the president of a concrete pipe company, so Don and his brother were very familiar with the industry. In the early days, my involvement with the company entailed successfully pleading with the banks to help finance Duracon's expansion. This was a tough and competitive industry, but Duracon did well. Twelve years later, it was sold to Lake Ontario Cement.

Next, Don and I invested in a self-storage facility in Burlington, Ontario. We rounded up a number of other investors, and we now have eighteen facilities, all in the United States except for the original Burlington unit. Don was also one of the original investors in Trimark as was Vern Howe, who had been my supervisor at Clarkson Gordon.

In 1980, just before we started Trimark, Vern spotted a small ad in the *Globe and Mail* offering for sale a woolen mill located in Brandon, Manitoba. Although he knew nothing about the woolen business, he flew out to Brandon and bought the company, White Buffalo Woolen Mills Limited. The operation had been established in the nineteenth century and the factory looked to be right out of Charlie Chaplin's movie *Modern Times*. There were long black belts operating old carding and spinning machines. The noise was deafening, big fluffy balls of wool were flying everywhere, and the whole place seemed to be shaking. In spite of the ancient equipment, there was a lot of activity and spirit, and everyone seemed to know what they were doing.

Compressed raw wool arrived from New Zealand to be washed, dried, carded, and loosely spun. The wool was then dyed, a process that was something to behold. A worker dumped wool into one of the big vats of dye and proceeded to swish it around with his hands, then set it out to dry. The wool was used to create a Cowichan style of sweater, which was all the rage, particularly on the west coast of Canada, where hand knitting with unspun bulky wool was extremely popular.

Vern described the extraordinary popularity of hand knitting this coarse bulky wool as a fad, and he likened it to the hula-hoop craze. White Buffalo wool was a competitor to the Cowichan brand. As soon as the wool arrived at Woodward's, Eaton's, or the other department stores in the Canadian west, there would be lines of knitters eager to buy it up. Sometimes the wool never even made it to the shelves.

The wool was so thick that it didn't take too long to knit a sweater, which probably contributed to its popularity. Vern became adept at designing patterns, and, for three or four years, White Buffalo Woolen Mills was an outstanding financial success. We seemed to spend most of our time at our board meetings deciding how big the dividend should be.

Just as Vern had predicted, the product was a fad. Demand for the wool started to diminish. The Chinese were shipping ready-made sweaters to North America, which may have had something to do with the fall-off in demand. By the mid-1980s, the mill was unprofitable, so we sold the land and equipment. But while this fad lasted, it was an interesting and successful investment.

Before White Buffalo, Vern, Sonia, and I invested in another start-up company named E.D. Johne Design Ltd. It was the brainchild of Edie Johne, the wife of one of my business colleagues, Hans Johne. A former fashion model, Edie was also a designer and knew a great deal about Toronto's garment district, near Spadina and King Streets. When people learned that I was an investor in Edie's company, they exclaimed, "My goodness, I didn't know you were in the *schmatta* business." I later learned that this is the Yiddish term for the garment industry.

Our whole family helped out in many ways at E.D. Johne Design. We worked in the shipping room, sent out invoices, and did the payroll. It was a great experience for everyone to learn what is involved in designing and marketing ladies' fashions. We discovered that it's a very difficult and demanding industry; in fact, at that time, the entire garment business was in the process of having to compete internationally, due to the removal of protective tariffs for the Canadian industry.

One enterprise I supported in 2009, and continue to fund, is a Montreal-based firm, Voti Inc. Its products comprise a family of 3D X-ray scanners capable of detecting a wide range of materials – explosives, weapons, narcotics, contraband, cell phones, etc. The company was founded by William Awad, an electronic engineer who describes himself as an inventor. I agree with his description, but hasten to point out that he is also a good businessman and a superb salesman. William was born in Lebanon and speaks fluent Arabic, Spanish, French, and English.

Although Voti is still waiting for approvals from European, Canadian, and U.S. governments for sales to airports, the company is already selling to embassies, jails, nuclear facilities, military bases, and other high-risk installations. Currently, a high percentage of Voti's sales come from the Middle East. Whether we like the way the world is going or not, this is a fast-growing industry, and Voti has state-of-the-art products with very competitive prices.

Over the years, I got involved with a number of other small enterprises. Retailing and prospecting were two of these that went nowhere. I took a pass on investing in restaurants, although I had many opportunities; I couldn't understand how the business could make any money on a sustained basis.

For a long time, another area I steered clear of was the movie industry, although making movies had always intrigued me. Then, in 2008, Sonia and I took the plunge and invested in a movie called *The Wicker Tree*. This film was a sequel to *The Wicker Man*, a cult movie released nearly forty years ago, produced and directed by our good friend Robin Hardy. Robin is the husband of Vicki Webster, a Montrealer who became a close friend when we lived in Paris in the 1960s. This new film is based on a book written by Robin called *Cowboys for Christ*, a title that was too much for some potential American investors, although it accurately described the movie's theme.

The storyline involves an attractive young evangelical couple from rural Texas who are dispatched by their church to a small village in Scotland. Their intention is to convert the local population to their particular brand of Christianity. The movie is both a horror film and a comedy, and we hope it catches the attention of the cult following that was created by *The Wicker Man*. The movie opened in January 2012 to good reviews.

Venture capital is another entire area of investment opportunity. Venture capital investors are institutions and individuals that are willing to invest in small start-ups that have no proven track record. Another term used for this is "angel investing." During the incredible run-up in the high tech industry in the 1990s, a number of venture capital funds appeared. Money was flooding into these funds, both in Canada and the U.S. Harvard MBAs who traditionally gravitated to Wall Street and investment banking were now starting their careers at relatively small venture capital firms. By the end of the 1990s, there were almost three hundred venture capital groups in Canada.

In the mid-'90s, I invested in a venture capital fund run by a couple of bright ex-bankers. Of the ten investments made by this fund, only the last one was a success. This winner nearly made up for the losses taken by the first nine.

The popularity of venture capital evaporated, however, when the dot-com bubble burst in 2000. Both institutional and retail investors lost a lot of money, and private investors were not willing to give venture capital a second chance. These days, the funds that remain are much more demanding of budding entrepreneurs who are looking for capital.

Investing in these funds was quite different from the kind of angel investing I had pursued previously. In venture capital, or angel investing, I learned a new language, terms bandied about that I had never come across in my years as a chartered accountant. When looking forward, you didn't talk about an anticipated "return on investment," you said, "This could be a ten bagger!" Also, when the hoped-for profitability did not materialize within a reasonable period of time, the venture capitalist simply indicated the project needed "a longer runway."

So great has been the fall-off in interest, that while in 2000, $6 billion was raised for one thousand Canadian startups, in 2011, there were fewer than a dozen VC firms operating in Canada with just over $1.1 billion raised and roughly one-third of that came from American investors.

In 2006, Sonia and I acted as angel investors in backing Greg Philpott, who had done some excellent work for Trimark as a consultant. Greg founded a company that he named mDialog. Broadcasters and cable operators use mDialog to deliver commercials in video formats to tablets, smartphones, Internet TV, and computers.

Greg has established excellent relationships with a number of big names in the computer business, including Cisco, Apple, Android, Adobe, Akamai, and Roku. In the summer of 2011, BlackBerry Partners Fund (now called relayventures) invested $5 million in mDialog. That fund describes Greg as a pioneer in Internet video and digital asset management. John Albright, who is the managing partner of BlackBerry Partners Fund, and everyone connected with mDialog see great potential for the company in the years ahead.

This type of investing is exciting and unpredictable; you can know the outcome only a few years down the road. It is not for everybody – certainly not the faint of heart.

X EARLY FAMILY DAYS

Toronto

MY upbringing was in a house in London that stayed in the family for about fifty years, and all of my summers were spent at the same cottage at Port Stanley. In my married life, on the other hand, our family led a mildly itinerant life, because of frequent moves due to business: from Toronto to Montreal, then to Paris, then back to Toronto. Our three children came to remember living in ten different houses and as many as seven country properties. In recalling events in the life of the family, I tend to associate them with the house we were living in at the time. I believe this is how Sheila, John, and Jacquie would also remember stories from their formative years.

Brentwood Towers

In the summer of 1958, before our September wedding, Sonia and I went hunting for our first home in Toronto and found an attractive one-bedroom apartment in the Brentwood Towers. This was a new development within walking distance of the Davisville subway station on Yonge Street. We were on the sixteenth floor and had a great view looking south to Lake Ontario. Many Clarkson Gordon employees lived in this area, all trying to look businesslike in shirts and ties and fedoras. Sonia was finishing her degree at the University of Toronto and wore bobby socks and saddle shoes. I was never sure whether her attire was appropriate as we sauntered to the subway along with aspiring "suits" going to their place of business.

Since we were both studying, we each had our own desk – one in the bedroom and one in the living room. We had my small upright piano, and I had purchased a banjo a few years earlier; I suggested to Sonia that she take lessons on the latter so we could work up an act. She closed the bedroom door and plunked away on this rather large, noisy instrument. One day, I received a telephone call from the banjo academy on Bloor Street where Sonia was taking lessons. A very nice gentleman, who was probably just going through the list of students, asked if he was speaking to Mr. Labatt. I assured him that he had the right person. He then asked if I was pleased with my child's progress. I said that I certainly was, but that Sonia was my wife, not my child.

When Sonia was writing her final exams, she was pregnant with Sheila and had a bad case of morning sickness. Since she had always been such a good student, I tried to encourage her to tell the school about her situation; I hoped they would let her skip some of the exams. However, she persevered and wrote them all, receiving her BSc (Honours) with flying colours.

Around this time, my brother, Jack, who was living in Winnipeg, shipped us a large wooden crate containing a trophy from one of his hunting trips: a huge set of moose antlers with considerable flesh still attached. We were both away for a couple of weeks at that time, so the superintendent placed this crate in our living room. On our return, we were overpowered by the odor of putrefying moose flesh. We dragged the crate out to the balcony, where it remained for the rest of the winter. These antlers, cleaned up and properly mounted, are still hanging above the fireplace at my sister-in-law's cottage on Smoke Lake in Algonquin Park.

20 BELGRAVE AVENUE

With the arrival of Sheila in November 1960, we moved to a three-bedroom house on Belgrave Avenue, near the Cricket Club, in the Avenue Road and Wilson area. It was a nice house with a finished recreation room in the basement and cost $25,000. It had one major defect, which only became apparent the following spring. The basement flooded, and we had to put the furniture on wooden platforms because the water reached three inches deep. This would have been bearable except that we had a Jamaican nanny living in the basement at the time, and she had to wear rubber boots to get around.

In December 1962, when Sonia was in the hospital expecting our twins – John and Jacquie – my mother and her housekeeper, Truce, came from London to help look after Sheila, who was two years old. One day, I heard Mother running around calling out to Truce because she couldn't find Sheila. They both called her name, but there was no reply. Then they called out "cookies" and "candies." Still no reply. However, they did detect a faint noise of something breaking. It was Sheila, sitting behind the Christmas tree, plucking ornaments off the tree and dropping them on the hardwood floor, to watch and hear them shatter.

When the twins first came home from the hospital, they shared one crib, both lying crossways, with big blanket pins holding the covers in place, and them apart. Eventually, we bought a second crib, with both children still sharing the same room. As they grew and could stand in their cribs, Jacquie did something that really surprised me. Once, when John threw his teddy bear out of his crib, Jacquie climbed out of her crib, retrieved the teddy, gave it to John, and climbed back into her crib. This eventually developed into a game of toss and retrieve.

When the twins were eighteen months old, we decided it was time to find a larger house, as we only had one bathroom on the second floor, and there seemed to be diapers everywhere. Like many of the houses built after the Second World War, ours was poorly insulated, and the diapers stored in a diaper pail in the closet froze solid in the winter. Also, having our Jamaican housekeeper living in the flooded basement was less than perfect.

We sold the house to Don Fullerton, who ultimately became the president of the Canadian Imperial Bank of Commerce. I later met Don and told him I had always felt guilty that I had not reported the spring flooding to the agent when selling the house. He told me I should not have been concerned because he never lived there. He was transferred to New York right after he bought it.

Next, we found quite a large house in Forest Hill on Dunvegan Road, which was much closer to downtown Toronto. It had a third floor, which would be ideal for our housekeeper. We were sure she would love it. On the contrary, she found the house too big, and, missing the coziness of our former house, she quit.

This house had quite a steep driveway sloping toward the street. One time we left our large station wagon parked in its usual place in the driveway at the side of the house but forgot to put it in park. The big car started moving and finally rolled down the driveway and across the street, smashing into a large tree on a neighbour's lawn. The car was badly damaged, but fortunately no one was injured. The tree also survived the impact.

Our immediate neighbour to the south was P.T. Molson, the manager of Molson's Toronto brewery. His children were a little older than ours. One day, the Molson kids threw some Molson bottles into our backyard. So, with a little help from me, our kids retaliated by throwing a couple of Labatt empties into the Molson yard, which they found very amusing. The first time this happened, we all had a good laugh. However, when it happened again, the adults decided the game was over.

This new house had plenty of room for our growing family, with an extra room on the second floor. This room had no furniture. We thought we would turn it into a playroom with a few little tables and let the kids run around and draw pictures on the walls if they felt so inclined. We left the door open and put a baby gate across the doorway. When we handed the kids cookies and juice boxes over the playroom gate, it felt a bit like feeding animals at the zoo.

Not all of our memories of Dunvegan are happy ones. Sadly, Sonia's father died there of a massive heart attack. We were having coffee just after dinner on a Saturday evening. Mr. Armstrong had recently retired after fifty years with the Bell Telephone Company and a few weeks earlier had returned from a very enjoyable two-month European holiday with Madame Armstrong.

Montreal

W HEN I was working for McLeod Young Weir and requested a transfer to their Montreal office, Sheila was turning four and the twins were two years old. When I suggested the Town of Mount Royal or the West Island, my sister Mary convinced us that this would be a mistake and that we should live in Westmount. She had lived in Montreal since the mid-1950s and had recently married her second husband, Rusty Lamb. At that time, Rusty was a senior partner with the law firm of Lafleur and Brown. He was later appointed a judge of the Quebec Superior Court by John Turner, who was then federal Minister of Justice in the Liberal government – despite the fact that Rusty was campaign chairman for a Progressive Conservative candidate in Westmount. Rusty had been born in Montreal. He and Mary seemed to know everyone.

3114 Daulac Road

We bought a lovely old stone house in Westmount, on a short street partway up Mount Royal, giving us a panoramic view of the city and the Saint Lawrence River. For us, Montreal was a welcoming city with a small and somewhat cliquish English-speaking minority. Sonia and I met dozens of new friends and felt very much at home. The twins were still too young for school, but Sheila attended kindergarten at Miss Edgar's and Miss Cramp's School. It was so close, she didn't have to cross a street to get there. Sheila remembers taking some chalk from school and writing her name on a wall with it on the way home. Sonia made her return the chalk.

The twins were too young at the time to remember much about our three years at that house. I recall taking John to the doctor after he stuck the end a paper clip in a light socket. Fortunately, he was not hurt badly, but his hand was burned, so the doctor put a huge bandage on it, completely enclosing his hand. Jacquie and Sheila were quite distraught at the sight of it.

The children all had mild cases of chicken pox when we lived on Daulac Road and passed the disease on to me. I was thirty years old and had never been infected with this childhood disease. I was covered from head to toe with pox and was medicated with a variety of lotions. I stayed in bed and didn't want the kids to see me in this state. However, Jacquie did get into the bedroom and saw hundreds of pox on my leg. I remember her precise words: "Oh Daddy, them are lots!"

THE LAMBS

My sister lived a few blocks away on Picquet Road. Mary and Rusty had two girls – Jennifer, who was the daughter of her first husband, David Morgan, and Brenda, Rusty's daughter, who was about Sheila's age. Mary was active with the Society for the Prevention of Cruelty to Animals (SPCA) and solicited funds in her best French accent at local gas stations. "Donnez-moi quelque chose pour les pauvres bébés phoques" (seals). She also rescued baby raccoons and went on the radio to look for a good home for them.

The Lambs also had a house just across the border in Vermont. It was a charming old farmhouse – with a mouse problem. Mary trapped mice in live traps and let them out at her barn. After a few days, she thought she recognized some of the mice, so she decided to paint their nails. Sure enough, mice with painted nails were back in the house nearly as quickly as she was. She then decided to transport them in a cardboard box and release them across the border in a field in Quebec. When she opened the box, she discovered that some of the mice had given birth, so she took them all back to her barn.

One evening, the Lambs and the Labatts were having dinner at the Beaver Club in the Queen Elizabeth Hotel. After many "bird bath" martinis, Mary and Sonia excused themselves to attend the ballet at Place des Arts. Rusty then announced to me that he was going to divorce my sister. He insisted that this was not a joke and that he was fed up with transporting three dogs and two cats in a station wagon to their house in Vermont each weekend.

I acknowledged that I understood the situation. He then went on to say that Mary could not stand another divorce. I told Rusty that Mary was a very strong woman and that, in my opinion, she could handle five divorces and not to worry about it. Rusty then announced that he had to get back to the office and we said good night. That was the end of Rusty's pronouncements on the subject.

RIDING DAYS

Neither Sonia nor I had grown up with the "horsey set," yet somehow, after moving to Montreal, we got scooped up by Herb O'Connell, Master of the Lake of Two Mountains Hunt, in Hudson. He was a forceful individual who never took no for an answer. He had founded a major construction company in Quebec and was very close to Maurice Duplessis, the founder and leader of the Union Nationale and premier for most of the period from 1936 to 1959.

Over the course of my life and our marriage, I have observed that when you get caught up in a new leisure activity, the new pursuit often takes precedence over everything else. For me, this has certainly been true with regard to flying, sailing, tennis, and golf. It was not true with skiing, as I've had a love/hate relationship with this sport over the years.

Riding was a new sport for both of us, and it seemed to take over our life during our three years in Montreal. We ended up owning horses, a horse trailer, and a house in riding country. We had a new circle of friends who were a wonderful mix of English- and French-speaking Montrealers.

Although we became reasonably proficient riders, we were always over-horsed and under-skilled. Our ability and our horsemanship did not, in my opinion, qualify us as sufficiently competent to handle the difficulties and dangers encountered in the "hunt." Nevertheless, we did receive our colours as full-fledged members of the Lake of Two Mountains Hunt.

Mr. O'Connell and his good friend Dini Appleton invited us to join them and other members of the Hunt for a hack. Sonia and I didn't even know the meaning of the term. We looked it up in the dictionary and found it to be "exercising a horse on the trails." The dictionary also describes the British hacking jacket in considerable detail. We arrived at the Club on that beautiful summer day with every clothing accessory known to man, so we would not embarrass our host – or ourselves.

The ride was organized for our benefit before we became members of the Club, to allow us to observe an actual hunt. We were at the back of the pack on horses borrowed from Mr. O'Connell that were accustomed to being up at the front with the Master of the Hunt. A small group stayed at the rear with us. I was having difficulty keeping my horse in a controlled canter. The horse wanted to do a flat-out gallop. Even in a semi-controlled

Dressed and ready at the Lake of Two Mountains Hunt in Hudson, Quebec.

state, I was moving pretty fast. The very moment I looked to my right to see where Sonia was, she passed me like I was standing still. Sonia charged across a paved road with me chasing her. The next thing I knew, she had steered her horse through an open door into a barn, where the horse finally halted.

When I caught up, Sonia, still in the saddle, let me have it verbally with both barrels: "You're going to get us both killed. I don't care what Mr. O'Connell thinks; I'm not doing any more of this crazy sport."

At that moment, Mr. O'Connell appeared at the open door on his big black horse and asked Sonia how things were going.

She smiled politely and replied feebly, "Oh, fine."

We then rejoined other members of the group, and Mr. O'Connell approached Judge François Auclair, who was riding an old police horse by the name of General.

"Remember, François, when I sold you General for one dollar on the condition that if I wanted the horse back you would return it?" O'Connell said to the judge. "Well, I would like General back right now. Would you please let Sonia ride General and you can have hers."

The judge graciously obliged, and Sonia got on reliable old General. Judge Auclair mounted Sonia's horse, which reared, ditched the judge, and took off.

The next time, Mr. O'Connell lent us two well-behaved horses, and we joined about twenty-five members of the Hunt on a fifteen- to twenty-mile cross-country ride to the Stone House. I am not sure who owned the house, but it was the finishing point for many of these group rides. After a leisurely ride, we dismounted, and cocktails and food were served. There was singing, and the whole post-hack party was quite festive. Usually the horses were trucked back to the stables and transportation arranged for the riders. Even in the depths of winter, we got bundled up and went for a hack or a sleigh ride, with Mr. O'Connell driving a four-horse team.

Our first real hunt, complete with hounds, had a somewhat unusual ending. By this time, Sonia and I had our own horses, Silver and Gribouille, and we were somewhat in control. We held our horses back a bit and were not at the head of the pack when there was a kill. The hounds had cornered a fox, and the huntsman dismounted and walked into the pack of hounds. Tradition calls for the huntsman to place the mask (the whole head) of the animal on his saddle.

As he passed us, I said to Sonia, "That's not a fox, it's a wolf."

"Don't embarrass us; of course it's a fox," Sonia whispered.

Well, it turned out I was right. It was a wolf. This was quite an unusual occurrence in this area, and dangerous for the hounds.

These riding days were exciting but produced a lot of anxiety for both of us. I worried all week about the Saturday hunt. When we went "cubbing" (training young hounds) at the end of August, I poured Scotch into our coffee cups at five a.m. as we left our house to go the stables. Bo Lewis, a genial stockbroker, beckoned me over on one of our first hunts to tell me that my bridle needed adjusting. I followed him into a wooded area where he offered me a drink from his flask. He said he felt I needed a bit of false courage, and he was right. I didn't tell him that I'd already taken a dram. When I dismounted later in the day, happy to be alive, the stirrup cups showed their effect. My knees buckled, and I crumpled to the ground.

When we moved to France, we sold our horses and the trailer. We kept our saddles and rented our country house on Rang St. François to an American couple. I was not unhappy to sell the horses, which had taken over our lives. On the other hand, this was an exciting time of our life, and we fully intended to return to Montreal and our house in riding country.

PARIS

OUR move from Toronto to Montreal had been somewhat disorienting to our family, but moving to Europe was a much greater challenge. Sonia's French was already quite good, but for the rest of us, the new language was a problem. A former Montrealer, Fred Wanklyn, met us at Orly Airport and helped us arrange taxis for the ride into town. Fred was working in the commercial section of the Canadian embassy in Paris and was married to our good friend Vicky Webster. John, then six, elected to travel in Fred's Mercedes; after we arrived at our hotel, he commented on how well Paris taxi drivers spoke English.

We stayed for a few days at the Hotel Vendôme, a small hotel bordering Place Vendôme in central Paris. After an overnight flight from Montreal, we were all excited, exhausted, and hungry. The hotel restaurant was not open mid-morning, but the staff offered to serve us fruit and croissants in the bar area. We installed ourselves on footstools circled around a low coffee table, and awaited our first French meal. We were all very content, and John leaned back to enjoy his first croissant on French soil. Backwards he went, heels over his head, nicking the table top, spilling the drinks, and landing on his back on the oriental rug, all the while still hanging onto the croissant.

16 Avenue de Breteuil

Finding an apartment was an adventure. At one address, we had a brief conversation with the tenant of one of the apartments, Françoise Sagan, who wrote the famous French novel *Bonjour Tristesse*, when she was nineteen. After much searching, we rented a furnished apartment on Avenue de Breteuil in the seventh *arrondissement*, but elected to stay at the hotel until our belongings arrived from Montreal. The owner of our apartment was a fussy aristocrat who lived in the suburbs and liked to be paid in cash on a monthly basis. The apartment was stuffed with oversized furniture as well as many glass-encased cabinets full of fragile antique pottery and silverware. We were always nervous that we would break the glass.

Our apartment comprised the fourth floor (*troisième étage*), which we reached in a tiny elevator. The kids were not allowed to use the lift, with its complicated set of doors, so they ran up the spiral marble staircase instead. During the oyster season in the fall, we walked around the corner and bought *belons*, which were shucked and sitting on crushed ice. When we had guests and ran out of gin, Jacquie got a string bag and, even though she was just a child, bought a bottle of Beefeater from the local grocer. In addition to the grocer, there was a butcher and a small hardware store. On our last trip to Paris, in 2009, we visited our former neighbourhood and saw that, so typical of Paris, all of these local shops were still in business, and the neighbourhood had not changed.

During the two years we lived on Avenue de Breteuil, the kids became very familiar with their surroundings and rode their bikes to a coffee shop across from Les Invalides and Napoleon's Tomb. Tourist buses stopped at this shop and the sightseers took pictures of the monument. Many of the tourists were American. Our three kids engaged them in conversation, instructing them in purchasing postcards and stamps, speaking to them in broken English with a strong French accent. I overheard a gentleman from Texas telling his wife that these little French kids could speak English "real good."

AUNT ANGIE

Every year that we lived in France, we looked forward to a visit from Aunt Angie, the grande dame of the Labatt family. She was the widow of my father's only brother, Hugh, and usually spent two months in the winter travelling in Europe. In London, she always took a suite at the Dorchester, and we often visited her there. In Paris, she stayed at the

Aunt Angie with Sonia and the kids in Paris.

Hôtel Ritz on Place Vendôme, which is now famous as the hotel from which Princess Diana departed just before she was killed in a car accident in 1997.

In 1968, Aunt Angie arrived in Paris well before Easter, and we joined her for lunch at an elegant restaurant. After we were seated at our table, John reached toward his side plate, and with a clenched fist pounded a decorative square of butter that had been placed on it. We were a bit in shock at this activity, especially in front of Aunt Angie, and asked him why he did that to his butter.

"Oh, sorry, I thought it was cheese," was his answer.

Aunt Angie's visits always brought a touch of adventure and excitement. With the student protests becoming very worrisome that spring, the hotel slipped daily notices under her door, warning of new developments. On one occasion, she was advised to fill her bathtub in preparation for a water shortage. On another, she was informed that all commercial flights had been cancelled. She dealt with these obstacles with flair and confidence. With respect to the water shortage, she filled every vessel in sight, thinking we might need some, too. The flight back to London was solved by gaining passage through her contacts at the BBC on their charter flight from a private field. It was a small aircraft; she was obliged to hold on her lap the cans of television film that had recorded the student riots.

FRENCH DOCTORS

Doctors in France seemed to be cut from a different cloth than the physicians we knew in Canada. We were used to thinking of our doctor as a god with a comprehensive knowledge of our condition. In France, the doctors liked to discuss a patient's symptoms with the patient.

"What do you think your problem is?" they often asked.

I felt like saying, "I have no idea, and anyway that's your job."

Sonia and I went to a GP who had an office right across the street from our apartment. He sat in his consulting room on a chair with rollers, discussing our concerns. Once he was ready to write a prescription, in a flash, he rolled his chair to his desk about fifteen feet away, typed up a lengthy *ordinance* on an old-fashioned typewriter, then rolled back and handed over the prescription.

Once when I was complaining of a bad head cold and fever, he began by asking me if I could *supporter l'alcohol*. I wasn't entirely sure of the relevance of this question but said that I could. He then proceeded to type his prescription, which read something like this: "Buy a bottle of Beefeater gin and go to bed. Boil water and add some lemon juice and sugar, then add a significant amount of gin. Stay in bed and keep drinking the potion until you feel better."

SCHOOLING IN PARIS

The kids' schooling was rigorous. The days were long, and there was little in the way of exercise. At first, Sheila was enrolled at L'Ecole Active Bilingue, while the twins attended a boys' pre-kindergarten school, Saint François Xavier, which was just across the street. John later attended L'Ecole Active Bilingue, and the girls transferred to the Cours Victor Hugo, a girls' school, very close to our second apartment on Blvd. Flandrin in the sixteenth *arrondissement*. We walked to school with the girls wearing their little berets and handed them over to Madame La Surveillante Générale, who announced their names to the teachers on a walkie-talkie, which in French is called a *talkie-walkie*.

When Sheila and Jacquie attended L'Ecole Active Bilingue, they were taught basic French from an illustrated book called *Blackie et Mousie*. The same cat and mouse characters were employed at the Cours Victor Hugo teach French kids how to speak English. Sheila one day complained to Sonia that her English teacher could barely speak English, and had asked Sheila to help her out, enlisting her to teach the story.

Some time later, Sonia was invited to have tea with the headmistress of the school and was asked if she was pleased with the girls' progress. Sonia replied that she was very happy but did mention Sheila's negative observations pertaining to the English teacher. It turned out that the headmistress was in fact Sheila's English teacher.

On returning to the apartment, feeling mortified, Sonia exploded with the words, "Sheila, why didn't you tell me that your English teacher was also the headmistress?"

"But Mommy, you didn't ask," Sheila responded calmly.

Renting in France

It seems to me that the rules pertaining to renting things in France are quite different for foreigners. The French assume that foreigners know what they are doing. And if they don't, *tant pis* (too bad)! No one ever asks the foreigner for proof of competence. Three instances of this come to mind.

I once rented a horse and buggy with Fred Wanklyn and proceeded to drive the family through a beautifully wooded park outside Paris. Although I had done a considerable amount of riding in Montreal, I had never actually "driven" a horse. It requires quite a different skill set than riding on its back. You have to make sweeping right turns or you will catch the right wheel of the carriage on a post. Fortunately, I avoided this hazard, but we did get trapped in a parking lot mainly because we had no idea how to make the horse back up. Our answer was to have everyone disembark from the carriage and, while someone held the horse's head, we lifted the carriage and turned it 180 degrees.

Another example was the time we signed the kids up for sailing lessons in Sainte-Maxime on the Mediterranean. The instructors put the kids in little square-ended dinghies, and in a moderate offshore wind, set them free. Our three children had no idea how to sail, and the next thing I knew, they were heading out to sea with the nearest landfall being Algeria.

Then there was the time our good friend John Frankel was visiting us in Sainte-Maxime. We decided to rent a cabin cruiser and take it about thirty miles to St. Tropez and the famous nude beach La Plage de Pampelonne. At this point in my life, I had little navigational skill and no idea how to anchor safely; basically, I should never have been handed the keys to a medium-size powerboat.

We dropped our wives off at the beach and, after failing to anchor the boat properly, finally tied the cruiser up to someone else's permanent buoy and swam to shore. To the surprise of our spouses, John talked me into taking off our bathing suits, whereupon he threw mine up on the beach. Fortunately, Sonia threw it back to me in the water so I was able to go ashore properly attired.

SUMMERS IN FRANCE

Our last two summer holidays in France (1970 and 1971) were spent at a charming housing complex called Les Mas de Guerrevieille, just outside Sainte-Maxime, on the road to St. Tropez. One owner of a villa in this compound was Jean-Claude Killy, who won three gold medals in downhill skiing at the 1968 winter Olympics in Grenoble.

Jean-Claude was married to the beautiful French actress Danièle Gaubert, and they had two young children. Jean-Claude and wife ran a swimming program for young people at the community swimming pool. This is where our kids really learned to swim, and as they got better, they entered swimming races run by the Killys.

Because of our proximity to St. Tropez, there were sometimes

Our family in St. Tropez.

discussions at the dining room table regarding the nude beaches. One day, when I was puttering around the Mediterranean in a paddle boat with our son, John, he asked me to alert him if I ever saw a *femme nue*. I assured him that I would.

Jennifer Lamb, my sister Mary's eldest daughter, visited us at Sainte-Maxime. I teased her, telling her that at a famous restaurant on the Plage de Pampelonne called La Voile Rouge, ladies who lunched removed their tops. Poor Jennifer nearly had a heart attack on the spot. We later did visit the restaurant; Jennifer wore at least three shirts and a poncho, despite the ninety-degree weather.

Those summers on the Côte d'Azur were perfect for all of us, and although the area was very busy during the month of August, the whole family got to know the south of France very well. Years later, when our children were in their teens, Sonia and I spent three weeks driving through Provence with a view to buying a place, in order to escape the Canadian winters. For all kinds of reasons (distance, climate, and economics), we decided against it and proceeded to build a house in Tucson.

When we lived in Paris, I asked friends how many weeks of vacation they had each year, and they replied that six weeks was the norm. I later realized that these six weeks were in addition to the month of August, which everyone takes off. I concluded that the three things the French loved most were their wine, their five hundred kinds of cheese, and their holidays.

When we first moved to Paris, Sonia and I decided we could spend the month of August right in the city and didn't need to find a vacation spot. When we mentioned this to Jean and Albane Huyghues Despointes, French friends from Montreal who had returned to France, they said it was absolutely unthinkable to remain in Paris during August. They suggested that we rent a little house on Île de Ré, where they had been vacationing for many years. And so we did.

Île de Ré is a small, low-lying island off the west coast of France, near La Rochelle in the Bay of Biscay. It is one hundred and sixty miles from Paris, which was not too long a drive for the kids. The island is about fifteen miles long and only about two to three miles wide. It was a lovely, quiet vacation. All of us spent considerable time at the beach as well as riding our bicycles around this flat yet picturesque island. It was quiet and charming, although friends who visited the island recently tell me it is now both busy and commercialized.

The next summer, we rented a house in the town of Saint-Jean-de-Luz, situated just south of Biarritz on the Bay of Biscay, close to the Spanish border in Basque country. My ancestors, whose name was Labat (with one "t"), were Huguenots originally from the Pays Basque. They eventually migrated to Ireland before coming to Canada.

John Dinnick's daughter, Vicky, lived with us that August, and helped look after the kids. Sonia and I often played at the beautiful tennis club in Saint-Jean-de-Luz, where we met René Lacoste on a number of occasions. Monsieur Lacoste had been an outstanding French tennis player in his younger years and founded the famous sportswear line with the crocodile logo. Sonia and I had joined an exclusive club in the Bois de Boulogne in Paris, the Polo de Paris, not to play polo but to learn to play tennis.

TRÉON

For most of our time in France, we rented a small cottage in a tiny village called Tréon, sixty miles southwest of Paris, and close to the cathedral town of Chartres. We spent nearly every weekend at the cottage, which was situated next to the village church and looked out onto an acre of land enclosed by a five-foot-high stone wall. The cottage was owned by Monsieur Trocmé, a French diplomat living in San Francisco.

Our kids remember every detail of their weekends in Tréon. The characters we met there were people from the countryside and not at all like Parisians. I think we were the first foreigners that the locals, including the parish priest, had ever met. One day, Sonia day asked the priest if he had ever visited North America. He replied that not only had he never been abroad, he had never even been to Paris.

Madame Jourdan was the property manager as well as our housekeeper. She was a large woman with a very loud voice who walked with a pronounced limp. Nearly every time I met her, she began the conversation with, "Pendant la deuxième guerre mondiale," and then told me that during that war she had been wounded in a bombardment.

Someone, perhaps Monsieur Trocmé, must have told her that I was an investment guru, because she then proceeded to tell me she had hidden a stash of gold somewhere in her house and cash under her mattress and would ask my opinion as to what to do with it. I always gave her the same advice, and that was to put the gold and the money in the bank, and she always replied that she didn't trust the banks. Everyone in the village seemed to know that Mme Jourdan had some gold hidden away. I was truly worried that she would be robbed.

The Pelletiers lived next door and had three children who were a little older than ours. There were two boys, Alain and Bruno. Both Sheila and Jacquie have since told me that they received their first kiss from these two lotharios. Monsieur Pelletier was definitely a "wino," always walking around with a bottle of red wine. He was strict with the boys. I recall him marching Alain home from our place holding him by the ear and kicking him in the backside.

On Bastille Day, July 14, the townspeople got dressed up and, accompanied by a small brass band, marched to the local cemetery to pay their respects. We were invited by the locals to join them and were flattered to be included. As we started out, one of our kids asked us not to speak English as they wanted us to blend in. After we were on our way, I asked one of our kids a question in French and was asked not to speak French either since my accent was quite pronounced. Nor did the kids want Sonia to buy their friends a bottle of Orangina after the parade, because this gesture made us stand out. The children felt quite accepted as long as Sonia and I kept out of the picture.

DRIVING IN FRANCE

For most of the time that we lived in France, we owned a top-of-the-line Citroën, a DS 21. Its pneumatic suspension created vertical movement when stopping and starting, which tended to make Jacquie carsick.

I never did try to obtain a French driver's licence, because I was advised that I wouldn't pass the test. On the few occasions that I had been stopped by the police for speeding or parking, I got by with a Quebec driver's licence, which was bilingual. However, on returning to Paris from Tréon one Sunday evening, I was pulled over by the police for speeding. The required sudden stop caused a big bowl of spaghetti in the trunk to spill its contents all over everything back there.

My licence was in my jacket in that same trunk, so the policeman and I were confronted with the horrible spaghetti sight together. When he saw the Quebec licence, he proceeded to tell me about the time he was stopped by the police in Montreal and how his fellow "policeman" (the only English word he used) gave him a ticket. He then told me he was going to tear my licence in two and mail the other half to a Montreal address.

After his long story he looked at me and said that I gave him the impression that I didn't understand a word he was saying. I understood that part and had to admit to him that his impression was more or less true. During this fractured exchange of accusations and apologies, Jacquie was throwing up at the side of the road. With the spaghetti-covered contents of the trunk and Jacquie's *mal-de-mer*, the policeman apparently concluded that I had been sufficiently punished and let me go with a warning.

Hunting in Ireland

France is not known for outstanding dentistry, so a friend from Toronto, Marion Morange Selig, who lived in a beautiful townhouse in Paris, recommended a dentist who had been trained in California. Jacques Vettier was one of the best. He looked after us professionally and later introduced us to his new Californian wife, Candice, who, at that time, was struggling with the French language. When he heard that we were Canadian, he assumed we were hunters. Soon we were shooting skeet and trap at a local club and became the proud owners of two double-barrelled shotguns.

Jacques and Candice became friends, and the four of us took two trips to Ireland to shoot snipe, woodcock, and ducks. We flew from Paris to Cork, rented two cars, and drove up the west coast of Ireland. Jacques had arranged that we would hire a ghillie, who would join us, accompanied by his dog, which would flush out the game. Sonia shot a "double" and brought down two plover, a protected species. The ghillie was worried that she would shoot the swans, which were floating everywhere on the Shannon River.

On one occasion, we exchanged cars, and our guide took us to a different location from where Jacques' ghillie took Jacques and Candice. I ended up with his set of twelve-gauge matched Purdeys, a very expensive gun. I went out with our ghillie, promising to be very careful not to damage these treasures. We were walking on bouncy grassland when all of a sudden the ground gave way and I began to slide into a peat bog. All I could think of was saving the Purdey, so as I sank further I held the gun above my head. I was up to my waist when the ghillie thrust the end of his walking stick at me and hauled me out of the bog. Without his help, I think I would be there to this day.

I was soaking wet, covered by bog dirt and a bit shaken. So we dropped into a pub where I sat in my underwear in front of a peat fire with one young fellow drying my pants and boots and another running to a store to buy socks. I asked our ghillie if he would like a whisky or a beer.

He thanked me, and said, "Don't mind if I do," and then called out his order: "A whisky *and* a beer, please."

AFRICA

As a family, we took a number of holidays in Morocco. On our own, Sonia and I visited Tunisia, the Ivory Coast, and Senegal. In Southern Tunisia, we stayed on the island of Djerba, which was our introduction to the Arab world. While we were there, we got to know a famous

Sheila, John, and Jacquie in Morocco.

With Sonia on the island of Djerba in Tunisia.

French broadcaster, Léon Zitrone, who was the news anchor on the French government network. His face was as familiar to fifty million Frenchmen as Walter Cronkite to Americans or Peter Mansbridge to Canadians. He was charming.

Sonia asked me if I could stand a twelve-hour bus trip into the Sahara, departing at six a.m. I said okay, thinking I would learn a lot about the tribes that lived underground in the desert. What we discovered at six-fifteen a.m. was that this was a totally German tour, to be conducted in German. Fortunately, a German-American couple was sitting in front of us, and they passed the gist of information on to us.

In 1970, during our second winter in Paris, Sheila, Sonia, and I were feeling quite depressed by the greyness and pollution of Paris. A doctor told us that we badly needed some sunshine. We took his advice, and in February, spent about ten days in Agadir, in southern Morocco, a town that was very popular with northern Europeans. It is unlike most Moroccan cities in that it is modern, having been totally rebuilt after a disastrous earthquake in 1960. The old town was destroyed in a matter of fifteen seconds and more than twenty thousand were killed.

The next year, the twins joined us in Morocco. This time, we visited Marrakesh and the Atlas Mountains. We drove into the mountains and took a chair lift to snow-covered peaks. The Moroccan army was being trained to ski; it was quite obvious from their skiing skills that these fellows were not in their usual habitat. When the five of us visited a busy souk in the old part of town, Sonia whispered to me that she was feeling claustrophobic and was going outside. The kids and I continued to walk around looking at native merchandise. Jacquie suddenly asked me what "Christ of Arabia" meant. She then explained that Mommy had told her that she needed some fresh air because she had "christofarabia."

Just before we were about to return to Paris from Morocco, I suffered the worst case of food poisoning I have ever experienced. The plane stopped in Casablanca on the return flight. I was tempted to go straight to the hospital but decided I had to get home to Paris. I was able to call a doctor from the Paris airport and he made it to our apartment shortly after we arrived home. I had a high fever, and was curled up in a fetal position under many blankets, shivering badly, when the doctor arrived. I well remember his first words: "*Pauvre petit.*" He then announced that he was going to give me an anti-spasmodic needle, which would help a lot. It was the biggest needle I have ever seen and the injection was so painful that I forgot all about my original condition. I required a number of follow-up shots, which were administered by nursing nuns. In France, one buys the medicine at a pharmacy, and the Grey Nuns come by to give injections. I finally recovered but was out of commission for nearly two weeks. The diagnosis was shellfish poisoning.

On another trip, Sonia and I visited the Ivory Coast and Senegal in West Africa. In the early 1970s, Abidjan was by far the most vibrant city in the region, and La Côte d'Ivoire was the most successful of all the old French colonies. I'd had a bad reaction to a yellow fever shot, and, when we arrived, I couldn't wait to get to the hotel. However, the travel agent had not advised us that, as Canadians, we needed a visa. The police chief at the airport was adamant that he was going to send us back on the next flight.

It was obvious that he was looking for some cash, but I was apprehensive about paying him. I called the manager of the Hotel Ivoire, who said he would come pick us up. The chief continued to give us a hard time and put us under guard at the airport. In hindsight, I should have paid the policeman and shaken his hand because he took our passports away and we spent the next five days trying to retrieve them. Despite the delays, it was an interesting experience. After recouping our travel documents, we flew on to Dakar in Senegal.

We then toured some of the slave-trading houses on the Île de Gorée, just off the Senegalese coast, and got a good feel for this West African nation. This area was the largest slave-trading centre on that coast. Because of our experience in Abidjan, we skipped our planned visit to Upper Volta and Niger and returned to Paris.

XI LATER FAMILY DAYS

138 Dunvegan Road

IN the fall of 1971, after an exciting four years in Paris, we returned to Toronto. Although we tried hard to find a house in Rosedale, we settled in Forest Hill Village, back on Dunvegan Road, this time at number 138. After living in Paris among beautifully ornate eight-storey-high buildings, the Eglinton Avenue and Yonge Street area, with its bland two-storey structures, seemed considerably less picturesque. However, we were all quite happy to be back home in Canada and living in a less stressful environment.

This was our second home on Dunvegan Road. With its Spanish tile roof, it was quite charming. I had a big, brown Mercury, which was our first car with air conditioning. The garage set-up was unique. It was tucked behind the house. To get the car into it, you had to drive onto a revolving turntable, then get out and push it around 180 degrees. This monster of a car barely fit on the turntable, but everything worked out well once you got the hang of it. Workmen asked if they could park their truck on the turntable and take a picture.

Shortly after we moved in, we bought a large white abstract painting by John Craven, a Toronto contemporary artist. We hung it in the dining room and invited Sonia's mother over for dinner. We had just given Granny a tour of the house, which she appeared to like. However, after dinner, she remarked that to her mind, it seemed a bit unusual to have the garage door right in the dining room. To this day, that's how we refer to the Craven painting.

One day, during our first winter back in Canada, the kids were playing in the back garden where there was an incline that was great for sledding. Sonia and I were enjoying a quiet moment in the kitchen, when we heard a heated argument in which our three kids were shouting at each other and exchanging obscenities for all of the neighbours to hear. The most distinct and oft-repeated epithet was the "F" word.

We called them into the kitchen for a scolding. We told them how wrong it was to use this word, and queried whether any of them knew what it meant. John, then ten, professed that he had no idea, while Sheila, twelve, responded with a sideways glance and smirk that implied, "sort of." We then turned to Jacquie, who said not a word, but tried to illustrate her knowledge by passing the extended index finger of her right hand in and out through a circle formed by her left thumb and forefinger.

Sonia and I were momentarily stunned by this graphic display, but quickly collected our thoughts and barked, "Now that we all understand what it means, you are being sent to your rooms for the rest of the afternoon."

Over the grumbling that ensued as the kids made their way up the stairs, we could hear John muttering, "I still don't know what it means."

The children took the Forest Hill bus and then the subway to school. The bus passed right in front of our house, after a stop at the nearby corner. The bus driver became accustomed to seeing one or other of the kids rush frantically out the front door and race up the street to the bus stop. Over time, he became most accommodating, slowing and even stopping in front of the house to let the kids on, mid block.

On one memorable occasion, the driver saw Jacquie racing out of the house. He kindly slowed down and stopped to let her on. However, not only did she climb aboard, but so did Amber, our clueless golden retriever. Amber was always seeking attention, picking up any item that was lying on the floor and running around the house with it. On this particular morning, Amber had chosen to pick up my underwear just as Jacquie was leaving.

Seeing this, Jacquie shrieked, "Amber, go home!" Amber looked up in shock at this sharp order, dropped the underwear, and scurried off the bus. Jacquie was not far behind, clutching the embarrassing clothing and vowing, as she retreated into the house, never to go to school again.

Sonia and I decided to make some major renovations to the house and discussed our thoughts with Gord Smeaton, the architect who had designed our cottage at Smoke Lake. Gord's very wise counsel was to look for another house rather than try to remodel this one.

60 OLD FOREST HILL ROAD

IN 1975, we moved a few blocks to an elegant older greystone house with a slate roof, at 60 Old Forest Hill Road. It was owned by the children of the late George McCullagh, a well-known businessman and the former owner of the *Globe and Mail*. His daughter, Ann, was a classmate of Sonia's at Havergal College. An unforeseen problem arose when we got possession and tried to move in. His widow, who was still living in the house, refused to move out. We gave her an extra two months because we didn't want to upset her or her children. I never did meet her, but I understand that considerable discussion with her children was required before she agreed to vacate.

Our new home was rather large, with four bedrooms on the third floor that were used for storage until the arrival of our housekeeper, Marta. The furnace was an ancient steam boiler fuelled from a one-thousand-gallon oil tank. The archaic heating system was somewhat dangerous, horribly inefficient, and required the regular services of a Swiss gentleman to keep it operational. On one occasion, Sheila's bedroom filled up with steam, causing the wallpaper to peel off. Another unique feature of this house was a screening room in the basement with two ancient 35 mm projectors that could be operated only by a qualified projectionist. During our ten years living in the house, we used them once.

I had two famous first cousins in the entertainment industry. One was the actor Hume Cronyn, who was married to Jessica Tandy (also an actor) and was very well known to fans in the U.S. and Canada for his movie roles. Hume, born in London, Ontario, in 1911, was one of six children of my Aunt Frances, my father's half-sister. Hume starred in dozens of movies and produced, directed, and acted in many stage productions, often with Jessica.

The other cousin was Robert Whitehead. Bob was born in Montreal and was the son of Father's sister, Mary Selina Labatt. He married the well-known actress Zoë Caldwell, and until his death in 2002, lived in Pound Ridge, New York, close to Hume and Jessica, as well as another famous Canadian actor, Christopher Plummer. Bob was not as well known to the general public as Hume was, but was highly regarded in the New York theatre scene as a successful director and producer of dozens of Broadway productions.

Shortly after moving into this home, I received a call from Bob explaining that he and Zoë had the most wonderful nanny helping them with their two sons. Her name was Marta, and she was from Haiti. She was working in the States illegally. Although he had tried to get a work permit for her, he'd been unsuccessful. However, he said that a friend of his at the Canadian embassy in Washington would be able to get her into Canada if she had a sponsor. Sonia and I told him that we would be happy to sponsor Marta and that we could use her help at our new house.

Marta's age was a mystery. She had worked in the Netherland Antilles and spoke a number of languages. Her English was quite acceptable but not always grammatically correct. She was full of energy and always upbeat, and the kids liked her.

Marta loved it when we had parties. Sonia was working at Butterfield & Robinson doing travel research and was often away on fam (familiarization) trips. Marta looked forward to these absences. When she heard that Sonia was going on a trip, she suggested to me that we have a dinner for ten because she loved organizing these parties. Knowing many of our friends by this time, Marta either agreed with everyone on my list of invitees or occasionally vetoed a guest. There was one gentleman that she definitely disliked. "No, don't invite he, I don't like he," she would say, and I obediently struck him off the list.

While not at all shy, she sometimes liked to over-dramatize her maid's role. She had purchased what I would describe as a French maid's black dress with a frilly white apron. Wearing this uniform, she greeted the guests as they arrived and then took their orders for a cocktail. She then approached me, and in front of the guests, said, "Mr. Labatt, would you like a Beefeater martini straight up with a twist, very dry?"

Whether I wanted one or not, I always nodded. She also set the menu, which was always the same: roast leg of lamb, *haricots verts*, potatoes and gravy, dessert, and coffee.

Another of her jobs was feeding Amber, who was always wagging her tail and looking for tidbits.

"If she say she no eat, don't believe she," Marta always told me.

Having worked for Bob, she had met many celebrities in the entertainment world. Katharine Hepburn, who was playing at the Royal Alex, invited Marta to the performance. She gave her two house seats, so Marta invited Sheila to join her. Sonia lent Marta one of her best theatre outfits. Then Marta and Sheila were picked up by limousine, enjoyed the show, were invited backstage, and were delivered home.

On one occasion, Marta was very ill with an upset stomach and stayed in her room. When she was feeling better, she came downstairs and explained something to me.

"I was so sick. I look in the mirror and I was so black. When white people sick they get very pale – more white. When black people sick, they get more black."

Another time, Marta told us that her father was coming for a brief visit. When I got home from the office one evening, I heard her say, "Daddy's home." I asked Sonia if her father had arrived and she replied, "No, you're her Daddy."

Marta eventually returned to Haiti and married Rodney, who ran a small art gallery in Port au Prince. The last time we heard from her, she was living in Miami and had obtained her green card. We're not sure what happened to Rodney.

29 Browside Avenue

THE property on Old Forest Hill Road went right back to the street behind us, Browside Avenue. Bordering our backyard was a stone cottage owned by an elderly widower, Mr. Wallace. A retired engineer, he had put a considerable amount of energy into designing his home along the lines of a French-Canadian country cottage. He was also an accomplished artist; we have some of his paintings. Although the three kids often did the grocery shopping for Mr. Wallace in Forest Hill Village, which he appreciated, he realized that he needed a housekeeper. He found a capable woman who moved into his home.

Six months later, Mr. Wallace told me how pleased he was with her and that he wanted to marry her. In discussing this idea with him,

I determined that the reasoning behind this major initiative was that he wanted to give her some money and, for some reason, thought he had to marry her to do so. I told him this was not the case and asked him if he had a lawyer and/or a trust company. He told me that he had dealt with Canada Permanent Trust and gave me permission to discuss the situation with them.

With the help of a lawyer and the trust company, a new will was drawn up with the housekeeper included. He was so appreciative that he wanted to give me the house. I told him that he should not do this, but the trust company suggested that I be given right of first refusal at market conditions. Mr. Wallace died shortly after his new will was in place. The trust company had three independent appraisals of the property performed, and, to make a long story short, Sonia bought the house from his estate. The balance of Mr. Wallace's estate went to charity, as he had no heirs.

The house on Browside was in poor repair and we fixed it up at great expense. Sonia decided to rent it, although she was not too keen on becoming a landlady. In July 1978, we were on our sailboat on Georgian Bay when I received a call from our real estate agent telling us that a couple from Montreal were interested in renting the house. They needed an answer promptly because the house they thought they had purchased in Toronto was not available.

We were given the names of this couple – Michael and Ruth Moffat. They were former Torontonians. Michael was a long-time employee of the Bank of Montreal, and Ruth was a broadcaster. We quickly accepted Sonia's first tenants.

Sonia and I have had a long and close relationship with Michael and Ruth, both in the city and at Lake of Bays. Michael joined Trimark in 1986 and retired from Invesco Trimark in 2004. A year after they moved in, they made an offer to buy the house, because, as Michael pointed out, the landlady was very tough. Sonia agreed that a sale was a good solution due to the fact that she had been exposed to difficult tenants like the Moffats.

As it turned out, while the four of us played lots of tennis followed by dinner at the Mayfair Tennis Club and the Granite Club, the Moffats were plotting all the while how they could get Sonia to sell the house. Michael told me that after many glasses of wine, one evening, they asked Sonia for a right of first refusal if she ever decided to sell. Sonia said that she would happily sell it but had no idea regarding price. Michael suggested finding two reputable real estate agents and averaging the price. It took a lot of wine, but the house was sold!

During our years on Old Forest Hill Road, we spent most weekends, year round, at our farm in Beaver Valley. On many occasions, one or more of the kids stayed in the city, and Sonia and I went to the farm. The Moffats' daughter, Andrea, who was about twelve, had a bedroom that overlooked our swimming pool. At dinner at the Moffats one evening, she regaled us with a story about one of John's wild parties that took place in our absence. She described chairs being thrown into the pool and loud music. All the while, her father was kicking her under the table, trying to shut her up.

Sheila and Jacquie also had some pretty loud parties with their friends from Toronto French School (TFS) but were not reported on.

The Moffats were very good neighbours and helped us out by passing a bottle of gin over the back fence if we ran out.

I was totally addicted to cigarettes and tried many times to quit. As described earlier, I finally did succeed in quitting cold turkey, in 1970, when we were living in Paris. Seven years later, however, I took up this bad habit again, but tried hard not to smoke in front of the kids, or in Sonia's presence. Both Sheila and Jacquie were also closet smokers, and we all thought we were fooling Sonia and each other. I used our upstairs guest bathroom as my secret smoking den; Sheila and Jacquie used their respective bedrooms with their doors shut, as theirs. All of these dens of iniquity opened onto the upstairs landing.

One afternoon, Sonia found the house extremely quiet and went upstairs to see what everyone was doing. As she stood in the upstairs hall, she could see and smell smoke seeping out under the doors of the three aforementioned rooms.

She gathered her thoughts and announced in a loud voice, "I am calling a family meeting. Here in the hall. Now!"

The three of us sheepishly opened our respective doors, and made some lame comments such as, "Hi Mom," or "Oh, it's you, Sonia." The only ones left unscathed were John and the dog.

John never took up cigarettes, but when he was attending Dalhousie University he bought a pipe. On one of my visits to Halifax, he was showing me his living accommodations. He was wearing a sports jacket with leather elbows and sat back in a rocking chair and proceeded to light his pipe. I asked him if he enjoyed smoking his pipe. He replied that, frankly, he didn't, but he felt it made him look like a true academic.

On this trip, I bought him a pair of good-quality shoes with thick soles and we proceeded to walk all over town. We then went to a pub, got pretty hammered, and then had a great steak dinner. When we finally got back to his room, his poor feet were bleeding profusely because of his new shoes.

The three children lived on Old Forest Hill Road for most of their schooling. Sonia and I felt they should go to university outside Toronto, but still in Canada. If they wanted to go on to postgraduate work, that could be in the U.S. or elsewhere.

Sheila and Jacquie switched from TFS to Havergal College in grade seven. Jacquie stayed at Havergal until she completed high school, but Sheila later transferred to Jarvis Collegiate before going on to university. John boarded for two years at Lakefield College but preferred to live at home, so he transferred to Royal St. George's College in Toronto, then spent his last year of high school at Lawrence Park Collegiate. John was at Lakefield at the same time as Prince Andrew, although Andrew was a couple of years ahead of him. John told me he got to know the bodyguards better than he did Andrew.

Sheila attended Queen's University and graduated with a major in Russian. During her university years, she spent four months at the Pushkin Institute in Moscow. This was during the Cold War, when few students attended from outside the Communist bloc. After Queen's, she obtained her law degree from York University's Osgoode Hall Law School.

John graduated from Dalhousie University. After working for a number of years, he moved to Tucson with his new wife, Diane, to obtain his MBA from the University of Arizona.

Jacquie went to McGill University in Montreal and worked for a few years before attending Harvard Business School, from which she graduated with an MBA.

For many summers, the kids went to the Taylor Statten camps: Ahmek for John and Wapomeo for the girls. They were all interested in canoe tripping and experienced some very long and difficult canoe trips in Ontario and Quebec, as well as in the Lake Superior region, including Minnesota and Lake of the Woods.

They progressed from campers to staff and made many lifelong friends at camp. Sheila ended up as a riding instructor, John as a guide at the girls' camp, and Jacquie as a babysitter for the camp director's children.

In September of 1983, the three children organized a wonderful surprise party to celebrate our twenty-fifth wedding anniversary. They were able to keep it a secret with the help of neighbours, relatives, and good friends. Sonia and I had absolutely no idea that a big party was about to take place at 60 Old Forest Hill Road until a stream of colourfully dressed characters marched out of the Moffats' house next door and entered our back garden. At the head of the parade was our friend and cardiologist, Doug Wigle, playing "When the Saints Come Marching In" on his trumpet.

The celebration took place around the swimming pool, and after a few speeches, George Butterfield pushed me into the pool. I don't think our kids have ever forgiven George for this. The party was a happy event. To this day, Sonia and I are grateful for the initiative taken by Sheila, John, and Jacquie.

49 HAZELTON AVENUE

WHEN the kids all went off to university, we were left in a house that was much too large for the two of us. It also needed some major upgrades, such as a new heating system and a new slate roof. In addition, I had just started at Trimark and depended on the venture succeeding. I simply could not afford to maintain Old Forest Hill Road. In 1984, the housing market was returning to health, after the 1981–82 crash, so we put it up for sale with the intention of finding something smaller – maybe a townhouse close to Bloor Street.

We quickly found what we thought we were looking for. It was a semi-detached, three-storey townhouse on Hazelton Avenue, about five blocks north of Bloor Street in the trendy Yorkville area. It was owned by a famous Toronto decorator and therefore presented extremely well. We did a major renovation of the third floor and made it into a master bedroom with a fireplace, and designed a totally new, elaborate bathroom. There were steep stairs all the way from the street level to the third floor, so the climb was great for cardiovascular exercise. We had a small black marble swimming pool in an enclosed back garden, but no garage. This lack of a garage bothered me a great deal and was probably the main reason we lived in this house for only two years.

There were other problems with 49 Hazelton. The principal one was that, with the children having now finished university, they all returned home. Each had a room on the second floor that was so tiny there was barely enough room to swing a cat. It didn't sit too well with me that drunks walking up the street from the Yorkville restaurants and bars often threw beer bottles around. The noise coming through the wall from the attached house next door also helped us decide that perhaps living in a townhouse in fashionable Yorkville was not for us. There were quieter residential neighbourhoods not far away.

Our golden retrievers.

21 Ormsby Crescent

FORTUNATELY, we were able to sell Hazelton for a good price in a matter of days. On the other hand, 1987 was not a good time for finding homes in Forest Hill. Sonia and I lived in a rented condo on Bloor Street for three months until we found a sensible place on Ormsby Crescent, just two blocks south of Eglinton. This two-storey house looked out onto a ravine and was the right size for the family and our golden retriever Timi (whose name was the acronym for Trimark Investment Management Inc.). Timi had replaced Amber, who was really Jacquie's dog; Jacquie took her back once she finished university.

While we lived on Ormsby, each of our offspring decided it was time to get married. Sheila married Dominic Barton at Grace Church on-the-Hill on June 9, 1989, with the wedding reception at the King Edward Hotel. Jacquie and Bruce Randle were married at Grace Church on September 21, 1991, with the reception at the Four Seasons Hotel. John married Diane Desjardins in Montreal at the Church of Ascension of Our Lord in Westmount, on May 30, 1992, with the reception at the Royal Montreal Golf Club. All three weddings were extremely happy events.

It was comforting to know that on Ormsby we were surrounded by doctors, should the need arise. Although I did not have a life-threatening disease, I did pass a kidney stone and can attest to the excruciating pain of the experience. Some equate it with having a baby, but I'm sure that's a gross exaggeration. I had no idea what was happening, but I was in terrible pain, and Sonia called two doctors, one who lived next door and the other from across the street. They both looked at me, asked a few questions, and then told me the pain was *not* caused by a kidney stone.

When the ambulance arrived, the attendants were not strong enough to carry me downstairs, so I descended on foot and promptly threw up. On the way to Toronto General Hospital, a chatty ambulance attendant asked me what I did for a living and I told her I was in the mutual fund business with a firm called Trimark. She then said that she owned some Trimark funds and dealt with a financial planner by the name of Coby Kobayashi. Coby had explained to her his concept of a money tree that kept your money growing. I grunted that I indeed knew Coby. She then asked if she was talking too much. As politely as I could, I responded that, yes, she was doing just that.

After our arrival at emergency, I was parked on a gurney in the hallway, then in various adjoining rooms, for what seemed like an eternity. The pain was excruciating. All of the nurses seemed to think I had a kidney stone, but they couldn't do anything for me until I was examined by a doctor. When the doctor arrived, she asked if I was in pain and I truthfully said that I was no longer in pain. Then all of the nurses jumped on me and said that I must take advantage of the doctor's presence. They had tried very hard to get her to examine me. The doctor then handed me a little paper cup and directed me to urinate into it. I did this and out popped a jagged little moon rock. I felt perfectly fine and said to Sonia that if she could find my clothes I felt like going out for a good Italian dinner.

The only other medical emergency on Ormsby happened over a game of bridge. Sonia had been after me for years to take bridge lessons (and she's still trying). I did take a series of lessons over a three-month period and became somewhat proficient at bidding. However, I had no idea how to play the cards. We decided to have a few couples over to practice what we had learned. Three couples joined us, including Peter Turner from McLeod Young Weir and his wife, Rayma, both of whom had attended the same bridge classes.

Everything was fine until Peter said he was feeling quite unwell; we called for an ambulance and subsequently found out that he had suffered a mild stroke. I still blame his "event" on the pressure bridge puts on the human body. It's almost as bad as golf!

While we were still living on Ormsby Crescent, Sonia decided to return to the University of Toronto for postgraduate studies in the environmental field. After taking a catch-up year, she learned that the Geography Department offered an excellent program. She gathered her transcripts and met Joe Whitney, the head of the department.

After reviewing and accepting her documentation, Joe stated that usually the department required a letter of recommendation from former advisors. "But," he said, "your teachers are probably all dead by now."

Sonia had graduated from U of T in 1960, in Honours Science (Food Chemistry) and was still using her original library card. It had an unbelievably low code number, and she was forever having to explain its provenance. In 1990, she obtained her M.A. from the Geography Department.

After Sonia graduated, her advisor, Virginia Maclaren, and Joe persuaded her to continue her studies with the goal of obtaining her doctorate. This was a great challenge, and there were a few occasions when Sonia questioned why she had done this to herself. However, she graduated in 1995 with her PhD in Geography. The entire family is very proud of this accomplishment, the only person in our extended family to have done so. I should also add that since her graduation, all of our mail from academia is addressed to Dr. Sonia and Mr. Arthur Labatt.

In the PhD world, the defence of the dissertation is a formal and in-depth examination of the PhD-elect's work, by her committee, in a boardroom setting. This takes place at the School of Graduate Studies (SGS). Sonia's defence went smoothly, and her dissertation, entitled "Corporate Response Toward Environmental Issues: A Case Study of Packaging," was immediately accepted.

Part of the formality of the occasion includes the signing-off of the written work so that the library can include a copy on its shelves. Sonia and her advisor left the room and were ushered into a small antechamber where the signing was to take place. As they sat down, Sonia noticed that the signature document had been put in front of Virginia, and the advisor's approval in front of her. Because of the difference in their ages, the authorities thought Virginia was the student and Sonia the professor!

Since 1996, Sonia's title has been Adjunct Professor, Centre for Environment, University of Toronto. From 1996 to 2005, she taught a course at the Institute for Environmental Studies entitled Corporate Perspectives on the Environment. She has also co-authored two books, *Carbon Finance* and *Environmental Finance*, with fellow professor Rodney White.

A senior banker who knows Sonia well asked me what the books were about.

"They're about carbon trading," I said.

To which he responded, "What does Sonia know about carpet trading?"

In addition to her work at the University of Toronto, Sonia has been active on a number of boards. These include the National Ballet, the Clarke Institute, Wellesley Hospital, the Art Gallery of Ontario, and the World Wildlife Fund. And for ten years, she was a trustee of the Hospital for Sick Children.

Warren Road

As was the case with a number of other houses we have owned, Sonia and I had a long discussion about completely remodelling the kitchen at Ormsby, including strengthening a large back veranda, which I worried might fall into the ravine with a load of guests on it. While we were thinking about this, our real estate agent, Janet Lindsay, phoned and told us that an outstanding home in the neighbourhood, designed by Napier Simpson, had just come on the market and that we should look at it right away.

Within an hour, we had toured the house, and that evening we put in an offer, which was accepted.

We moved into this house in 1994, and are still there. It's a great house for entertaining, with only two floors and three bedrooms. The previous owner had added a beautiful garden room at the back of the house and had upgraded everything. All we had to do was move in and decorate.

Tucson, Arizona

During the 1990s, Sonia and I went several times to Canyon Ranch, a health spa in Tucson, Arizona. This spa has a fairly balanced clientele of men and women (most spas cater to women) and is the perfect place to get fit and lose weight. Canyon Ranch introduced us to hiking in the mountains – Tucson is surrounded by four mountain ranges – as well as biking. We played tennis, took cooking classes, worked out with weights, didn't drink, and cut down on our food consumption.

In 1993–94, we had a particularly harsh winter in Toronto. We longed for a place in the southern sunshine where we could escape at least part of the Canadian winter. Our family had taken many winter vacations in warmer climes, so by a process of elimination, we decided that Tucson might be the place. Southern France was too far away and not warm enough; the Caribbean was expensive and complicated; in Mexico the chance of getting Montezuma's revenge was very high; and the topography of Florida didn't appeal to us – *et voilà!*

On our last visit to Canyon Ranch, I met with a real estate agent and toured most of the gated communities around Tucson. We finally settled on a neighbourhood containing nearly six hundred properties, two golf courses, a Loews Hotel, dozens of tennis courts, and a lodge for extra guests at the Ventana Canyon Golf and Racquet Club. There was one lot left on the second hole of the Canyon Golf Course, and it just happened to be next door to other Torontonians, Boyd and Rose Matchett. We ended up buying this lot on Desert Moon Loop. When the kids heard this, they wanted to know when the house would be finished.

Before we settled on Ventana, Sonia and I considered Canyon Ranch. In addition to the spa, there were many lots available for building vacation homes called *casitas* on spa property. I decided I didn't want anything to do with this approach to a winter home, because I recalled, when staying at the Ranch, having to go "over the wall" to get a drink. In my opinion, you can have too much of healthy living!

The five-bedroom house was finished within a year. Our decorator from Montreal, John King, did the interior design. Most of the furniture had a southwestern motif but was made in Quebec. In Tucson, the builder asks where the client would like to store his guns. I had to admit that I didn't have any.

Apart from the furniture arriving by van from Canada, we had to buy all of the beds, sheets, towels, blankets, etc. to make a five-bedroom house habitable. Apart from the bedsteads, Sonia and I went shopping at Bed, Bath and Beyond and with the assistance of a very helpful sales lady filled sixteen huge shopping carts with merchandise. We had a brand new Wells Fargo chequing account and presented a cheque for payment. This was refused because it hadn't been printed with our names on it.

We had a bit of an exchange of words with the store, and I was on the verge of giving them a Canadian credit card. However, Sonia was dead set against doing this because we had gone to a lot of effort to open this account. She told the store manager that we would shop elsewhere and suggested they put everything back. I must say that this got some action; their minds quickly changed regarding our cheque. Thousands of dollars of goods were sent to a storage facility because the house wasn't finished. The clerk, who was on commission, was quite relieved by the happy turn of events.

When we started building the house, we opened an account with a branch of the Bank of America located close to the architect's office, but far from our new home. Once the house was nearly finished, we discussed opening a chequing account with Wells Fargo, which was closer to home.

One day, we were hiking close to the original Bank of America branch and decided spontaneously to go in and close the account. We entered the branch wearing hiking boots, unkempt T-shirts, sunglasses, and wide-brimmed felt hats. Sonia remarked that we looked like Bonnie and Clyde.

We had been using this account to pay the builder so there was usually a fairly large balance.

I told the teller that we wanted to close our account, and take our $32,000 with us. I expected some raised eyebrows because of our appearance and our request to close out the account. She said she would be right back. When she returned she had a worried look on her face, and I thought that perhaps she couldn't imagine the two of us dusty characters having that much money. However, the reason for her anxiety was that the cheque-printing machine was out of order. She asked if we would mind taking the $32,000 in cash. We didn't feel comfortable stuffing that much cash in our hiking shorts and were able to pick up a cheque at another branch. No one ever asked why we were closing the account.

As the construction of the house was proceeding, Sonia and I made a number of trips to Tucson. We observed golfer after golfer driving their carts on the par five second hole that our house backed onto. We are 150 yards from the green, but far enough from the tee box that we have never had a problem with golf balls landing on the property. Neither Sonia nor I had ever been golfers. Golf is so time-consuming; we couldn't figure out how you could play golf and lead a normal family life.

As we stood gazing out at the mountains beyond the beautiful fairway, Sonia turned to me, and with a very serious demeanour, stated, "I guess we're going to have to learn to play this stupid game."

Golf is not an easy game at the best of times, but it is particularly difficult if you take it up in your early sixties. Fifteen years later, we are still struggling but do enjoy it if we are playing with others who don't take the game too seriously. We take the odd mulligan and use a foot mashie if the ball is behind a tree, rock, or cactus.

Our house in Tucson is large enough to accommodate everyone in our family– eight adults and six children – but the entire group has been there only once. Sheila's family has lived in the Far East for the last fourteen years, and John's family has lived in France for nearly six years. Jacquie's

Top: Sonia's t-shirt pretty well sums up our relationship with golf.
Bottom: If one is going to take up golf, one must have a
golf cart – as we do, compliments of our kids.

family, who stayed in Toronto, has been closer at hand. John and Diane have now moved back to Canada, and Sheila and Dominic have moved to London, England. But everyone is always welcome.

When the kids are in residence, they spend most of the time playing in the swimming pool or the hot tub. There are tennis clinics and golf lessons for those so inclined. We do a lot of hiking with the kids, all of whom are faster and more agile than their grandparents. I can visualize Sheila and Dominic's children, Fraser and Jessica, jumping from rock to rock, crossing the river on the way to Seven Falls.

One day, when we were hiking with the Barton and Randle grandchildren, we walked by a large sign that read WARNING – HIGH MOUNTAIN LION ALERT. We entered into an animated discussion of the word "high." Were the lions "high in the mountain" or was there "a high alert?"

Fraser, who was ten, tried to end the controversy by declaring that we were probably okay because "mountain lions are much smaller than African lions."

To which six-year-old Courtney, who had been off on her own train of thought, exclaimed, "Lions? What lions?"

When Jacquie and Bruce's son, Dylan, was six, we took him out on the golf course for the first time. On the first hole, which was a par four, Dylan had some good hits and, like all of us, some not so good ones. After we had all sunk our putts, we each reported our scores. Sonia and I announced that we both had a six, and Bruce said he had a five. I asked Dylan for his score. He smiled and reported that he had a fourteen, and he figured that he had won the hole. Bruce then explained to him that in this game the low score wins.

On the next hole, a par five, three of us announced our scores, which varied from a five to eight. We then asked Dylan for his, he smiled and said that he had a four.

We said, "Great Dylan, how did you do it?"

"I carried it in my pocket most of the way," was his reply.

A very honest golfer!

Mary and Rusty visited us in Tucson on a number of occasions. Although I have told our gardeners and the fellows who look after the pool that the Labatt family no longer owns the brewery, they refuse to believe this story, or don't want to. When Rusty arrived, they thought he was my father and the patriarch of the Labatt clan. With his flowing white hair and his cane, he used to take leisurely walks around the Ventana neighbourhood, making many friends.

HIKING

THE move to Tucson really got us into hiking. Dr. John Evans, a friend and director of Trimark, who began his career as a cardiologist, told me that it was the best exercise for the heart. Hiking is not a stop-and-start sport (like tennis) and strengthens the heart muscle with steady, ongoing demand. That is my amateur unscientific recollection of what he said. Sonia and I still hike twice a week in the mountains around Tucson, and I do believe this activity is keeping both of us in reasonably good shape.

CHILKOOT PASS, ALASKA/YUKON

Probably the most difficult and memorable hike I have ever experienced was a five-day trek over the Chilkoot Pass from Skagway, Alaska, to Whitehorse in the Yukon. Departing the first week of September, Sonia, John, and I flew from Toronto to Vancouver and on to Skagway. We carried all of our gear and our food with us. As we left Skagway, the Rangers warned us to beware of grizzlies, to camp in approved sites, and to hang our food in trees, well off the ground. They went into considerable detail in explaining the difference between black bears and grizzlies (their shape, their paws, and their capacity to climb trees). From our point of view, we wanted to avoid both.

We saw few if any hikers on this famous route. As a bit of background, the Klondike gold rush began in July 1897, when ships carrying miners with bags of gold returned to the U.S. from the Yukon. Soon, other miners, called stampeders, were on their way to the gold fields. Within six months, approximately a hundred thousand set off for the Yukon, but only thirty thousand completed the trip. Most stampeders knew little or nothing about where they were going. The most common route to reach the fields was by boat from ports on the west coast to Skagway, over the Chilkoot to the Yukon River at Whitehorse, and then by boat five hundred miles to Dawson City. ·

The Chilkoot Pass trail is steep and hazardous. Rising a thousand feet in the last half mile, it is known as the "golden staircase" – fifteen hundred steps carved out of snow and ice to the top of the pass. The miners usually travelled in the winter, in order to use the ice steps. It was too steep for packhorses, so stampeders had to cache their goods, moving their equipment piecemeal up the mountain. Those who gave up, often did so here. Those who went on, found themselves in Bennett, British Columbia, where boats had to be built to run the final five hundred miles down the Yukon River to the gold fields.

For our trio of adventurers, the first couple of days were pleasant ones. We walked in forests amidst enormous pine and fir trees. We saw no one and rounded bends in the path to see salmon jumping in small streams. We did see bear scat and were always nervous that we would run into a grizzly about to wade into the river to catch a salmon. We wore tin cans around our necks containing pebbles, the idea being that a bear could hear us coming and stay clear. We stayed at designated campsites, cooked our meals, set up a tent, and carefully hoisted our packs high off the ground and well away from the tent, as instructed.

While we saw a few hikers the first day, after that we were alone in the wilderness.

As we got farther from Skagway, the forest started to thin out and the climbing became more strenuous. On the fourth day, we had to cross the ridge bordering the Yukon. It was here that the miners cut steps out of snow in winter in order to cross the divide. At this point on the trail, the treeline disappeared and it was seventeen miles until we were back in forested country in the Yukon. This part of the trip was really a killer. Since it was late summer, there were no ice steps cut out for us. Instead, we had to climb over huge boulders and through deep crevices, sometimes dragging, and other times pushing, the packs.

As we approached the highest point on the trail, we were travelling in mist and light rain. Although the temperature was perhaps fifty degrees Fahrenheit, we were alternately overheated and then cold. After we pitched our tent, I suffered a bad case of hypothermia. I got into a sleeping bag with Sonia cuddling me for warmth. It was many hours before my body temperature started to go back up to normal. I felt truly miserable.

The next day was another long day of hiking, often slogging through sand, to the train station in Bennett. The White Pass & Yukon train arrived from Skagway about ten p.m. All of the passengers got off and we joined them for a meal in the station. We certainly enjoyed it and boarded the train for the continuation of the trip to Whitehorse. We arrived at four a.m. and walked down the middle of the road in the fog from the station to our hotel, which offered hot showers and comfortable beds.

After resting up, and seeing the sights in Whitehorse, we rented a car for the drive to Dawson. On the way, we passed the new road that goes all the way to Inuvik. After spending a day in Dawson, we took the Top of the World Highway that continues on to Fairbanks, Alaska. We didn't quite make Fairbanks, but did a giant loop and returned to Whitehorse before flying home. The roads in this part of the world were all gravel and we blew two tires during the trip. We may not have discovered gold but we brought back some amazing memories.

THE GRAND CANYON

When Jacquie was at Harvard, we planned a five-day holiday to hike in the Grand Canyon. Jacquie's fiancé, Bruce Randle, joined Jacquie, John, Sonia, and me on the adventure.

On the floor of the Canyon, there is really only one place to stay other than pitching a tent. This is Phantom Ranch, and to be there in the busy winter season, you have to reserve a year in advance.

On a cool February day we headed down from the south rim of the canyon. On the floor of the canyon, near the Colorado River, the tempera-ture was a very pleasant seventy degrees Fahrenheit. Jacquie followed and didn't arrive until two p.m., so it was too late to hike the ten-mile Bright Angel Trail down to Phantom Ranch. We decided that the only way we could make it before dark was to take the South Kaibab Trail. The distance on this trail is only seven miles but it can be very steep in places. On both trails, there is a drop in elevation of 5000 feet.

On the way down, Sonia's knees almost gave out, and we had to wrap them in tensor bandages. Jacquie, John, and I seemed to stand the strain of the steep decline reasonably well, but Bruce also found it rough going. Today, he is as fit as can be, but at that time, he was a former hockey player who was somewhat out of condition.

About three-quarters of the way down, Bruce sat on a rock and

Hiking in the Grand Canyon.

motioned me to join him. He said in all seriousness that none of us was going to make it out of this canyon on our own steam. He said he was going to ride a donkey out. I told him that you cannot ride a donkey if you are over two hundred pounds. Bruce must have weighed at least two hundred and thirty at the time.

He then said that he would hire a helicopter. I pointed out that this wouldn't work either, because I had read that the rangers had even prevented Sylvester Stallone from using his own helicopter. You would have to be at death's door to get permission to fly out.

"Okay," said Bruce, "if that won't work, I'll hitch a ride on a raft going down the Colorado River."

After this conversation, we stumbled on, and managed to reach Phantom Ranch before dark and before the second dinner sitting was over. The staff had waited for us and served us a wonderful steak dinner. We were shown to our private one-room cabin, which had a toilet attached and air conditioning – not exactly roughing it. Bruce and I were asleep before the sun went down. We all slept in one large room with multiple bunk beds.

During the next few days, we hiked along the canyon floor as well as some trails that led up to the north rim, which is 1000 feet higher than the south rim and not accessible at this time of the year because of heavy snow. These day hikes, with a lunch packed by the Ranch, were truly impressive. The problem for me was that some of the trails were along the edge of the canyon and had terrifying vertical drop-offs. I have always been nervous of heights. I was once advised, when in such situations, to put a piece of cardboard, or my hand, over the downhill eye to fool my senses. I did this and it got me past the worst parts of the hike. It's the equivalent of being a carriage horse with blinkers on.

After a few days of exercise, we all felt extremely fit – even Bruce. We had all helped Jacquie carry down a heavy load of schoolbooks, but they were never opened. For the trip out, we packed them in a dunnage bag and had a mule lug them to the top for us. On our last day, Bruce and Jacquie headed up the Bright Angel Trail at daybreak and completed the trip in record time. Sonia, John, and I departed a little later and had no trouble whatsoever walking the ten miles out. I recommend this area, as well as Havasu Falls, as an ideal place for a family vacation.

SOROK SAN, SOUTH KOREA

On one of our visits to Seoul, Korea, to visit the Bartons, we flew with Sheila, Fraser, and Jessica from Seoul to a mountainous region near the North Korean border. Dominic and some friends from the McKinsey office in Seoul took a later plane and caught up with us on the trail to Mount Sorok.

Unlike the hiking trails we are used to, this one, starting in the town of Sorok, resembled a two-lane highway but without pavement. On the lower stages of the trail leading to Mount Sorok, thousands of hikers marched along, chatting away in many languages. Koreans and Japanese are avid hikers and dress up for the occasion. The Japanese groups wore brightly coloured jackets with argyle socks to match. Everything was orderly, and, every now and then, a temporary "town" of merchants appeared. They sold everything from food to clothing, as well as trinkets. It wasn't exactly a serene and tranquil stroll in the woods.

As we got higher into the mountains, the crowds started to thin out, and the trail became narrower and steeper. It was here that Dominic and his friends caught up with us. We climbed a series of extremely long ladders, which made me quite nervous. As we approached the summit of Sorok San, I was ready to call it a day, but the kids wanted to get to the very top. A self-appointed guide, wearing regular walking shoes with no treads, appeared from nowhere and said he would take us to the summit by a better and shorter route. This involved using ropes to pull ourselves up steep rock faces. I asked him if we had to come down by this trail, and he told me that there was an easy way down, on the other side.

There was no simple way out of this challenging predicament, so I started the descent sitting on my rear end and holding onto someone's hand. It was all very embarrassing. I kept asking myself how I got talked into this escapade. After having said a few Hail Marys, I finally made it to a more forgiving path, having torn major holes in my pants.

Tucson

Hiking the four mountain ranges around Tucson can also be adventurous. Our house looks out onto the Santa Catalina mountain range, where the peaks rise to 9000 feet. Our home at Ventana is at about 2700 feet, and our normal elevation gain on a four-hour hike would be between 600 and 1400 feet. Sonia and I have hiked many of the trails in the Catalinas as well as the three other mountain ranges close by.

Sonia loves hiking and encouraged many of our house guests to go for "a little hike." The trouble was that she was taking people who were not used to hiking on strenuous trails, and often in very warm temperatures. I was afraid someone might expire. The footing on some of the steepest and most popular hikes has been dramatically improved in the past few years, so some of these hikes are not as difficult as they were. Still, I now lead these expeditions and set a considerably slower pace than Sonia, not only for our guests' sake, but also for mine.

The only frightening experience Sonia and I had on any of our hiking trips occurred a number of years ago on Mount Lemmon. In reading the Tucson Hiking Guide, I spotted a suggested hike called Box Camp Trail. It was described as "an excellent hike beginning in ponderosa pine forest and ending in saguaro (pronounced sawaaro) cactus desert."

There is now a highway that climbs almost to the peak of Mount Lemmon at 8500 feet. The idea is to drive to milepost 26, which is close to the summit, and leave a second car at the Sabino Canyon visitors' parking lot in Tucson, about fifteen miles away. The downhill descent is described as "difficult, mostly continuous steep downhill."

The Box Camp Trail was originally a packhorse route to the higher elevations of the Catalinas. In the old days, Tucsonans rode horses up to summer cabins situated in the cooler climate of the high country. In hindsight, I agree with the guidebook that it is one of the most dramatic trails in the Tucson area. The only thing that our guidebook didn't tell us was that the upper third of the trail is pretty well marked, as is the lower third; however, the middle section is never used, is completely overgrown, and is very hard to follow.

We set off downhill from milepost 26 with some modest equipment, a little food, lots of water, a guidebook, and a topographic map of the Catalinas. The November weather was cool and sunny, and for our first two hours, the trail was reasonably well marked. The path switchbacked through tall ponderosa pines to the head of a small stream. As we progressed, the stream became larger and we crossed and recrossed it many times.

We were making out all right until we came to Apache Spring, an ancient campground of the Apache tribe. I think this is where knowledgeable hikers turn around and head back up to the summit. The vegetation had totally obscured the path and several trees had fallen across the trail. The guidebook kept warning us to beware of a number of faint trails going off to the right where other hikers had descended into Box Camp Canyon. This canyon is 3000 feet to the bottom, with no way out but to retrace your steps. We had read of several hikers who had ventured into this canyon, never to be seen again.

This put the fear of God into us as we debated turning around and going back up. However, now we couldn't find the trail, in either direction. We were lost, but could see the valley thousands of feet below.

By this time, it was well past noon, and we realized that even if we found our way down, we would miss the Sabino Canyon Shuttle bus that would take us the last three and a half miles to our car. We now thought that we might have to spend the night in the mountains. I asked Sonia if she had remembered to bring her long pants. She told me that she had left them in the rented car at the top of the mountain. We had no matches, cell phone, or flashlight, and only a few warm clothes. I felt if we couldn't find our way out, we had to at least get to a lower elevation, because the nights can be very cold. We started bushwhacking toward a line of green cottonwood trees we could see in the distance below, trees that we believed (correctly) marked the Sabino Basin. In the process of making our own trail, each of us fell a couple of times and were scratched and bleeding. We looked like the wrath of God, with bruises and bloodstains everywhere. Fortunately, there were no broken bones or sprains.

Eventually, we reached a sizeable creek that was bordered by the cottonwoods we had seen from above. We scrambled across the rocks to the other side, then proceeded a little farther until we came across a path and a signpost telling us exactly where we were. It was now four p.m., and we had about two and a half hours to reach the top of the Sabino Canyon road before dark. When we finally arrived, it was nearly dark and we spotted a cyclist about half a mile away. This was the first person we had seen since leaving the summit ten hours before.

When we finally arrived at the paved road, our feet were so sore that we took off our boots, put the insoles between two pairs of socks, and walked the last three and a half miles in the moonlight in our stocking feet. When we reached the car park, our Jeep was nowhere to be seen. We thought that after all this struggle, someone had stolen it. Actually, it was still there – behind the only bus left in the lot.

In retrospect, as I recount some of our hiking adventures, I realize we're probably lucky to be alive.

XII ALL CORNERS OF THE WORLD

SONIA and I have had the good fortune to travel extensively on every continent. There are a number of reasons for our wanderlust, including the fact that our family lived in France for nearly four years and we took advantage of the proximity to other European countries, the Middle East, and North Africa. Also, our eldest daughter, Sheila, and her family lived in the Far East for fifteen years, and we tried to travel across the Pacific annually to visit them. From there, after a few days, we picked a country in the region and made plans to do some sightseeing. They moved to London, England, in 2010, so our Far Eastern junkets will be fewer in number.

Another reason for our many trips is the fact that Sonia worked for Butterfield & Robinson from 1978 to 1987. Before that, she helped organize trips for the Art Gallery of Ontario, the Royal Ontario Museum, and many other organizations. Her duties involved travel research and group coordination. For a number of years, Butterfield & Robinson ran extremely successful and popular student trips to Europe, so shortly after her arrival, its owner, George Butterfield, decided to try marketing adult bicycle trips in France.

The first B & R adult biking venture was in the Beaune region of Burgundy, and the leaders of this trip were Richard Meech and Sonia. Richard, who had led a number of student trips in France, scouted out the route. I participated in this inaugural expedition, as did our close friends Chuck and Nancy Kennedy. On the first day, we set out from Beaune in a very heavy rainstorm. Nobody could find Richard. He was terribly disappointed with the weather and was sound asleep, so we left without him.

At the Temple of Heaven in Beijing.

At the Great Wall of China.

Top: On our African safari.
Bottom: Our transportation in Egypt.

Top: Burmese temples.
Bottom: On the move in Bermuda.

I had researched the route out of town by car the night before and became the leader of our group on the first day. A truck followed us, carrying the baggage. At the next hotel, Sonia had me carrying heavy valises up to the third floor. I rebelled, pointing out that not only was I a paying guest, but many of the guests were younger and stronger than I was.

In addition to biking in Europe, Sonia began to do a great deal of travelling to scout out tours and hotels all over the world. She often invited me to tag along, and I started to think of myself as a half-priced spouse. On a trip to Costa Rica, we found ourselves aboard the Costa Rican airline's inaugural flight from Miami to San José. The aircraft had a "new car" smell, and, as we boarded, each passenger was handed a nicely boxed bottle of Pinch Scotch as a promotional gift. No sooner had we taken our seats than a flight attendant examined our boarding passes and politely asked for the Scotch back, because we were flying on a discounted fare.

I accompanied Sonia to India twice, both times in the month of April. There were lots of empty seats; I later found out that this is because April is the hottest part of the year. I could actually smell the soles of my shoes melting.

On one of the flights, we had to fly through New York in order to transfer to an Air India flight to Delhi. As Sonia handed me the tickets, I noticed that she was travelling first class and I was in steerage. I was a bit taken aback by this and hoped if I handed the tickets to the agent with the first-class one on top, she wouldn't notice. After this lovely lady in a beautiful sari finished typing furiously into her computer, she informed me that I could join my wife in first class. I was so grateful I could have kissed her. I then had the nerve to ask her if there was any possibility of returning first class, knowing full well that she couldn't arrange this.

Of course, Sonia took many trips without me. On a trip to Baltimore with the Art Gallery, she was standing in a hotel lobby when Jimmy Carter and his entourage came through the door. At this time, he had not yet been nominated as the Democratic contender for the presidency. With television cameras rolling, he walked over to Sonia and shook her hand. She had no idea who he was, but realized that he was an important politician. He then asked Sonia if he had her support and Sonia answered that she was a Canadian and unfortunately could not vote. He was a good listener and went on to say what good neighbours Canadians were, and how much he admired our country.

We decided to be even more adventuresome in our travels, so we contacted Eugen Koenitz, an Australian who now lives in Hong Kong. Eugen, whose impressive list of clients includes former Canadian Prime Minister Pierre Elliot Trudeau and American industrialist David Rockefeller, specializes in trips to out-of the-way destinations.

BURMA (MYANMAR)

WE had met Eugen on many occasions when he was visiting Toronto to meet with our travel agent, Kathii Benn, to discuss potential tours. We settled on a three-week trip to Myanmar, formerly known as Burma, in April 2000, for us as well as six like-minded friends: two couples from Toronto, John Moore and Elaine Solway and Bill and Meredith Saunderson, and Texans Jim and Claire Woodcock.

Since the British departed in 1948, Myanmar has been isolated and ostracized by the international community because the army has ruled in a tough and undemocratic manner. Its people are gentle and considerate. In spite of the military presence, we felt very comfortable visiting the country.

Eugen knows the country well and has many friends, including a goddaughter, who are permanent residents. Though he is a soft-spoken individual, he can be quite forceful when giving his clients important instructions. For instance, on arriving at Rangoon (now called Yangon), he clearly told us to stand in a specific area while he handled the passport and visa formalities. When one of our group went over to him as he was talking to an immigration official, he told the person that he had been instructed to stay in a specific place. He dealt with us much like a master giving orders to a dog: "Sit" and "Stay." We learned our lesson!

Yangon had been the capital of the country for many years, but in 2005, a new capital called Nay Pyi Taw (Royal Capital) was announced. Located two hundred miles north of Yangon, the building of the capital is scheduled for completion in 2012. Yangon, with four million people, is the largest city in the country and the most important commercial centre. You can see the British influence in the older colonial buildings, which are gradually being demolished. After the country became independent from Britain, many south Asians and Anglo-Burmese were forced to leave.

We had dinner with Priscilla A. Clapp, the chargé d'affaires who was the head of the U.S. mission in the country. The U.S. had not had an ambassador in Myanmar since 1990. This dinner was arranged by Frank "Pancho" Huddle, the U.S. consul general in Toronto who lived right next door to us, and who had previously been the chargé d'affaires in Myanmar.

After listening to Priscilla, who was very open in her remarks, I came away feeling that the relationship between the U.S. and the governing

Burmese woman.

military was better than you would expect. She talked about playing golf with various generals. Hillary Clinton visited Burma in 2011 and met with Aung San Suu Kyi, who had been released from house arrest in 2010. This famous woman is the daughter of Aung San, who led Burma to independence after more than a century of British rule. In 1988, she became the symbolic leader of those opposing the generals and spent fifteen years under house arrest. Clinton announced in 2012 that the two countries have begun the process that will lead to exchanging ambassadors.

On this trip, we also visited Mandalay and Bagan (formerly Pagan). Some of the most beautiful Buddhist temples and pagodas in the world are located in these two cities. There are literally thousands of temples and, of course, many thousands of monks in their colourful robes.

We also visited Inle Lake, a large, shallow lake in the middle of the country. Getting there by local airline was a bit challenging. The old Russian-built aircraft didn't instill us with a great deal of confidence, but we made it. The lake is at an elevation of 3000 feet, so the temperature was very cool, but we had only light clothing, since April is one of the hottest months. There was no heat in our lovely room overlooking the lake, so the manager managed to find us some ski parkas that had been stashed away. There are a number of different tribes living around the lake; their traditional farming methods made for picturesque scenes. It is a special place.

John Moore had mentioned to Eugen that we would like to do some serious hiking for two or three days. It was challenging, but proved to be a highlight of the trip. We found ourselves in a remote jungle that was mountainous and damp. We all had proper hiking boots and rain gear as we headed out to visit tribes nestled high up in the hills.

We did see authentic village life that was not just created for tourists. In one village, we met a woman with an elongated neck caused by placing an increasing number of brass rings between the base of her neck and her chin. This practice is found in some parts of Africa; how it came to Burma is a mystery. Adding to the anomaly was the fact that she was a Catholic, having been converted by an Italian priest who had lived most of his life in the area.

On the drive back from the hill country, we passed a small store that sold wooden carvings to tourists. Prominently displayed on the front porch was a large metal sign advertising Labatt's beer.

Incongruous sight in a small Burmese town.

At the time of our trip, I was part of the small group at Trimark negotiating the sale of our company to Invesco. A conference call was scheduled for three p.m. local time. We were hiking that day, and I had our guides lead us to a small hut in the middle of the jungle where a satellite phone was available. We were successful in making a connection with Toronto, and, in the rather lengthy conversation that ensued, the deal was finalized. John Moore commemorated the occasion by taking a picture of me standing in the telephone shack wearing an orange crate that fell on my head while I was talking.

UZBEKISTAN

SEVEN years later, our same group of adventurers asked Eugen to propose another interesting trip to an out-of-the-way place not frequented by tourists. He suggested that we explore the Great Silk Road that caravans have used for two thousand years to transport goods between Europe and China. Much of this route passes through what is now Uzbekistan, a landlocked country that has been occupied many times by various conquerors, including Alexander the Great, Genghis Khan, and Timur, known in the West as Tamerlane. It has been invaded by Huns, Turks, and Arabs, the latter bringing a new religion – Islam.

Our first port of call was Istanbul, and after a day of sightseeing and buying Turkish rugs for our home in Tucson, we mentioned to the merchant that we were leaving the next day for Tashkent in Uzbekistan.

"Why in God's name would you want to go there?" was his reply.

It was a five-hour flight to Tashkent. When we arrived in the former Soviet Republic, it seemed that we were back in the cold war era. Only a few bare bulbs lit the airport building, and the immigration officer looked at us with suspicion and wonderment.

In order to obtain visas for this visit, each of us had to contact the Uzbekistan embassy in Washington, D.C., by telephone. We had carefully filled out all of the paperwork; I wondered why the interview with the officer was even necessary. Did we appear to be hippies or terrorists on the visa applications?

What I hadn't realized was that two years earlier, Uzbekistan's military had opened fire on protesters and killed hundreds if not thousands in the city of Andijan, which is located just east of Tashkent. Although Andijan was an important stop on the Silk Road, we opted not to visit this part of the country; it had become increasingly unstable following the withdrawal of the Soviets. Poverty and an upsurge in Islamic fundamentalism led to the massacre in Andijan. Some Westerners had been accused of helping the protesters; perhaps this was was why the Brooklyn-accented man at the Uzbek embassy in Washington was interested in finding out more about our background.

Unfortunately, there appears to be rising support for Islamists in the entire country, and there were (and probably still are) roadblocks about every forty miles. Our group of eight, plus Eugen and a local guide, travelled throughout the country in an air-conditioned Mercedes bus. In addition to visiting most of the major cities, such as Samarkand, Bukhara, and Khiva, we passed close to what used to be the Aral Sea. The Soviet master plan was to grow cotton and grain in the region. Beginning in 1960, they diverted two major rivers that fed the Aral Sea. The use of vast quantities of water and the overuse of chemicals poisoned the land with salt. What used to be the fourth-largest inland sea in the world is now twenty percent of its former size, with the rest mostly desert.

In Urgench, we visited three *madrassas* (Islamic religious schools for boys) located within the walls of the old town. We were given a tour of the schools by a pleasant English-speaking teacher. The boys start attending as young as nine or ten. After learning to read and write, they spend countless hours memorizing the Quran, and sit around wearing skullcaps with bowed heads. These young boys often come from families who cannot afford to send them to a secular school and are being indoctrinated at a very impressionable age.

Many of the *madrassas* in Pakistan, Afghanistan, and Uzbekistan are financed by Saudi Arabia to teach an austere and rigid form of Islam. These schools are seminaries designed to produce Muslim clerics. However, in Afghanistan, many of the schools are not as concerned with religious scholarship as with training religious fighters. The enemy is no longer the Russians; it is the Americans. I find all this disconcerting.

We decided, probably at John Moore's suggestion, to do some yurt camping. A yurt is a nomad's tent, which essentially is a large, colourful dome made of felt. The camp was set up in the middle of nowhere, and a number of camels were tethered outside. We felt like we were on a desert safari.

There was a yurt for the ladies, one for the gentlemen, and a third for dining. The dining yurt was decorated with bright colours and had a stage that was set up for an after-dinner performance by belly dancers. The food table seemed to be about eight inches off the ground, and although there were big pillows available, you had to eat half lying down. I am sure that dining in a yurt would have been much easier if I had been taking yoga lessons for the past fifty years.

Following this experience of "roughing it," we travelled to Tashkent,

Souvenirs from Uzbekistan.

the largest city in Central Asia. While many of its people live in Third World conditions, Tashkent is a First World city (almost) with an opera and ballet theatre, the only subway system in the region, sizeable parks, well-laid-out thoroughfares, and a few modern hotels and commercial buildings. The subway system is modelled after the Moscow subway, and many of its stations have elaborate decorations, including crystal chandeliers. We were able to get tickets to an opera and found that nearly all of the patrons were speaking Russian.

In Uzbekistan, security is very tight. When leaving the country, you have to park about three hundred yards from the airport terminal, and a porter brings the luggage. There is currently a travel warning from Ottawa which states that Canadians should exercise a high degree of caution. They further mention that terrorists may be planning attacks on foreigners.

When we departed in the middle of the night, the customs people gave Eugen a hard time by examining each and every item he had purchased in the many bazaars we visited on this exciting trip. For a while, I was afraid they were not going to let him go, but it all worked out.

Train Ride in Ecuador

MOST exotic travel is rewarded with exhilarating experiences, but sometimes they come with a few frightening ones, too. One was a near robbery on a train in Ecuador. We were en route from Quito to the port city of Guayaquil, to catch a plane to the Galapagos Islands. This trip was in the mid-1970s, before much of the track between Quito and Guayaquil was permanently wiped out by the devastating *El Niño* floods of 1982–83. We were advised to take a bus from Quito to Riobamba to catch the train for the most exciting part of the trip.

After passing through some picturesque towns and beautiful countryside, the train began the hair-raising descent of the *Nariz del Diablo* (Devil's Nose). When the rail line was built in the early 1900s, it was described as "the most difficult railway in the world." It drops thousands of feet as it descends precipitously through a series of tight zigzags down the mountain. The rickety old tracks cross a 400-foot-deep gorge and pass through dozens of low tunnels.

With Sonia in Ecuador.

Top: *The hair-raising train ride in Ecuador.*
Bottom: *Riding atop the train.*

Passengers are encouraged to ride on the top of the train cars for a better view but are warned to hang on tightly. Usually the tops of the cars are very crowded with tourists as well as locals selling fruit and trinkets. The day we took the train and elected to sit up on top, there were few people – perhaps only four or five individuals per car.

This is a spectacular and terrifying ride. As Sonia and I were perched up top, hanging tightly on to the centre bars, two ominous-looking individuals started walking slowly from the last train car toward the one on which we were riding, eyeing each passenger very carefully. At the same time that we noticed these two characters, the other two passengers on our car, an attractive French couple, got up and asked if they could join us, because they had the same reaction we did, and felt that we were all in danger of being robbed. There was safety in numbers. The two men jumped onto our car and, after giving us a hard look, moved on. We then chatted with the couple and they took our picture. We offered to reciprocate, but they did not want their photo taken because, they explained, they were both with Air France and were *un couple illigitime.*

HORSEBACK RIDING IN PATAGONIA

THE southern portion of Chile and Argentina is a unique and beautiful area. We have visited there twice and I would love to return. It seems like the end of the earth with bleak, windswept plains, majestic snowcapped mountains, and forbidding glaciers. There are also some incredible lodges that offer hiking, skiing, horseback riding, and just plain sightseeing.

We were on a five-day visit to Explora Lodge in Torres del Paine National Park, located close to the southern tip of Chile. At lunch one day, a striking young woman, who was wearing low-cut blue jeans and had a bare midriff, approached our table and asked if everyone had plans for the afternoon. As she walked up to where I was sitting, I turned my head and looked straight into a big belt buckle. It appeared that I was the only tourist with time on my hands; she told me to put on some jeans and meet her at the front door in five minutes. I suddenly found myself joining a group of twenty riders who were far more fit and experienced than yours truly. While I had done quite a bit of riding when we lived in Montreal, I hadn't been on a horse in thirty years.

The horses were all saddled up, skittish, and ready to go. The saddles, half way between English and Western style, sat on a beautiful sheepskin and were very comfortable. So far, so good. With yet another attractive Englishwoman leading the group, we all took off at a gallop. Miraculously, I did not fall off. Soon, we were fording rushing rivers with the water coming up to the horses' stomachs. We climbed up and down some very steep embankments and then back to the open plain where we resumed our full-out gallop. When our group paused for a short break, seven of us fell to chatting, marvelling that we were all still alive. Our leader informed us that the ride back was to be at a fast clip, but there were vans ahead, so if we wished to drive back, we could leave our horses here. Our group quickly decided to jump in the van and thank God that we were all still in one piece.

The next day, we boarded an expedition ship sailing to the island of South Georgia. I was so stiff and sore that, for more than a week, I could barely get out of my bunk.

WINDSURFING IN LAMU

SONIA and I were visiting Uganda for the African Medical and Research Foundation (AMREF) annual meeting, and before leaving East Africa, were invited by one of the senior flying doctors, Dr. Anne Spoerry, to visit her on the island of Lamu. She flew us in her Piper Cherokee Lance, a fast and powerful aircraft. She was an experienced pilot, with over eight thousand hours of flying time.

Once we had reached our cruising altitude, she put on the autopilot, closed her eyes under her Toronto Blue Jays baseball cap, and proceeded to have a little nap. After about ten minutes, I gave her a nudge, to make sure we were on course. She claimed she was not *really* asleep. Anne is very well known and loved in Africa and wrote an autobiography, *They Call Me Mama Daktari* – her name in Swahili. She was a great friend of Sir Michael Wood, one of the original flying doctors. Anne died in 1999.

When we visited Lamu in the mid-1970s, there were few tourists. Lamu is a small island off the Kenyan coast, close to the border with Somalia. There are no roads on the island, just alleyways and footpaths. Everyone moves around on foot or by boat; donkeys are used to transport goods. The port was founded by Arab traders as early as the fourteenth century and it prospered on the slave trade.

After much effort, a couple of years before this trip, I had learned to windsurf. On the beach in Lamu, I spotted a young fellow who was renting windsurfers. The sun was shining, and the wind was moderate. He did mention that the wind was stronger beyond a point of land that he indicated in the distance. His reference to wind strength was a serious understatement, which I was soon to discover. He also pointed out an island, in case I wanted to take a rest before returning.

I started off successfully, then the wind gradually began to pick up. Once I rounded the aforementioned point of land, the moderate breeze turned into a gale, and the sea was quite rough. I hung on for dear life and made it to the island for a much-appreciated rest. I doubted that I could make it back through the high winds and waves, not to mention an ocean current that was running out to sea, but I had to try. As I feared would happen, I eventually fell into the brine. I wasn't attached to the board, nor was I wearing a life jacket. With the current going one way, and the wind the other, there was no way I could catch the board. I was being drawn out to sea and was beginning to think about sharks. There were no boats in sight. I hoped Sonia would notice my absence and alert the surfboard gentleman.

I then saw a powerboat in the distance and frantically waved my arms. Luckily, someone on board spotted me, and a boatload of British tourists rescued me, as well as my surfboard. When I was returned to the beach, Sonia did mention that she had just alerted the man in charge of surfboard rentals. Had I not been rescued, the next port of call would have been India – two thousand miles across the Arabian Sea.

PARASAILING IN PUERTO VALLARTA

AFTER returning from Paris to Toronto in 1971, our family took a number of winter vacations in Mexico. Puerto Vallarta was one of our favourite destinations. Until the mid-1960s, it was a remote fishing village on the Pacific coast. What put it on the map was the filming of the famous movie *The Night of the Iguana*. The play on which the play was based was written by Tennessee Williams; the movie was directed by John Huston and starred Richard Burton, Ava Gardiner, and Deborah Kerr.

The movie was a great success but it was the love affair between

Richard Burton and Elizabeth Taylor that really caught people's attention. Burton brought his soon-to-be-wife to view the filming. By all accounts, they both fell in love with this seaside town, with its winding cobblestone streets. Burton bought a house in the middle of town called Casa Kimberly and gave it to Elizabeth for her thirty-fourth birthday. He then bought a house across the street and built an attractive overpass, known as a "love bridge," between the two structures. Casa Kimberly became one of Mexico's most famous celebrity landmarks. Elizabeth Taylor owned the house throughout their two marriages (and divorces) and for about ten years after Burton's death in the early 1980s.

Mismaloya, a small village about a twenty-minute drive south of Puerto Vallarta, was the location of the filming. We stayed at an excellent hotel called the Garza Blanca, very close to Mismaloya beach. Because of the notoriety of the area in the early 1970s, a planned gated community was being promoted, offering lots on the steep hillsides overlooking Los Arcos, a spectacular island about three miles offshore. Bryson Farrill, a colleague of mine at McLeod Young Weir, had just finished building a spectacular house just outside this new community. Bryce called his new vacation home Casa Helga after his new wife.

The creation of this new development was in the very early stages, so there were few roads. However, with a four-wheel-drive Jeep and on foot, I began looking for a lot overlooking Los Arcos. I finally found a small lot and gave a $250 down payment. I knew once I got back to Toronto I would likely see the light and not go through with this purchase. Years later, with the help of a Mexican lawyer, I did officially get out of this commitment, but for many years I kept getting letters saying that my payments were getting lost in the mail. Fifteen years later, I visited the area and found that the development never really got off the ground. My lot with its beautiful view was still available.

Our hotel had a beautiful beach with soft white sand that was long but not very wide. Parasailing had become popular, so I decided to take a ride. I was impressed at how you could be gently lowered onto the narrow beach without getting wet. At this beach, there is a strong onshore wind, so you must descend steeply to avoid hitting hotel buildings and palm trees. However, there were many strong boys available to catch you if the landing was going badly. The ride was exciting. Nobody told me that parasailing could be dangerous.

The next day, I decided to take my camera to take pictures of Los Arcos, because I knew, of course, that it would not get wet. Up I went, taking many photos. When it came time to land, the wind was blowing hard. As I approached the buildings and the trees at a steep angle, I started drifting sideways at a pretty good clip, just before touchdown. The catchers were nowhere to be found. I should have allowed myself to fall sideways, as parachutists do, but I tried to stop myself and heard a bone in my left leg snap as I hit the ground.

The catchers finally appeared, put me on a chaise lounge, and carried me through the hotel dining room. My foot looked terrible; it was turned ninety degrees to the left, but the skin was not broken. I was transported in a dump truck to the closest hospital, which happened to be a maternity hospital, and examined by a father and daughter pair of doctors. They told me no X-ray equipment was available but they knew the ankle must be repaired without delay or all circulation to the foot would be cut off.

The hospital was quite clean, though there was blood on some of the plastic sheeting covering the beds. There seemed to be a number of women giving birth, and there were kids riding bikes in and out of rooms and through the hallways.

They concluded that I had dislocated my ankle and broken the fibula, the small bone in the lower leg. I was very happy to be there and in the hands of medical staff who knew what they were doing. Sonia had arrived at the hospital, and, after a brief discussion with her, I was given a general anaesthetic and woke up with my foot straightened out in a walking cast, feeling no pain. The doctor told me he could not repair the fibula but that I should be able to travel the next day if we could arrange a flight.

Of all people, John Dinnick walked into my room. I was working for McLeod Young Weir at the time, and John was the president of the company. I had no idea he was in Puerto Vallarta and was very pleasantly surprised to see him. He asked if there was anything he could do to make me more comfortable. I thought for a moment and said that I was still wearing my bathing suit and it was full of sand. Could he help me take it off and then see where we could find some dry underwear? There was President John standing on the bed, working away at pulling my bathing suit over my big cast. The two of us never forgot that incident.

Although no patient should fly the day after a general anaesthetic, the doctor and his daughter escorted us to the plane and signed something stating that I was fit to fly. They found me some crutches, though I was barely strong enough to climb the stairs to the plane.

The day after arriving home, I was examined by Dr. Allan Gross, a senior surgeon at Mount Sinai Hospital. Dr. Gross said that, because fever blisters had developed around the ankle and up the leg, it was too late to operate, but he could set the fibula manually while giving me injections of valium. As a nurse gave me 20 mg. injections, he manipulated the bone through the skin. In spite of the valium, it was very painful. I ended up receiving 80 mg. of the drug before they finished and wheeled me out into the hall, directly under a phone. In my drugged state, I called everyone I could think of, carrying out, I am sure, some very incoherent conversations.

Pickpockets in Nairobi

ANOTHER memorable scare occurred in Nairobi, during one of our trips with AMREF. Margi Zeidler, the managing director of AMREF Canada, was walking with Sonia and me along Jomo Kenyatta Boulevard in the middle of the day when we turned up a side street to find a store that Sonia had visited the day before. After a couple of blocks, as I was pointing out that the neighbourhood was deteriorating, we were suddenly confronted by a rather big man.

As I moved to the right, he moved the same way, until I put my hands up to stop from bumping into him. At that moment, I felt a hand in my back pocket and realized that my wallet had been stolen by someone right behind me.

Margi saw this pickpocket throw the wallet to a third individual, and, being a strong person, she lifted this little guy right off his feet. I made a big commotion and attracted quite a crowd. I pointed to the big guy who, by this time, had my wallet. As he and his two accomplices started backing up, he threw the wallet on the ground, and I pounced on it. Everyone, including me, started chasing the three thieves. I quickly dropped out of the race, since I had no idea what I would have done if we had actually caught them.

We told this story to our driver, whose immediate comment was,

"I hope you were not there when they caught them." He explained that the crowd would have killed them on the spot. In Kenya, the police turn a blind eye to vigilante justice. The crowd's attitude would have been that these were not Kenyans (they were most likely Somalis), and they were destroying Kenya's tourist industry and its economy.

In Shanghai.

Karate Chop in Shanghai

WHEN our daughter, Sheila, and her family were living in Shanghai, we visited them at least annually, occasionally acting as babysitters when either she or her husband, Dominic, were travelling. On occasion, when I had time on my hands, I wandered around Shanghai on my own and became somewhat knowledgeable about this bustling city of nearly twenty million people. Because my Mandarin is non-existent, I carried half a dozen business cards from major international hotels, so that I could direct taxis back to familiar territory.

One day, I was walking from the Bund, central Shanghai's historic waterfront area, to the Ritz-Carlton – a distance of just over a mile. Young men and women would suddenly appear, slap some shoe polish on, and proceed to polish my leather loafers. By the third time, I had become quite exasperated, so I grabbed the young guy by his shirt collar, and raised my hand as if to give him a karate chop to the top of his neck.

I actually stopped short of striking him. Half a dozen young shoe-shine boys who witnessed this fake chop burst out laughing and I became their hero. When I told my son-in-law what I had done, he was amazed. He pointed out the possible consequences of my actions, as it could have escalated into a serious incident. After this incident, I switched to wearing running shoes and started carrying a briefcase in an attempt to look less like a wandering tourist.

Garden Route in South Africa

IN the early '80s, Sonia and I enjoyed a three-week visit to South Africa. This was in the days of apartheid and, although things were unsettled, we saw a great deal of the country. One uncomfortable incident occurred on a driving trip we took from Cape Town to Port Elizabeth. This scenic four-day drive is known as the Garden Route and is very popular with tourists.

We rented a car and left our hotel in Cape Town around nine o'clock. The concierge suggested that we take a picnic lunch because there wasn't an ideal place to dine. He then showed us a turnoff on the map that would lead us to a beautiful spot overlooking the ocean. We set off, driving carefully on the left-hand side. Leaving Cape Town and navigating the roundabouts and expressway ramps was a bit disconcerting, but we finally made it to the highway that follows the coast.

At noon, we studied the map carefully and turned off the highway onto a dirt road that led to the picnic site. The first mile was straightforward, but then the road became narrower and the pampas grass on either side seemed to be getting taller. At this point, we became worried that we had taken the wrong road. Rounding a bend, we were suddenly confronted with an armoured truck blocking the road. The back of the vehicle, which appeared to have been customized in an unprofessional manner, was reinforced with a half-inch steel plate, and the back doors were secured with a giant padlock.

We were sure we were going to be robbed – or worse. There was no way to turn around, so I slammed the car into reverse and backed up about three miles, as quickly as possible. We had indeed taken the wrong road and although we were not harmed, this incident left us a bit shaken.

LOCKED IN A FRENCH MEDIEVAL TOWER

OVER the years, Sonia and I have taken many bicycle trips in Europe. The first was Butterfield & Robinson's inaugural adult trip in the early 1980s, which I described earlier. Later, we joined a Toronto group put together by David and Debbie Beatty. These trips are run by Glenn Ford, a charming and witty Englishman and an Oxford graduate, now living in Alsace. Glenn has a pronounced Cockney accent, which is still discernible when he is speaking French.

In 2010, we joined nine other couples for a cycling tour of Provence. After arriving in Avignon, we were driven to the Château de Massillan, where we changed into our biking attire and did a nine-mile warm-up tour near the château. Our room was at the top of one of the towers. We had a bit of difficulty opening the two sets of doors, but managed to let ourselves in, then changed for cocktails and dinner.

Sonia had left something behind, so she left me and walked down a long winding staircase to the front desk. When she returned, neither of us could open the door. The owner of the château came up with one of the staff and tried all of his keys. Nothing seemed to work. Finally, after banging too hard with his hammer, he broke the lock.

Biking in Provence.

I was locked in the tower, and the village locksmith could not be reached. I felt trapped. Moreover, this was a terrible dilemma because it was the cocktail hour. I thought of tying bed sheets together, but when I looked out the window, I realized the ground was hundreds of feet down. Sonia sat outside on the stairs drinking her cocktail while I consumed the entire bottle of champagne that was in the mini-bar. Chatting through a double set of doors, we tried to pretend we were having fun. Eventually, the locksmith was located but he was unable to fix the ancient lock. The hinges holding the steel door had to be cut with a blowtorch in order to rescue me. An interesting start to a wonderful, and otherwise uneventful, ten-day trip.

La Défense in Paris

WHEN we lived in Paris in the late 1960s, there was an eighty-acre district consisting of factories, shanties, and a few farms known as La Défense. It was named after the statue, La Défense de Paris, which was erected in 1883 to commemorate the city's defence during the Franco-Prussian War. Since our return to Canada, seventy-two glass-and-steel skyscrapers had been built on this land, as well as an extension of the Paris Metro, making the district accessible to one hundred and eighty thousand workers daily. The area is now Europe's largest purpose-built business district, comparable to London's Canary Wharf.

Sonia and I had never set foot in this new centre of commerce, so on a visit to Paris in 1998, we took the Metro and proceeded to the district, with the intention of strolling through the lobbies of the high-rise buildings.

Few people were in the area on this bright Sunday morning, and the small shops were closed and shuttered. We obviously looked like tourists and noticed that we were being observed by small groups of young men, most likely French of Algerian ancestry. There were a few security people in the buildings but they were not always in evidence.

We saw, as we started up a long three-storey escalator, that not only had a group of these men boarded behind us, but another had formed at the top. We frantically scanned the area for a security person, knowing we were headed for a confrontation. Sonia put her purse over her shoulder and, as we got close to the summit, we put our heads down, shouted, and barged through the group. We then spotted some security guards, and the groups vanished.

Lesson learned: Don't visit La Défense on a Sunday.

Polar Regions

The Canadian Arctic – July 2001

SONIA and I had made a number of trips to the Arctic, but it was challenging, logistically, to get to the High Arctic, as there was no commercial air service. This is that vast area north of Resolute Bay, which is the second most northerly community in Canada, after Grise Fiord. Located on Cornwallis Island, Resolute is at about seventy-five degrees north latitude. It has a gravel runway long enough to accommodate commercial jets, and acts as the termination point for regular scheduled flights from southern Canada.

With a population of two hundred and fifty, Resolute is a cold, windy, and desolate place. Surprisingly, it gets very little snow. It became an Inuit community in 1953 with the controversial relocation of several families from northern Quebec and one family from Pond Inlet on Baffin Island.

When I indicated my interest in visiting the High Arctic, George Butterfield, of Butterfield & Robinson, suggested that I contact Richard Weber and his wife, Josée Auclair. They specialized in travel to Arctic regions, and also ran a wilderness lodge called Arctic Watch, which is located on the northern tip of Somerset Island, a half-hour flight south of Resolute.

Richard and Josée, both champion cross-country skiers, had led numerous trips to the North Pole, and Josée had also led an all-women excursion to the South Pole. Their sons, who had also been to the North Pole, helped their parents run the lodge, making this wonderful family Nunavut's largest outfitter.

With the help of Richard, Josée, and our good friend and travel agent *extraordinaire* Kathii Benn, we created a ten-day Arctic safari, designed for us to see as much as we could of the High Arctic, and, we hoped, to get as close as possible to the stepping-off point to the North Pole.

Sonia, Kathii, and I arrived in Resolute and flew south to Arctic Watch in a de Havilland Beaver aircraft with a huge radial engine. The Inuit pilot of this old workhorse made a superb landing on a small gravel landing strip, right beside the lodge.

The lodge consisted of a large white igloo made of some composite material. The bedrooms were smaller igloos of the same material and design, connected by walkways to the lodge. It looked a bit like a futurist's idea of a settlement on the moon.

We spent three days there, hiking and riding great distances in all-terrain vehicles. Anytime we went to a far-off location, we were accompanied by a staff person with a gun, in case we were attacked by a polar bear. No bears crossed our path, but we did encounter many muskox that looked at us menacingly if we got too close. We were also treated to the inspiring sight of hundreds of beluga whales that had recently arrived with the breakup of the sea ice. On one occasion, we drove a considerable distance to a landlocked lake, which was teeming with arctic char. We caught many fish to take back to the lodge for dinner.

We then returned to Resolute and joined three other adventurers for our trip north. One was a charming Englishman who had come all the way from London for this trip; rounding out the group was an American woman and her son. The charter company, Kenn Borek Air, had to restrict the number of passengers because the plane needed to carry maximum fuel. We soon found out that the operators of aircraft in the Arctic have fuel stashed in hundred-gallon drums all over the region. Some of us became quite proficient at climbing up on the wing and pumping jet fuel from the drums into our Twin Otter.

Upon leaving Resolute, we headed north to Axel Heiberg Island. En route, we spent many hours crossing Devon Island, which is described as the largest uninhabited island in the world. It is interesting to note that all of these extremely large islands in the Far North, with the exception of Ellesmere Island, are devoid of permanent settlements. Some had been attempted in the 1920s and '30s, but due to wind conditions and an extremely cold climate, the Inuit families chose to leave Devon to return to Baffin Island.

Axel Heiberg is the third largest in the Queen Elizabeth Islands group. Unlike most of the islands in the High Arctic, which are relatively flat, over half of this island is mountainous, and it has extensive ice fields and glaciers. Our first destination on the island was the McGill Arctic Research Station, established in 1960, at Expedition Fiord. The station is on the western side of the island, where the mountains rise precipitously from the sea, reaching a height of 6500 feet. The weather station is one of the longest-operating seasonal facilities in the High Arctic and can accommodate up to twelve people during the short summer season.

Landing our plane at this destination was an exciting experience. We proceeded up a long and steep fjord with Sonia convinced that our wings were going to graze the mountains. The captain of the plane assigned to the co-pilot the task of landing in this difficult and remote place. We made two attempts that were aborted; then the captain took over. We had to make a very tight left turn on our final approach over water, then ice, and, finally, permafrost. The soft muskeg brought us to an abrupt stop, as our big balloon tires got stuck in the muck. Since Kathii and I both have a pilot's licence, we were truly impressed with the skill of both our pilots. Sonia was just glad to have landed safely. We enjoyed a pleasant one-hour visit with the researchers at the station, who were happy to see us because, as they pointed out, "Visitors seldom drop by for a chat."

We were able to get the plane turned around; then, with full power, we seemed to literally jump into the air. We headed northwest, toward the famous fossil forest. In 1985, tree stumps and fallen trees were discovered on Axel Heiberg; they have since been dated at forty million years old. This fossil forest is not petrified wood, but contains all of its organic matter, which provides a unique look into an ancient ecosystem. There is evidence that some of this wood and other prehistoric animal material is being removed, probably by other tourists. Plans are in the works to protect these artifacts.

We then headed northeast to Eureka, on Ellesmere Island, which is a small research station that was set up in 1947 as a weather station and is the second most northerly permanent research community in the world. The only one farther north is Alert, also on Ellesmere Island. However, Alert is classified as a military base and does not welcome visitors. Eureka boasts of having the lowest annual temperature of any weather station in Canada. It is manned by eight staff, in continuous rotation, and is supplied by one ship a year from Montreal. We were warmly welcomed by the staff, handed some blankets and a towel, and told to take any room we wanted, since all of them were unlocked. There was a small cozy lounge with satellite TV that had beer and liquor for sale. We enjoyed an excellent buffet-style dinner with the staff – very civilized!

We all had a long sleep (especially the pilots) because our circuitous flight from Resolute had probably lasted twenty hours. The next leg of our trip was likely to be even longer; there would be no other accommodation available to us until we reached Grise Fiord, located on the southern tip of Ellesmere Island.

When it is light twenty-four hours a day, you tend to forget about nighttime. Before departing on our journey, we had asked the charter company if we could take tents for overnighting but were told that this was not possible. They did say we could be left somewhere for a week and be picked up; however, because of changing weather conditions, the plane was not allowed to remain on the ground overnight, except at a weather station.

We took on maximum fuel at Eureka and headed for Ellesmere National Park, which is located on the northern part of the island and is now called Quttinirpaaq National Park. Our destination was Fort Conger, located on Nares Strait, a deep waterway separating Greenland from Ellesmere Island. The strait is perhaps twenty miles across; we could see Greenland and its ice cap clearly during our two-hour stopover.

Fort Conger, at eighty-one and a half degrees north, is approximately six hundred miles from the North Pole and is well known as the site of the Greeley expedition of 1881 to 1884. This expedition was originally known as the Lady Franklin Bay Expedition and is one of the most interesting, but also most tragic, expeditions ever sent to the Arctic. It was led by Lieutenant Adolphus Greeley of the United States Army.

Many excellent books have been written about this ill-fated expedition, which was supposed to last one winter in the High Arctic but ended up stretching over three long and difficult years. Nineteen of Greeley's twenty-five-man crew died from starvation, drowning, or hypothermia, and one was executed. Just about everything that could have gone wrong, did. Poor planning, inexperience, and bad weather all contributed to the tragedy. Cruelty, violence, and even cannibalism darkened the picture during the last days before rescue.

There are very few visitors to this historic place, but I had read a great deal about the failed expedition and was anxious to see the site of this terrible tragedy. Our pilots had never visited Fort Conger. On arriving, we observed that there were huge boulders everywhere. The pilot made a number of passes before setting the plane down in a very constricted area.

The only sign of habitation was a collection of five small wooden buildings that were virtually derelict. One of the reasons for building the camp on this site was the presence of an open coal seam about a half-mile away. I walked up the hill and got a look at the source of the coal.

There is an effort currently under way to save this site from further deterioration, as it was a staging point for American explorer Robert Peary's three attempts to reach the North Pole. It was also used by many other explorers and by the Inuit and other groups until 1937.

Our plan, after leaving Fort Conger, was to fly to Lake Hazen, a base camp and air access point to Ellesmere National Park. This small landing strip is the stepping-off point for anyone wishing to hike in this vast area at the northern tip of Ellesmere. When we landed at Lake Hazen, the sun was shining; it was pleasant and even a bit warm. However, the pilot told us that there was a snowstorm to the north and we couldn't proceed any farther. We were about five hundred miles from the Pole and one hundred and fifty miles from the Ward Hunt Island ice shelf, from which Polar expeditions leave Ellesmere Island. This was somewhat disappointing because we were hoping to get to the most northerly point of land.

We spent many hours at Lake Hazen before departing for the six-hundred-mile flight to Grise Fiord on the southern tip of Ellesmere Island. Canada's third largest island, Ellesmere covers 76,000 square miles. The Arctic Cordillera mountain system, with peaks as high as 8500 feet, covers most of the island. It is extremely rugged with vast ice fields, glaciers, and long, deep crevasses. We did not fly directly over the highest peaks but enjoyed incredible views of the mountains and ice fields. We made at least one refuelling stop before arriving at our destination, after another twenty-hour day.

At seventy-six degrees north, Grise Fiord has a population of 168, with the only other inhabitants of Ellesmere Island being the staff at the weather station of Eureka and the military base at Alert. The community rests at the foot of 2500-foot-high mountains and overlooks Jones Sound. The winter temperatures remain consistently in the –30C to –45C range, and the earliest it gets above freezing is July. The extreme cold of the area causes the sea to remain solidly frozen for ten months of the year.

Our plane dropped Sonia, Kathii, and me at Grise Fiord and took off for Resolute with our three fellow passengers, who were ending their trip.

We were advised that an aircraft would be making a scheduled run to Grise Fiord the next day and would take us to Resolute, where we could connect to a commercial flight to Ottawa.

The question for the operators of our small guest house at Grise Fiord was, "What are we going to do to keep these three adventurers occupied?' One suggestion that appealed to Kathii and me, but not to Sonia, was to be taken by skidoo to the site of a polar bear trap that was used by the Inuit a thousand years ago.

This trip involved a fifteen-mile journey over sea ice that was in the process of breaking up. In fact, the ice near the shore had already done so, and the snow machines were parked on solid ice about a third of a mile offshore. Two Inuit guides accompanied us out to them, because the only way to get there was to jump from one floe to the next.

Kathii and I were squeezed into a little wooden sleigh that was connected by a long towrope to a skidoo on which the two guides rode. Their machine nearly went into the sea a couple of times before reaching solid ice, leaving the two of us wondering if we would be next. After about an hour, we arrived at a rocky point. With difficulty, we were able to get ashore by walking over unstable and shifting ice.

The ancient polar bear trap consisted of a large stone cairn, about three feet high and just wide enough for a bear to pull himself forward to reach a piece of seal meat that had been deposited at the far end of the trap. With no space to turn around, the poor bear was trapped after he reached the bait.

There were no major incidents on the way back until we parked the skidoos and started to walk back to shore over the breaking ice pack. I was wearing rubber sailing boots that had no tread. Just before reaching the shore, I fell through a bit of overhanging ice and slithered down an icy slope into the frigid water. The ice floes appeared to be four to six feet in depth. Straightening up, I was able to momentarily stop myself by putting my feet against the next ice floe. I became submerged up to my chest in a matter of seconds, but our two strong Inuit guides immediately grabbed my arms and pulled me out.

The shock of the freezing water was one thing, but it was secondary to my objective of avoiding a complete dunking. We arrived at our guest-house within five minutes, and my soaking wet clothes were put in a dryer.

As frightening as it was, it was not the most terrifying experience of my life because I knew our two guides were only a few feet away.

The next day, we flew back to Ottawa without incident. What an unforgettable trip!

THE ANTARCTIC – FEBRUARY 2004

Once we were knowledgeable about some regions of our Canadian Arctic, Sonia and I started thinking about the South Pole. We were introduced by our friend Kathii to a fellow Torontonian, Dave German, who had been running Antarctic adventure cruises, as well as trips to the European Arctic, for a number of years.

In 2004, we signed up for our first Antarctic voyage. This was a three-week expedition on a one-hundred-passenger ship, the *Polar Star*, which was designed to retrace the route taken by Ernest Shackleton and his crew aboard his ship *Endurance*.

After spending some time in Patagonia, Chile, we arrived in Ushuaia, in southern Argentina, to board the ship. Ushuaia and Puerto Williams, which is just across the Beagle Channel in Chile, are two of the southernmost settlements in the world. The Beagle Channel was named after the HMS *Beagle*, the ship made famous by Charles Darwin. Darwin was invited on the ship's second voyage as a gentleman's companion, giving him opportunities as an amateur naturalist.

After two days at sea in moderately choppy conditions, we anchored off one of the outer islands in the Falkland Islands. Going ashore in rubber Zodiacs, we enjoyed tea with two staunchly British families. The charming people who owned two farms confided that they did miss civilization and travelled by boat to the capital, Port Stanley, about once a month for provisions. Then a group of us took a long hike in rolling grasslands. Our leader assured us that the hike would be one and a half miles around the inner harbour – but it ended up being more like six and a half. This island contains extensive sheep farms and, like all of the Falklands, is devoid of trees, except for Port Stanley. This was the most desolate place I had ever visited.

The population of the more than seven hundred islands that make up the Falklands is currently estimated to be 3,140, but these permanent residents are augmented by a significant number of British troops (perhaps

1,500) who have remained on the Island since the end of the 1982 Falklands War. Everything in Port Stanley is very British, with pictures of Margaret Thatcher, Tony Blair, and other U.K. politicians everywhere. Many of the homeowners have painted a Union Jack on their roofs. Pubs with catchy names are in evidence in downtown Port Stanley, and most of the street names come from London, much as they do in my hometown of London, Ontario.

Leaving the Falklands, our ship headed for King Haakon Bay on South Georgia's coast, Shackleton's landing place. We sailed for two days, passing close to Shag Rocks where big whales are often spotted, although unfortunately not by us. The crossing was very rough, as demonstrated on the first night, when some of the many Antarctic specialists on board tried to make presentations in the ship's lounge. The first, a tall gentleman, tried to steady himself with one hand on the ceiling, but to no avail. Chairs were tumbling off the stage, curtains were falling down, and it quickly became apparent that the passengers might be better to find a good book and a comfortable, secure chair. When it started to look like some speaker might break a leg, Dave German announced that it was too rough to continue the presentation.

Sonia then asked if she could use the microphone. I had no idea what she had in mind. Did she want to abandon ship?

Taking the microphone, she said, "Since we have to remain seated, does anyone play bridge?"

When we arrived at the entrance to King Haakon Bay, the captain announced that those of us who wished to go ashore for the day would be taken into the bay in Zodiacs, while the ship would enter later with the crew. He explained further that only three ships a year enter the bay because of difficult ice conditions and uncertain charts. There were four separate passenger groups on the ship, and each landed on a different beach. We were deposited near the entrance, and our group leader was Dave German himself. He asked if we were game to hike up to the nesting places of the giant wandering albatross.

Although we gained less than 300 feet in altitude, it was a very difficult climb. The slope rose steeply from the beach and we had to press through wet and slippery tussock grass that could be six to seven feet high, making it difficult for us to see our footing. Small streams ran down the hillside,

Turkey-sized albatross chick.

and occasionally we stepped, with a jolt, into a two-foot gully. When we reached a plateau, we had incredible views of two large bays, numerous icebergs, and brilliant glaciers.

While up there, we also saw half a dozen large nests, each occupied by an albatross chick the size of an adult turkey. These chicks can weigh up to twenty-five pounds and they take twelve months to fully develop. The Wandering Albatross, with a wingspan that can measure up to twelve feet, lives to be eighty years old and can remain at sea for seven to ten years, always returning to the island where it was born. We didn't see any adult birds circling the sky above the nests, but earlier had observed petrels and albatrosses following the ship. We were careful not to get too close to the nests but could see these huge chicks, all covered in white fluff, sitting patiently waiting for their parents to feed them. They appeared to take no notice of our presence.

The island of South Georgia is also home to large numbers of the small and attractive fur seals. They can be quite aggressive as they approach you and try to bite your boots. These little seals have needle-sharp teeth designed for chewing air holes in the ice and are not afraid to use them, so most of us carried sticks, and chased them away with these, as we shouted at them. By the 1820s, the fur seal was nearly extinct, having being slaughtered by the whalers, but they are slowly rebuilding their numbers, especially on South Georgia.

We also encountered enormous female elephant seals (the males were out at sea). Sonia and I were walking on a beach away from our group when I quietly announced to her that I was just going to disappear behind a big boulder for a brief pit stop. As I started to slip behind this rock, I came face-to-face with an enormous seal that rose up on her hindquarters and bellowed at me. I was out of there like a rocket, mission unaccomplished.

At about seven that evening, as we were returning to the ship, we spotted some killer whales. After a beautiful, sunny day, the seas were calm and the passengers and many crew members had just sat down to dinner. Wine had been served and the ship was under way, travelling at about five knots. Leaving the bay, the ship was cautiously passing small icebergs. We were about to toast the captain for a very successful day on shore when suddenly we were interrupted by a loud scraping noise and the shuddering of the ship.

After perhaps twenty seconds, the ship came to a complete stop. As we listed to starboard, reaching a precarious angle, there was not a sound from the passengers or crew. We knew this was serious because the recently filled wine glasses were just on the verge of falling over. The silence remained, but before anyone could start heading for the deck, the Norwegian captain announced on the loudspeaker, in accented English, "As you have probably noticed, vee have grounded." He stated that we were not taking on water (he should have added "in the inner hull") and were to stay where we were until further notice.

We were already at high tide, so we could not wait for the tide to lift us off whatever had entrapped us. Our double-hulled Swedish research vessel had twin propellers at the bow as well as the stern, and the captain used these to try to rock the ship free and into deep water. After fifteen minutes, he succeeded, and we could feel the *Polar Star* slide off the pinnacle of rock thrusting up from the bottom of the bay.

Following our grounding, there was extensive radio transmission with the British Admiralty outlining our predicament. The ship was eventually given permission to sail around the island to the port of Grytviken, a former whaling station, a trip that took about twelve hours.

Fortunately for us, two Chilean divers were upgrading and repairing the station. They inspected the hull and reported that the damage to the outer hull was quite extensive with four major holes taking in tons of seawater. However, the ship was permitted to take day trips from Grytviken to visit extensive penguin colonies, some with over five hundred thousand birds in residence. We remained on South Georgia for an unscheduled five days while the divers completed temporary repairs. We were not allowed to proceed to Antarctica but returned instead to Ushuaia. Because of the rough seas in the Drake Passage, we were ordered to take a longer return route that followed the Argentinean coast.

The passengers chose a group of four to demand either a refund or a second voyage to Antarctica. We maintained that the operators of the vessel had not fulfilled their contract, which was to visit the Antarctic Peninsula, the South Sandwich Islands, the South Orkneys, and the South Shetland Islands. These last island groups were very important because thirty of the passengers were from England and Scotland and had a connection with these British islands in the South Atlantic. They were members of the Tom Crean Society, an organization that revered the explorer who was very close to Shackleton and had spent more time in this region than either Shackleton or Robert Falcon Scott. This group was particularly disappointed that we could not continue; they had been planning this trip for years.

Two years later, the shipping company did in fact offer a refund or a two-week trip on the same ship to the Antarctic Peninsula, including airfare. Sonia and I were delighted to return, as did eighty percent of our fellow passengers. My personal disappointment with the second trip was that the Drake Passage between Cape Horne and the Peninsula, reputed to be an extraordinarily rough channel, resembled a millpond on this occasion – both ways.

Our first stop on the second voyage was the notoriously hostile Elephant Island, an ice-covered, mountainous island off the coast of the Antarctic Peninsula. The Drake Channel seas were reasonably calm during this leg of the trip, yet what seemed like an innocent swell out on the Drake became a significant force where land was concerned. While we couldn't drop anchor, we could take the Zodiacs in to clearly see the forbidding small inlet and rocky beach where twenty-one of Shackleton's men landed in lifeboats in 1916, following the loss of their ship in the ice of the Weddell Sea. They spent four months in this desolate refuge before being rescued. And they wouldn't have been saved, if Shackleton, realizing there was no chance of rescue by passing ships, had not set out for South Georgia Island, where there was a whaling station. He left the island with five of his men on an eight-hundred-mile voyage in an open lifeboat, arriving at King Haakon Bay on South Georgia two weeks later. This voyage in howling winds and huge seas is one of the most incredible feats in the history of sailing and navigation.

Our two-week tour of the Antarctic Peninsula, where we enjoyed excellent weather, was spectacular. In addition to seeing many types of penguins and seals, we were fortunate to encounter dozens of minke and humpback whales, which playfully came very close to our Zodiacs. This second trip was well worth it.

Thousands of penguins on South Georgia.

Silhouettes.

Whales up close in the Antarctic.

The Norwegian Arctic – June 2008

Having enjoyed two successful adventure tours with Dave German, we booked a ten-day cruise with him on a small, twenty-five-passenger ship in the European High Arctic. The Svalbard Archipelago, administered by Norway, forms a group of islands well within the Arctic Circle, at eighty degrees north latitude – about six hundred miles from the North Pole. The largest island in the group is Spitsbergen. The principal town is Longyearbyen, which is where we boarded our small icebreaking vessel after a flight from Oslo. We were joined on this expedition by Carl and Jeanie Blöm and Joan Boswell, friends from Lake of Bays.

During the summer months, the west coast of the islands, warmed by the Gulf Stream, are free of ice, whereas the east coast is subject to a cold sea current from Siberia and is usually choked with pack ice, even in summer. Before entering the pack ice, we went ashore in Zodiacs on many occasions and observed reindeer herds and millions of migratory land and sea birds. On one hike, we came very close to perhaps a hundred walruses sunning themselves on a rocky island, grunting loudly. These huge mammals were nearly wiped out by hunters in the last century, but they are making a strong comeback in the Svalbard islands. Sonia tells me

On the island of Spitsbergen in the cold Norwegian Arctic.
Our small passenger ship is anchored in the background.

that climate change has caused fewer ice floes, which is why the walruses were crowded together on the rocks instead of out on their own ice floes, which they would have preferred.

We spent at least two days in the pack ice tracking polar bears. We successfully observed three bears at close range, watching them swim between ice floes as they tried to distance themselves from the ship. We were all invited to have a swim in the ocean, the temperature of which was slightly below zero. While neither Sonia nor I took advantage of this opportunity, others did. I'm not interested in water whose temperature is anything less than eighty degrees. At our cottage on Lake of Bays, the grandchildren all know my aversion to cold water and call me the president of the "chicken club."

For a number of days, Dave had been looking for a large and stable ice floe. His plan was to put the guests on the floe for a festive cocktail party and lunch. Wind conditions and currents were not favourable, but he kept hoping things would change. Finally, he announced that he would run some of our group to a floe in a Zodiac. A couple of boatloads of passengers were landed on the ice when suddenly two large floes collided. We barely had time to yank the Zodiac out of the water or it would have been crushed. Dave then called the ship on his walkie-talkie and asked for a second Zodiac to be sent, making it quite clear to the captain that we were abandoning the proposed cocktail party.

I then noticed a big crack across the floe we were standing on. This was truly frightening. I envisioned Sonia and me and some new-found friends drifting off to Siberia, never to be heard from again. We departed from the floe safely in the two Zodiacs, but I will never forget that feeling of imminent danger.

African Safari with the Family

ALTHOUGH Sonia and I had enjoyed viewing game in many parts of Africa, our children and grandchildren had never had this experience. It required three years of planning by Sonia to put this family safari together. Our children and their families were spread around the globe – in Shanghai, Singapore, France, and Toronto – and the only time we could all get together was during the 2010 Christmas holidays.

The grandchildren ranged in age from thirteen to nineteen. We felt they were certainly old enough to enjoy and remember the trip, but still young enough to be able to take nearly three weeks off from school or university. The fact that our son-in-law Dominic, who is a very busy individual, elected to take seventeen days away from the office pleased all of us. This family holiday presented a wonderful opportunity for Sonia and me to spend some quality time with everyone, and for our children and grandchildren to get to know each other a bit better.

Sonia worked with Kathii to devise a safari entirely in Tanzania. This plan allowed us to fly from Amsterdam directly to Kilimanjaro airport in Tanzania. Well, this is how it was supposed to work. However, our flight from Toronto was one of the last ones to land in Amsterdam because of a severe snowstorm that grounded most flights in northern Europe. Sheila and Dominic's daughter, Jessica, flew from Singapore and met the Toronto contingent in Amsterdam. Sheila, Dominic, and their son, Fraser, were to fly from London to board the same KLM flight to Kilimanjaro, however, their flight from London was cancelled, and our departure to Tanzania was delayed for four hours. Fortunately, the London group was able to fly to Kilimanjaro through Nairobi. This flight was the last out of Heathrow before most European airports were closed – some for nearly a week. We were all very fortunate to get to our destination.

We stayed overnight in Arusha and flew by chartered aircraft to the Sanctuary Kusini camp in the Southern Serengeti. This is a permanent tented camp established by Abercrombie & Kent and managed by a charming South African couple. The brand new tents, with excellent en suite facilities, were large and luxurious. We stayed three days at Kusini and enjoyed two game drives each day. Our three Toyota Land Cruisers were permitted to drive cross-country, enabling us to observe far more game at this location than at any other, including lions, wildebeests, gazelles, and hyenas. Our vehicles had four-wheel-drive and open roofs, so we not only could see lions, but also could photograph them feasting on their most recent kill. Our three guides were extremely knowledgeable about flora and fauna, as well as about African tribalism and customs.

Our next port of call was the Serena Lodge overlooking the Ngorongoro Crater. The lodge is at an altitude of 7500 feet and has an incredible view of an expanse of land thousands of feet below and more than thirty-five miles across. Ngorongoro is actually not a crater but a collapsed volcano

African Safari, Christmas 2010.

that erupted eight million years ago, spreading the ash that formed the Serengeti Plain.

We drove down to the crater floor and had a magnificent sit-down barbecue picnic under a tent, which the hotel had set up for this special occasion. The shelter was most fortunate because a torrential downpour occurred at one o'clock, just as we were about to eat. The party was a surprise celebration of the recent birthdays of our three children – Sheila, who had turned fifty on November 22, and the twins, John and Jacquie, whose birthday was on December 12. Sonia presented each with a large birthday card with their photo taken at age three. On the inside of the card was a collage of photos going back half a century. There were two other milestones that we celebrated at this get-together – our fiftieth wedding anniversary and my belated seventy-fifth birthday, for which our children proposed a wonderful toast. To cap the celebration, we were fortunate to see a rhino as well as a pool full of hippos on our return drive.

We then proceeded to Sanctuary Swala camp in Tarangire Park. It was a very long journey over poor roads but was well worth the effort. This camp was even more luxurious than Kusini and was situated in the central part of the Serengeti. This area is inhabited by hundreds of elephants, giraffes, and Cape buffalo. We were warned that the Cape buffalo is probably the most dangerous animal in the Serengeti, and that the large black beasts will charge for no apparent reason.

After dark, we were always accompanied to and from the dining area by a Masai guide who carried a long pointed stick. The buffalo that lived near this camp were much tamer than the ones found in a herd. There were perhaps half a dozen older males that had made the Swala camp their home. Our guide shone his flashlight in their eyes and gave them a poke, whereupon they ambled off. Also, elephants sometimes came right up to our tents, so you had to be cautious. Our three guides and most of the staff at the camp referred to me as *Babu* (grandfather) and Sonia as *Bibi* (mother safari).

In this region, the elephants rule and had driven the lions away. As one of our guides pointed out, the elephant is really the king of the jungle – not the lion. Elephants are very protective of their young. Although we saw very few big cats, we did spot a leopard walking along a branch of an acacia tree. Ten other vehicles soon joined us, but this beautiful spotted cat didn't seem to notice the convoy of tourists furiously snapping photos. It proceeded down the tree, head first, and disappeared into the tall grass, then reappeared beside the vans and sauntered past all of us down a dirt road. This behaviour was quite unusual, as leopards are hard to spot and generally stay out of sight.

We concluded our safari by flying directly to the Island of Zanzibar for a few days of beach time in a tropical setting, sightseeing, and celebration of New Year's. Most of the group spent considerable time upgrading their scuba diving skills.

This was a very special and memorable trip: It was the only one that has included our entire family. Following our return, our daughter, Jacquie, who is a photojournalist, collected the best of all of the photos taken by the family. With Sheila's contribution as a Photoshop technician and cartographer, and John's help in the final edit of thousands of pictures, Jacquie spearheaded a major project to produce a large, beautifully bound photo album that gives our three families a lasting memory of this great holiday together.

Above and following pages: Our African Safari, Christmas 2010.

My Italian restaurant look – in case I decided to give up my day job.

XIII OTHER PURSUITS

MUSIC

UPON retiring from Trimark in 2000, I envisioned having lots of time for hobbies, sporting endeavours, and travel. One particular activity I wanted to concentrate on was music. Playing and collecting various instruments is a hobby I have pursued since I was seven years old. I've mentioned my first music teacher, Mother de Chantal, a wonderfully kind Ursuline nun whom I will never forget. She taught me the violin as well as the piano, and although I played half a dozen instruments, I was most proficient with the violin.

When I was eleven, I switched violin teachers and took lessons for four years from Margaret Tremeer. Miss Tremeer had polio as a child. Although she was able to drive a car, she had considerable difficulty getting in and out. I became quite adept at assisting her and this helped me understand the difficulties that physically challenged people experience in everyday life. She was a great teacher and pushed me to enter competitions and music festivals in both London and Toronto. I don't recall winning any of the major ones, but was placed second or third on a number of occasions. I was never disappointed with the outcomes.

Miss Tremeer introduced me to Gordon Jeffery, a famous organist and conductor in London, as well a lawyer whose family controlled the London Life Insurance Company. Gordon had gutted an older building in downtown London and installed a massive baroque organ in a large high-ceilinged room that resembled a concert hall. I was thirteen at the time, and Miss Tremeer had instructed me in playing second violin in a number of classical pieces arranged for a string quartet. She played first violin. The violist and the cellist were adults, which made me the only young person in the group. Gordon set up our quartet on a small stage and was a one-man audience for our recital. He then played the organ for us and later asked us to play one of our pieces again and quietly accompanied us on the organ.

Besides having a massive baroque organ in his two-storey office, he owned a number of famous instruments, including two violins made by Stradivarius and one by Guarnerius. Upon his death, these instruments were donated to the Faculty of Music String Instrument Bank at the University of Western Ontario. The Gordon Jeffery Music Foundation sponsors concerts in London to this day.

At McGill, my violin was stolen, and I didn't replace it or touch one for decades. In the early 1980s, I received a phone call from the Dean of the Faculty of Music at the University of Western Ontario. He said he was calling on behalf of Margaret Tremeer, who had recently had a serious stroke. He asked if I remembered Margaret's violin. I replied that not only did I remember her violin, but I had always played it on important occasions such as the Kiwanis Music Festival. It was a far better instrument than mine. Although the violin I was then playing said Stradivarius, everyone was convinced it was a fake. I also told the dean that I would never have called my teacher "Margaret." She was always Miss Tremeer to me.

He went on to say he had been able to sell her bow for a good price but had not found a buyer for her violin, which was a genuine Testore (circa 1700). He had obtained three appraisals and had hoped to sell it to the concertmaster of the Detroit Symphony, but the arrangement had fallen through. So I agreed to buy the instrument to help Margaret out financially. I drove to London to pick it up and deliver the cheque. She was overjoyed to see me again, and couldn't wait to cash the cheque, which I delivered to the bank for her.

I didn't play this violin for at least a dozen years, but when people heard I owned a violin made by Carlo Giuseppe Testore of Milan, they said it was a tragedy that it was not being played. I had the instrument carefully restored by Geo. Heinl & Co. in Toronto. This firm, founded in 1926, had originally sold the instrument to Margaret's family in 1942, and its restoration took eighteen months. In the meantime, I acquired three more antique violins: a British one made by David Furber (1755), a French instrument by Joseph-Laurent Mast of Toulouse (1796), and lastly, an American violin made in Detroit in 1900 by N.L. Thomas.

As I was becoming a bit of a collector, I took violin lessons from the concertmaster of the Hamilton Symphony, Corey Gemmell. It certainly was a struggle to get back to a reasonable level of competence. One thing that has prevented me from practicing has been writing this book. The hours I have spent at the computer could have been devoted to practicing the violin or another instrument. At least, that is what I tell myself.

Another problem with my music is my desire to play many different instruments. The ten-thousand-hour rule espoused by Malcolm Gladwell in his book *Outliers* is one I should have understood when I was trying to gain proficiency in music. This is the number of hours Gladwell says are needed to train your brain to truly excel in any activity.

I tend to work hard to get to a certain level of proficiency (mediocrity

Adding to my collection of music instruments.

is perhaps a better word) and then am satisfied. This also applies to my level of play, be it in golf, tennis, or a musical instrument. I think it would be better to focus on a particular goal, aim high, and devote energy to becoming as good as possible. Of course, it's not just the ten-thousand-hours factor; innate talent counts for a lot.

Thus, in retrospect, I wish I had focused on one instrument when I was young, probably the piano. In high school, I played three different wind instruments, the trumpet, the baritone horn, and the sousaphone, all B-flat instruments. I still have two other beautiful instruments just waiting to be mastered – a mandolin and a Russian balalaika, given to me by my niece Brenda Makarova and her husband, Vitale.

In recent years, the accordion became my favourite instrument. It is difficult to play this instrument quietly, especially for beginners, and because of this, it was not exactly Sonia's favourite. In the mid-1980s, our family frequented an Italian restaurant on Eglinton Avenue called Sabatino Ristorante. It was owned by a wonderful man, Germano, who loved music. Not only was he an excellent singer, but he also played the guitar and the cello. During dinner, he strolled around playing the accordion. I thought, "Yes, I can learn to play that; it has a piano keyboard and somehow I'll master those 120 black bass buttons."

I signed up for lessons at the Caringi Accordion House on Dufferin Street, right in the middle of the Italian district. It was a bustling place, teeming with Italian mothers waiting patiently for their sons to finish their accordion, trumpet, or drum lessons. I certainly stood out in this environment. Pictures of former Prime Minister Pierre Trudeau hung on every wall; I quickly came to realize the influence and goodwill the Liberals had built up with the immigrant community in this part of Toronto.

I ended up buying the biggest and heaviest accordion known to man. It had electrical pickups internally and could be hooked up to the sound system in the Air Canada Centre. Luckily (especially for Sonia), I have since found smaller and quieter instruments – six accordions of various sizes and colours. Eventually, I stopped playing the accordion; then I took it up again, with my new teacher, Pasquale Lorello, coming to the house. I will have to decide whether I give Pasquale a call again or go back to taking lessons in what I describe as "cocktail piano."

Studying cocktail piano was an experience. In this approach, rather than learning to play the instrument the traditional way, you learn to play the melody line with the right hand, and, with the help of chord symbols, to fill in the harmony with both hands. I progressed quite well, mainly because my teacher, Norma, put the fear of God into me. In the 1960s, Norma had operated a very successful musical establishment on Bloor Street with the catchy name of 88 Keys.

She had her prescribed method of teaching chording and was very strict and demanding of her students. One certainly had to practice for fear of getting rapped over the knuckles. She often commented that I didn't apply myself as diligently as a friend of mine from the Toronto Golf Club, Strachan Bongard.

One day, she told me her teaching was not bringing in enough revenue, and she might have to sell her grand piano. I did my best to discourage her from selling her principal asset. At this point, I thought perhaps I should move on. What happened next convinced me. When I returned to my car, all of the hubcaps had been stolen – a clear sign that I should look for a new teacher, even though I still had five lessons to go.

SAILING

WHEN our family returned to Toronto from Paris in 1971, Peter C. Newman invited me to sail with him on his new thirty-five-foot C & C sailboat. I had sailed dinghies at Camp Ahmek but had never sailed a keelboat. I was very impressed with Peter's sloop and pleased with the opportunity to get to know him. He talked a great deal about Conrad Black and went on to write a biography of him, which was published in 1982. Newman tried to put Black and me together but never succeeded. I also tried, but failed, to meet Conrad with the idea of buying Crown Trust in the 1970s. In hindsight, it was fortunate that I never got involved in a major way in the trust industry.

Peter and I sailed a number of times out of the Royal Canadian Yacht Club, and, within a relatively short time, I bought an older thirty-six-foot (keel/centreboard) sloop from my cousin, Alex Graydon, which we called *Mistral*. Alex had retired from Labatt's and owned Talisman, a ski lodge in Beaver Valley, north of Toronto.

As the proud owners of a sizeable yacht, Sonia and I decided we had better learn to sail our new craft. We took a week's holiday in the British

Do I look happy?

Virgin Islands and hired a similar-sized sailboat with a young Scottish captain. The three of us lived on board. Our instruction to our captain was to teach the two of us as much as possible in five days at sea. It was a very enjoyable week, and we did learn a great deal.

A few days after returning to Toronto, we set sail for Kingston,

Ontario. The weather was breezy but not impossible. About three hours after departing, we were sailing at six knots and were four miles offshore. There was a terrific bang, which shook the boat. This was followed by two or three more bangs. I lowered the sails and had not a clue what was happening. We were in 200 feet of water, but the boat didn't seem to be taking on water. Sonia volunteered to dive in and inspect the hull. In the end, we both decided the water in Lake Ontario was too cold. We raised the centreboard, started our diesel engine, and headed for Port Hope.

Even with full power, we could reach a speed of only two knots. I imagined that we were towing hundreds of feet of fishing line. A diver in a wet suit inspected the hull and informed us that the pin holding the centreboard had broken. When we had been under sail, the heavy metal centreboard was hanging loose by its cable about ten feet below the boat. With the boat's forward movement, it sometimes flew up and hit the boat's hull. Hence the bangs.

After a year sailing in Lake Ontario, we took the boat to Georgian Bay and never returned to sail on the Lower Great Lakes. We moved up to a forty-two-foot sailing craft, which we called *Endiang*, and then to a thirty-three-foot powerboat, which was promoted as The Sailor's Motorboat. The boat was named *White Buffalo* and had three partners: Bob Krembil, Vern Howe, and me.

Our experience is that boating can run the gamut from dull to extremely nerve-wracking. Thunderstorms, especially in a sailboat, can be pretty frightening. Wearing oven gloves when holding the wheel may be a safe idea but it makes you look pretty silly. Being hit by the boom and nearly knocked out in very rough seas is terrifying; getting lost in dense fog can be unnerving, as is putting out five anchors when a tornado warning is broadcast.

In our early, pre-GPS days of boating on Georgian Bay, navigation was a real challenge. We enjoyed thirty-five years of recreational boating and shared numerous adventures with the kids and with good friends who put their lives in our hands.

Our last boat, *Ventana*, was a fifty-six-foot custom-built powerboat on which we made two trips to Florida and a visit to the Bahamas. This boat was large and complicated and required a captain. With a house in Tucson and a cottage on Lake of Bays, we had too many toys, so we sold it in 2009.

Flying

As mentioned earlier, my brother, Jack, obtained his commercial pilot's licence in his late teens and later took his baby brother with him on many occasions. Flying in light aircraft on warm summer days can be bumpy at times, and I was frequently airsick. One day, when I was eighteen, I decided that I was going to conquer this motion sickness problem, so, without telling anyone, I began taking flying lessons at the London Flying Club.

Flying lessons were heavily subsidized by the government. The total cost of obtaining a private licence was $280 and included thirty hours of flight instruction as well as ground school. My flight instructor was Ty Noble, who taught his aspiring pilots in a Fleet Canuck, a Canadian-made two-seater. I turned up at seven a.m. and didn't leave the airport until dinner time. I soloed at fifteen hours, and finished my required thirty hours within two weeks.

On Sundays, my mother noticed I was out of the house well before seven a.m. She assumed I had suddenly found religion and was at mass. She was delighted with this turn of events and didn't ask any questions. However, I knew that if I crashed and killed myself, she would be extremely upset. I wasn't afraid of dying; I was afraid of disappointing Mother.

When taking lessons from Ty, the question of when he would let me solo was uppermost on my mind. One day, when we were practicing "touch-and-go" landings and takeoffs, he casually suggested I let him off by the side of the runway.

"Take it around for one more touch-and-go yourself," he said. "I'll see you at the hangar."

My first solo cross-country flight was from London to St. Thomas, a distance of eighteen miles. The Fleet Canuck had no flaps, so the only way to lose altitude quickly was to "sideslip" and then straighten out the aircraft just before touchdown. There was no radio contact at the St. Thomas airport; signals were given by the tower by shining a green or red light in the pilot's eyes.

I made three attempts to land but found myself at an altitude of 300 feet at the end of the runway, and had to go around again. Then, out of nowhere, a single-engine Chipmunk aircraft appeared in front of me. It was my teacher, Ty, flying an RCAF trainer used to train air cadets. Obviously, he had been keeping an eye on me. I followed him in a left-hand circuit and landed successfully. The only thing Ty said to me afterwards was that some work on sideslipping was in order.

I continued flying for a number of years and eventually bought a secondhand four-place Cessna 170 on floats. I took float training from an Air Canada pilot on Grenadier Pond in Toronto west. This very small pond is no longer open to aircraft.

I flew my bright yellow Cessna, which was based at the Toronto Island Airport, up to our cottage on Smoke Lake in Algonquin Park. Dodging thunderstorms returning to Toronto on Sunday evenings was challenging, to say the least. We had little weather information, and on more than one occasion, I was forced to consider landing in a farmer's field – on floats! But someone must have been looking after me; I always made it to my destination.

This plane was a great two-person aircraft. However, even with its Franklin engine, with four on board and a full tank of fuel it was definitely underpowered and needed a long expanse of water to get airborne. My navigational skills were rudimentary, and I often used a road map for guidance. While there was no GPS, I did have a radio direction finder and could zero in on radio broadcast towers.

The two potentially lethal incidents during my flying years both involve my friend Don Greer. One took place in the spring, when the ground was very wet and muddy. We set out from London in a Fleet Canuck, landed on a small grass airstrip outside Goderich – and got hopelessly stuck in the mud. I asked Don to get out of the plane to lighten the load, but he refused because he was wearing expensive new Dack's shoes. He did eventually exit the craft, and, with the help of five strong farmers, we literally lifted the plane to the hangar.

Then the challenge was how to get the plane off the ground for the return flight to London. It was suggested that, since the ground around the hangar was relatively dry, we could start the takeoff run in a circle around the hangar and then, with full power, hope to keep the aircraft just above the mud until we had enough air speed to gain altitude. This seemed to be working, but the tail wheel kept hitting the mud and held us back. We jumped the plane over a fence separating the airstrip from a farmer's field and stayed a couple of feet above the ground, allowing the airspeed to gradually increase. At the end of this field was a row of tall poplars, a steep cliff, and Lake Huron. We had to keep heading straight for the trees to get enough speed before banking left, otherwise we would have stalled the left wing and fallen to ground. Fortunately, the speed did come up, we did a steep turn, and are here to tell the tale.

The second incident with Don was not as dramatic but is one I haven't forgotten. We were flying the Cessna floatplane well out over Lake Ontario. In order to stay under the clouds (since my lack of an instrument rating required me to stay below the clouds), we were flying at an altitude of 200 feet above the water, with very little forward visibility. Suddenly, there was a break in the clouds and there were the Scarborough bluffs, dead ahead. Fortunately, we had enough airspeed to quickly gain altitude and avoid the cliffs.

My good friend and commercial pilot, Bud Moore, and I set up a small prospecting syndicate and proceeded to explore for base metals on Baffin Island. Two of the members were pilots who were flying DC-3s in northern Quebec, and one was a prospector. I lent them my Cessna float-plane, which was fully insured for the Baffin region. The plane flew from northern Quebec, across the Hudson Strait, to Iqaluit, which was then called Frobisher Bay. The syndicate's base camp was on a small lake two hundred miles north of Iqaluit. The understanding with the control tower in Iqaluit was that the plane would report in at least every two weeks.

About a week after they set up camp, a small group was leaving for a prospecting trip to another lake when a weather front with high winds came through. Once the plane was pushed away from the shore toward deep water, the pilot couldn't get the engine started. Unfortunately, they had left the anchor on shore, so the plane continued to be blown across the relatively small lake onto a rocky shore. Serious damage was done to the floats, a wing, and the tail section. Since they could not call Iqaluit on the radio from this distance, the group tied the plane down, walked around the lakeshore back to their base camp, and patiently waited to be rescued.

Two weeks later, a search and rescue plane that had been dispatched to find them spotted the group and flew them and their supplies all the way to Seven Islands on the Saint Lawrence. The insurance company settled the claim as a writeoff, because of the remote location. However, I heard many years later that an aircraft salvage group had bought the plane from the insurance company and were able to repair it and fly it out.

Without a plane, I continued to fly rented aircraft from time to time but was too busy working at Clarkson Gordon to make it a meaningful activity.

Religion

I am not a particularly religious person, and it is not my intention to give the delicate subject of religion too much emphasis. However, religion definitely had an influence on my life, particularly in relation to my schooling.

During my school years, I was an altar boy, and served at many funerals, including the bishop's. While there has been much publicity in recent years about past scandals within the Catholic Church, I was never affected. Mother had concerns about certain priests, as well as other men who worked with young boys, warning me to "watch out for him" – but I didn't know exactly what to watch out for. She once gave Father Smith hell for teaching grade seven kids a little bit about sex, by recounting the virgin birth.

Once I was at university, religion didn't play a big part in my life. Sonia and I were married in the Catholic Church, although only at the foot of the altar, and without a nuptial mass, because she's Anglican. Sonia's father was an Orangeman, but he accepted me.

Religion even pervaded business at the brewery. Regardless of their excellent qualifications, only one or two token Catholics were hired, as Father didn't want too many of them in senior positions. He felt if he wasn't somewhat restrictive, they could take over. And Mother, the devout Irish Catholic, agreed with his way of thinking. In recent years, a number of female friends have told me that they were not allowed to go out with me in our younger years because of my religion. Fortunately, animosity between Catholics and Protestants has cooled down since then.

The 1956 theatre production of *Spring Thaw* (a McGill student musical) included a madrigal sung by three clergymen – an Anglican minister, a Catholic priest, and a Jewish rabbi. The line from this skit that always stuck with me was, "God is a gentleman through and through, and no doubt Anglican, too."

While I still go to the Catholic Church periodically, to check in on its progress (or lack thereof), I also attend the Anglican Church, mostly to keep Sonia company. Had I been given the choice, rather than being born into the Catholic religion, I would have chosen the Anglican Church, as I find it somewhat kinder, gentler, and less demanding,

As children, our Catholic upbringing shaped us in different ways. It is interesting that, while my brother, Jack, became very religious at the end of his life, my sister, Mary, profoundly dislikes the Catholic Church, or any organized religious group, for that matter.

The emphasis on confession has always intrigued me. I could never figure out what women like my mother might have to confess. I once came close to having the opportunity to find out when I was wandering around the Catholic cathedral in downtown Ottawa. I was killing time and observing the artwork, having arrived too early for the funeral of my cousin Eddie Galbraith. Dressed in a black suit and dark tie, and standing right next to the confessional, I was approached by a young woman who said she needed to confess. It was tempting to hear her confession. Perhaps I missed my calling.

There was hope during the time of Pope John XXIII for a more liberal attitude, to bring Catholicism into the twentieth century. Progress was made after he called the Second Vatican Ecumenical Council, but after he died, subsequent popes didn't continue the culture of modernization. I had always hoped there would be some kind of rapprochement between the Catholic and Anglican Churches, but I am quite sure I will not see it in my lifetime. I am working hard to arrange my funeral service in such a way that it will encompass clergy from both.

In recent years, I have noticed an absence of younger parishioners, and fewer people generally. Many Christian churches of all denominations are closing; it appears that we are becoming a more secular society.

Philanthropy

IN looking back at my parents' philanthropy, I realize that both my father and mother were exceedingly giving of their time and energy to individuals in need. Sometimes my mother, when delivering chicken soup to elderly people living alone, even went so far as to clean their living quarters for them. My father was on the board of the sanitarium in London for many years. Tuberculosis was a major problem in the 1930s and '40s and had a considerable stigma attached to it, just as, unfortunately, mental illness has today. My mother gave a great deal of her time to St. John Ambulance, as well as to church and hospital causes. However, my parents did not make major donations to institutions, and therefore, in London, one does not see their names recognized on landmark buildings. Large donations were mostly made by the brewery.

I did not inherit a significant fortune upon my father's death. With three children and their schooling costs, Sonia and I, in the early years of our marriage, were able to make only small gifts to a number of institutions. These usually involved schools or children's theatre, such as Young People's Theatre in Toronto. We also support the Canadian Opera Company, the Art Gallery of Ontario, and the Toronto Symphony. The extraordinary financial success of Trimark allowed us to look more seriously at giving back to the community. Although we were encouraged to set up a foundation, we decided instead to donate a significant portion of the proceeds of the sale of Trimark Financial Corp. on a more personal basis.

We first made sure that our children and grandchildren were well looked after. Then we studied the many worthy causes needing support, in Canada and in the developing world. We decided to concentrate the bulk of our giving on education, health, and research, mainly in Canada.

We continue to help fund arts organizations that are important to us, as well as a number of organizations in Africa and the Far East. This section is simply an attempt to explain the causes that are near and dear to our hearts.

Hospital for Sick Children (SickKids)

In the mid-1990s, Trimark Financial Corp. was growing at an amazing pace. The firm that Bob Krembil, Mike Axford, and I had founded in 1981 went public in 1992. In 1996, Dick Thomson, who was then chairman and CEO of the Toronto-Dominion Bank, dropped into my office and observed that Trimark's share price was doing exceptionally

CAMPAIGN LAUNCH: Sonia and Arthur Labatt talk with 5-year-old Justin and his mother Flora Pogmore at the launch yesterday of the Sick Kids Hospital campaign to raise $82 million for research projects.

$5 million for Sick Kids

Labatts kick off fundraiser with largest ever gift

BY PHILIP MASCOLL
STAFF REPORTER

Mitchell Taylor didn't seem to care that the couple feeding him a container of juice had just donated $5 million to the *Help Make Sick Kids Better* Campaign.

"Tilt it more, tilt it more," the 2-year-old outpatient urged Sonia and Arthur Labatt, who had just made the largest personal monetary gift the world-famous Hospital for Sick Children has received in its 123-year history.

Mitchell and the Labatts met at a party yesterday on the lawn bordering the University Ave. entrance of the hospital to launch the campaign aimed at raising $82 million for research projects.

The Labatts' $5 million will bring together scientists and clinicians from Sick Kids, the University of Toronto and the Toronto Hospital into one laboratory to study brain tumours.

Sonia Labatt, who teaches environmental management at the University of Toronto, said the research facility will take the top people from all these institutions.

"There is a critical mass of expertise in Toronto, in the diagnosis, treatment and cure of

brain tumours," she said.

Arthur Labatt, founder and president of Trimark Financial Corp., said he hoped their donation would be doubled by other sources. "We hope government agencies will react."

Sonia Labatt said she had been a patient at Sick Kids, and had been treated by Dr. Alan Brown, the inventor of Pablum. One of their children, a daughter, had been treated at Sick Kids. Their grandchildren had also been patients.

Arthur Labatt, though raised in London, Ont., had been treated with Dr. Brown as a consultant, he said.

The couple urged support for the campaign. "Every $10, every $25, helps," they said.

Earlier, an audience in the hospital auditorium was told by campaign chair Al Flood that they had already received pledges of more than $44 million, or 54 per cent of the target, since the campaign started last November.

Flood, who is also chairman and chief executive officer of the Canadian Imperial Bank of Commerce, praised the Labatts' contribution.

"You have helped raise the bar on giving in Canada."

Lieutenant-Governor Hilary Weston spoke to the guests in the auditorium and later launched the community portion of the drive on the hospital's front lawn as a huge banner was unfurled from the hospital's roof.

Announcement in the Toronto Star, *September 23, 1997,*
of our donation to the Brain Tumour Research Centre.

well. He also mentioned that he noticed that neither Bob Krembil nor I had sold any stock.

I had known Dick for a number of years, and the TD Bank had an established relationship with Trimark. Dick had raised money for SickKids faithfully for over twenty-five years and had approached me in the past regarding a donation to the hospital. On previous visits, I had told him that I didn't have any cash – only bank loans. I was afraid he would ask, "From what bank?" – but he never did.

When chatting with me about Trimark's success and the price of the stock, he suggested, in his low-key way, that I couldn't take this new-found wealth with me. At that time, I knew that Rob Prichard, president of the University of Toronto, and Drs. Charles Tator and Alan Hudson, of the Toronto General Hospital (TGH), were also seeking major endowments. I told Dick that if he could find a really important project that involved the University of Toronto, TGH, and SickKids, then I would be pleased to make a significant donation.

Dick soon came back with an excellent suggestion. An outstanding team of scientists and neurosurgeons from two of the University of Toronto teaching hospitals – SickKids and Toronto General – required substantial additional funding in order to establish an interdisciplinary research and training centre. The key members of the original team were Drs. Peter Dirks, Jane McGlade, Ab Guha, and James Rutka. The team was headed by the latter two and included five graduate students and research fellows.

In the fall of 1996, our donation helped establish the Brain Tumour Research Centre (BRTC) and assisted in keeping extremely talented researchers and medical specialists in Canada. Both TGH and SickKids are world-class institutions, and, in the collective opinion of the medical community, it was extremely important that SickKids remain a world leader in pediatric research. The centre is a collaborative undertaking by three extraordinary institutions; without it, there was a real possibility of losing exceptional scientists to major U.S. hospitals.

Brain tumours (even benign tumours) are extremely frightening. The trauma of tumours, especially in children, is heartbreaking and devastating. Sonia and I were very moved by an article by Kathy Douthart in *Owl* magazine in November 1998, entitled, "When a Child Dies – A

The formal opening of the BTRC at SickKids with Governor General Romeo LeBlanc.

Mother's Story." Kathy's son showed the special bravery that children possess when confronted by obstacles that many of us see as insurmountable. We all want to prevent such tragedies.

Sonia and I have met so many parents whose children have suffered pediatric brain tumours. In 1993, an organization called b.r.a.i.n.child was established. It is a group of parents, families, and friends who have the common experience of caring for a child with a brain tumour, or who are, themselves, survivors. This volunteer organization provides support and education, and also raises millions of dollars for research. It helps sponsor summer camps and endowment funds, such as Meagan's Walk and Rigatoni for Research, both in Toronto, and Jessica's Footprint, in Guelph, which we've been involved in. Hundreds of volunteers show a remarkable passion for the hospital and its staff.

Sonia and I are also trying to support researchers in order to better understand and eventually prevent brain tumours. As Sonia stated at the opening of the centre in January 1999, we all have causes we feel passionate about and want to help in a meaningful way. We feel very fortunate to have been able to do just that.

The formal opening of the Brain Tumour Research Centre took

place in the main auditorium of the Hospital for Sick Children, with Romeo LeBlanc, then the governor general of Canada, and Mrs. Diana Fowler LeBlanc in attendance. Later that day, the first annual Arthur and Sonia Labatt Brain Tumour Research Centre Academic Lecture was presented. This informal opening and a luncheon the following day given by Rob Prichard, with the governor general attending both events, were a significant acknowledgement to us of the importance of our contribution.

Medical advances and scientific discoveries made at SickKids inspired us to double our support for the BTRC, and further, eleven years later, in 2007, we donated substantially more to establish the Labatt Family Heart Centre. This centre, under the leadership of Dr. Andrew Redington, is a state-of-the-art facility that will help hundreds of children from across Canada who suffer from congenital heart disease. The quality and focus of the centre's cardiovascular research will further the understanding of pediatric cardiology around the world.

A gala reception was held at the MaRS Discovery Centre, which now houses the Brain Tumour Research Centre. Both Sonia and I were invited to say a few words. We commented briefly that we had witnessed results from Dr. Jim Rutka and his colleagues' work at the centre that were above and beyond anything we had anticipated.

We have come to know SickKids very well. Few organizations have created an environment where doctors and scientists work together so successfully, and where the best pediatric health care in the world is delivered with empathy and compassion.

During the years that we have been involved with the hospital, we have met a great many outstanding physicians, scientists, members of management, hospital trustees, as well as members of the foundation board. Hospitals are difficult to manage because there are so many stakeholders. Mary Jo Haddad, who was appointed president and CEO in 2004, joined SickKids in 1984. She came from a nursing background and achieved many honours along the way, including the Order of Canada. In our opinion, she has done a magnificent job.

Although SickKids has taken excellent care of one of our children, as well as a grandson and a young nephew, my association with the hospital goes all the way back to the winter of 1936, when my parents were travelling in Europe and I was left in the care of a registered nurse. During their absence, I became quite ill. My aunt and uncle (the Hugh Labatts), alarmed at my deteriorating condition, contacted the Hospital for Sick Children. Dr. Alan Brown, then the physician-in-chief (and co-inventor of Pablum), made a house call – driving the long, bumpy road to London. He pulled me through, relying heavily on Lyle's Golden Syrup and large doses of Kepler's Extract of Malt.

In November, 2010, I was featured on the front of a SickKids Hospital campaign flyer entitled "I'm a SickKids® kid," which mentions Dr. Brown.

Arthur Labatt, 76
Businessman, philanthropist, great-grandson of John Labatt, who founded Labatt Breweries

As a baby, treated for failure to thrive by Dr. Alan Brown, an inventor of Pablum.

I'm a SickKids® kid.

On the front page of the campaign flyer.

St. Michael's Hospital

In March 2006, I disclosed to Dr. Bob Francis of Medcan that I was waking up in the morning feeling lightheaded. An MRI confirmed that I had a fairly sizeable meningioma – a tumour of the lining of the brain. I was referred to Dr. Richard Perrin at St. Michael's Hospital. Dr. Perrin is an experienced neurosurgeon who had joined St. Michael's when it merged with the Toronto Wellesley Hospital in 1998. Dr. Perrin (whom I now call Richard) told me that he had some bad news and some good news. The bad news: Yes, I had a tumour. The good news: It was well positioned and in all likelihood was not malignant. He pointed out that these tumours are extremely slow growing, but his advice, considering its size, positioning, and my age, was that it should be removed.

I mentioned to Richard that I was the chancellor of the University of Western Ontario and my main concern was, "Will I be okay to preside at the convocation in June?" Richard thought for a moment and replied, "Well, we'd better get right at it." We waited a couple of weeks for operating times to become available. When a last-minute cancellation came up, I was in the operating room.

Before this procedure, I had signed two separate power of attorney forms, in case the outcome of the surgery affected the full function of my brain. This was somewhat unnerving, to say the least.

During the operation, dozens of health-care professionals buzzed about, and I was attached to numerous wires and tubes. I asked someone in a surgical gown if I was going to be given a shot of something to calm me down. After checking the machines monitoring my vital signs, he simply answered, "You don't need one."

In the recovery room afterwards, a nurse kept shaking my shoulder and saying, "William, William, are you awake?" When Sonia entered the room, she told the nurse that she should call me Arthur. The nurse had been reading my name band – officially, William is my first name. When she addressed me as Arthur, I immediately responded. She asked how I was feeling and if I was interested in having some lunch. I replied that I was a bit hungry and would like a little red wine with lunch. She was quite surprised with this response and said, in all seriousness, "I'm not sure we can do that."

Richard did a fantastic job as a neurosurgeon and even dropped around to the house a few weeks later to remove the clamps and stitches. He had brought his surgical tool to remove the clamps but had forgotten to bring scissors to cut the stitches in my forehead. So there we were in the kitchen, looking through Sonia's makeup bag for nail scissors. You can hardly see where the incision was made; Richard is also a plastic surgeon *par excellence*. My barber, Elias, was very impressed.

I confided to Richard that I had been nervous before the operation and thanked him profusely for the fact that I had come through the procedure with all my faculties. I also told him that this was my first brush with eternity. (My unconscious use of that word undoubtedly stemmed from my Catholic upbringing.)

He corrected me with, "You mean mortality!"

I then asked him if there was anything I could do to thank him and the hospital for a very successful outcome.

He told me he had been quite involved for a number of years with an organization called the Hassan II Foundation for the Prevention and Cure of Nervous System Diseases, which is headquartered in Rabat, Morocco. The King Hussein V Hospital in Rabat is one of three hospitals in Africa that trains neurosurgeons from sub-Saharan Africa. He asked if I could be instrumental in establishing a professorship in neurosurgery through St. Michael's Hospital and the University of Toronto. This program would offer six to eight months of hands-on training for qualified African neurosurgeons, after which they would return to their country.

The professorship has now been established, and one surgeon, Dr. Ismail Hassan, has successfully finished the program and returned to his native Nigeria. Another highly qualified surgeon is due to arrive in 2012.

In March 2011, Sonia and I joined Richard and his wife, Dr. Sandra Jelenich, also a physician, on a trip to Morocco to formally announce the creation of the professorship. It was a wonderful experience for both of us and took place shortly after the Arab Spring manifestations that began in Tunisia and then spread to Egypt. This was our third visit to Morocco, and although we saw a couple of organized rallies, we had no problems, and the country seemed prosperous and happy.

Sonia and I also have helped in the funding of the Centre of Excellence in Brain Injury and Trauma Research, located in the new Li Ka Shing

Knowledge Institute at St. Mike's, which opened in the fall of 2011. The Institute houses two nine-storey buildings and will be a world-class leader in innovative patient-care delivery. Everyone at St. Mike's seems to have an incredible spirit that sets the hospital apart. As a patient, you can feel it.

FOUNDATION FIGHTING BLINDNESS

In 2001, Sonia had the frightening experience of losing sight in her left eye. This sudden occurrence caused her to feel, first-hand, the great anxiety that accompanies visual impairment and sight loss. It turns out she had a hole in the macula. She was successfully treated at the Toronto Western Hospital and has recovered sixty percent of her forward vision and eighty percent of her peripheral vision in that eye. Fluid was removed from the eye and gas inserted, a procedure that relieved the pressure on the macula, allowing the hole to heal. The treatment lasted six weeks. During this period, she was required to keep her head bowed; at least that position allowed her to play bridge.

Two years later, Sonia was introduced to the Foundation Fighting Blindness. Its aim is to drive the research that will provide preventions, treatments, and cures for people affected by the entire spectrum of retinal degenerative diseases. Once Sonia understood the foundation's objectives, she was eager to set up an endowment to help fund vision research. We both found that there is a great need for research, not only in the field of age-related visual problems, such as macular degeneration, but also for genetic problems such as retinitis pigmentosa, which has a great impact on children and adolescents.

We have met a number of young people who suffer from the latter, a genetic degenerative eye disease that slowly causes blindness. One such person is a very impressive young man, Gavin Morrison, whose family has a cottage near us on Lake of Bays. As I write this, he is a second-year business student at the University of Western Ontario, but in 1998, his mother, Ann, was told something no parent wants to hear: Her five-and-a-half-year-old son was going blind.

Most people have 180 degrees of vision, but Gavin had only 18 degrees. As a young child, he had no night vision – one of the first signs of the disease. Ann decided to take action. She went to a patient conference to learn more about the disease and discovered the Foundation Fighting Blindness.

At that time, the organization was quite small, but Ann sent e-mails to her friends, and people started responding and making donations.

One friend, Meg Soper, who is a stand-up comedian and a nurse, proposed a fundraiser for the foundation. They were able to put together a group of stand-up comedians, and Comic Vision, a night of hilarity and the foundation's primary fundraising initiative, was born. Comic Vision started in Toronto but now also takes place in London, Oakville, Vancouver, and Calgary. In 2004, Ann became the director of philanthropy and has helped raise the foundation's profile.

Centre for Addiction and Mental Health

In 2003, Sonia and I were invited to dinner by our friend, Ted Tremain, to learn more about the Centre for Addiction and Mental Health (CAMH). The centre was established in 1998 as a merger of the Clarke Institute of Psychiatry, the Donwood Institute, 999 Queen Street West, and the Addiction Research Foundation.

With the strong support of the Ontario government, CAMH set out in 1995 to raise $100 million from the private sector in order to transform mental health facilities in the Greater Toronto region. Although this was a very ambitious goal at the time, as of mid-2011, $108 million had been raised.

Along with the Bob and Marilyn Beamish, Sonia and I made a substantial commitment to CAMH, because we were aware that twenty percent of Canadians suffer from mental health issues at some time in their lives. The Romanow Commission recognized that mental health has been the "orphan" of the health-care system. There is still a stigma attached to mental health issues, but in recent years, people are more willing to talk about them. As Dr. Catherine Zahn, president and CEO of the centre, said in an interview, "It's like the world of cancer in the 1960s, when there was developing an increasingly political and social voice to combat cancer, to bring cancer out of the shadows – and something similar is happening now in the world of mental illness and addiction."

Over the years, Sonia and I have both learned a great deal about CAMH. Sonia was on the board of the Clarke Institute for a number of years, and we have both attended many Courage to Come Back dinners. I feel I understand anxiety and depression to some extent, and I know how real and debilitating they can be. In my earlier account of the challenges I faced in moving to Paris and opening a new office for McLeod Young Weir in 1970, I described what I now believe was anxiety. Anxiety and depression can take a long time to develop and considerable time to treat. The embarrassment of depression or anxiety often keeps people from seeking help for what would otherwise be very manageable illnesses.

The redevelopment of the twenty-seven-acre parcel of land at 999 Queen Street in Toronto, the principal site of CAMH, is a ten-year undertaking, costing hundreds of millions of dollars. It will transform the face of mental health and addiction care. We are so fortunate to have this large property right in the middle of a major metropolitan area. This land was assembled in 1846. An ugly stone fortress of a building was constructed and named the Provincial Lunatic Asylum. This structure was torn down after the Second World War, in favour of equally unattractive buildings that were erected. In 1966, the name was changed to the Queen Street Mental Health Centre. The address of the new institution has been changed from 999 Queen Street to 1001 Queen Street to further disconnect it from its stigmatized past.

As of 2012, most of the old structures have been removed from the property, and a number of attractive new buildings have been opened, or will be opened within months. The new surroundings include shops, residences, businesses, and parks. This will stimulate a change of attitude by breaking down barriers and will help eliminate the shame associated with mental illness.

CAMH is one of the largest hospitals of its kind in the world. Twenty-five percent of all Canadian psychologists receive all or part of their clinical training here. It offers a broad range of programs, caring for two hundred thousand patients a year. When the transformation of the Queen Street property is complete, it will increasingly be recognized as a leader in its field.

There is incredible leadership at the hospital; I would like to mention five individuals who have given so much to the institution: Drs. Paul Garfinkel and David Goldbloom; Michael Wilson, Canada's former Minister of Finance and later our ambassador to the United States; Jamie Anderson, deputy chair of RBC Capital Markets; and Paul Beeston, the former president of Major League Baseball and now president and CEO of the Toronto Blue Jays.

L'ARCHE

Jean Vanier, the son of former Canadian governor general Georges Vanier and Pauline Vanier, founded L'Arche in 1964 when he welcomed two men with intellectual disabilities into his home in Trosly-Breuil, a small town near Paris. He named his home L'Arche, which is French for the Ark, as in Noah's Ark.

Sonia and I first met Jean in France in the fall of 1968, a few months after we had moved to Paris. My mother, who was a close friend and a great admirer of Madame Vanier, was visiting us at the time. She told us that Madame Vanier's son, Jean, had opened a home near Paris for adults with intellectual disabilities. The concept was for people with disabilities to live together, enabling them to live in a real community surrounded by assistants who live with them as friends.

We got in touch with Jean, and he accepted our invitation to join us for afternoon tea in our tiny apartment. He was a wonderfully gracious and modest man who believed deeply in what he was doing. The first of his communities in Canada opened the next year. We supported the international work of L'Arche for a number of years. Twenty-five years later, Dean Levitt (chair of L'Arche) and Nathan Ball (executive director) invited us to Richmond Hill to show us how a L'Arche community really functions. We were impressed by the length of time that Dean and Nathan, who were our contacts with L'Arche, had been involved. They were obviously deeply committed.

We met one of the original members of this community whose name was Bill (who, sadly, has since passed away). He was a great character who loved telling jokes. Bill asked if I was a board member. I told him I was not.

Then he turned to Dean and Nathan and told them they had to stop bringing people by. He pointedly said that he was in charge of the woodworking shop and had been given strict instructions to turn off the machinery every time a guest came in – since the buzzing saws and equipment were noisy and posed a danger to visitors.

"So," he asked, "with people coming through all the time, how are we ever going to get any work done?"

This visit was transforming for both of us.

Since we first met Jean in 1968, L'Arche has expanded around the world. Today, it is a very well-run international organization operating in forty countries, and on every inhabited continent. Sonia and I are so proud to have been able to support Jean and the wonderful organization he founded.

AFRICAN MEDICAL AND RESEARCH FOUNDATION

In the early 1970s, Sonia and I were invited to a cocktail party in Forest Hill, at the home of Bill Wilder, president of Wood Gundy. The invitation came from Dr. John Evans, president of the University of Toronto, and the purpose of the party was to introduce the African Medical and Research Foundation (AMREF) to potential supporters. John stood on a chair and explained AMREF to the well-heeled group.

AMREF was founded in 1957 by three surgeons who had lived in Kenya for many years. They were all pilots and realized that the only way to provide medical assistance to remote regions of East Africa was by plane. They encouraged other doctors to take up flying, and the Flying Doctors Service of East Africa was born. The founding doctors established a medical radio network and eventually introduced mobile health services to mission hospitals.

Following the party, John called and asked me to do a few things for

At an AMREF meeting in Uganda.

AMREF, assuring me that I didn't have to get very involved. Slowly and quietly, over time, he encouraged me to take on more roles with the organization. John is so pleasant and persistent that I soon found myself on the board, then treasurer of the foundation for a number of years, and eventually chairman of AMREF Canada. Many years later, I said to him, "You promised me that I wouldn't have to take on additional responsibilities when I joined the board."

"You're absolutely right," he replied with a smile, "but I lied."

John, a past chairman of the Rockefeller Foundation, did a great deal to reorganize and revitalize AMREF internationally. The founders had passed on, and there was a need to rethink the organization's goals and its internal controls.

AMREF has grown enormously over the past fifty years and now trains more than ten thousand health workers in forty African countries. I very much enjoyed my years with AMREF. Because the organization's headquarters were in Nairobi, Sonia and I attended a number of annual meetings in East Africa.

One year, the annual meeting was held in Mukono, a town in Uganda. It so happens that our son-in-law Dominic Barton and his brother and sister were all born in Mukono, where his father was an Anglican missionary. When Idi Amin took power, he personally took over most of the house the Bartons were living in. On one occasion, Dominic was playing in Amin's Land Rover when the dictator and his driver took off – with Dominic still in the car. They discovered him and returned him safely to his parents. Dominic's father, John Barton, taught at Bishop Tucker Theological College in Mukono; the school is now Uganda Christian University. During our visit there, Sonia was asked to address the students. She talked about Dominic's years in Uganda and brought greetings and a big suitcase full of clothes from the Barton family.

Together with a charming Swedish woman, an AMREF representative from Uganda, and a driver, we set out in a Land Rover to attend a meeting deep in the jungle, many miles from a main road. We were to attend a town hall gathering, to listen to local people who would outline their greatest needs. We got hopelessly lost and were at least three hours late for the meeting. Most of the participants attending the meeting were women who wore very colourful full-length gowns and bright head coverings.

We were so late that many of the women were heading home, but when they spotted the AMREF vehicle approaching, they ran through the bush and returned to the meeting place.

We learned so much that day. We toured a local clinic run by AMREF, visited a school full of AIDS orphans, and listened to the local people. Although their needs were wide-ranging, we discovered that their greatest need was fresh water. Many grandmothers told us they were each looking after at least a dozen grandchildren because a whole generation had been wiped out by AIDS.

The schoolteacher told us sixty to seventy percent of his students will never find work and that he teaches them how to be subsistence farmers because they have no parents to pass the skills along. The young man who ran the clinic had one year of medical training and supervised eighty to one hundred patients. He was doing an incredibly good job.

During our time in Mukono, we stayed in a suite in the best hotel in town. The only negative was that our room had no screens or air conditioning, and mosquitoes were constant visitors. When we returned to Toronto in mid-February, I came down with a fever. I had carefully studied the symptoms of malaria and was convinced I had it. Sonia, who believes that I am a hypochondriac, told me it was just the flu. Nevertheless, I called the tropical diseases department at St. Michael's Hospital and related my symptoms to a doctor. He first gave me hell for stopping my malaria pills too soon, then told me that it sounded like I had indeed contacted the disease. I went to the hospital the next morning for a blood test that found I did *not* have malaria. In presenting these varying results to Sonia, I insisted that it was nevertheless true that even hypochondriacs get sick sometimes.

KiBO Foundation

The history behind the KiBO Foundation could be a book unto itself. While I can't recount it all here, I am going to touch on some of it, because the background is both fascinating and inspiring.

In January 1990, John Evans introduced me to Abraham Temu, a nineteen-year-old who had recently emigrated from Kenya to study at the University of Toronto. John had met his mother, Margaret Emokor, through mutual friends at AMREF in Nairobi.

Abraham is now the managing director and co-founder of the KiBO Foundation, a remarkable initiative in Uganda that provides unemployed people, ages eighteen to thirty, with skills for becoming self-reliant. It emphasizes computer literacy and leadership training. The school also focuses on community service. In an area where unemployment can reach eighty percent, KiBO has trained more than eight hundred youths through its various programs. Of those who graduated from the two-and-a-half-month course, more than ninety percent are working in the region.

Operations at KiBO are getting close to being self-funded through a combination of tuition fees ($200 per student) and local corporate contributions. This is an important step in overcoming an aid-dependent mindset. Prospective students must complete an admission process that indicates whether they have the motivation to transform themselves and, eventually, their communities. Finally, all students must perform community service work and fundraise for a local charity. Ugandans helping Ugandans has become a source of pride among the students.

When Abraham came to Toronto, he already had a small circle of friends from East Africa, but I made a point of introducing him to our family and to a number of Trimark people. During his four years at university, he worked part-time for Trimark; he made many friends there and got to know our family very well.

After graduating with a BSc (Honours) in Quantitative Methods (Economics, Mathematics, and Statistics), he worked for State Street Bank and TD Asset Management, then returned to university to earn his MBA at the Rotman School of Management. After that, he worked for PricewaterhouseCoopers, in Financial Advisory Services.

In 1996, Abe returned to Kenya for three months and founded a pioneering youth program, Ungana, which is still a significant force in volunteerism in Kenya. During this trip to East Africa, he met his wife, Judith Butagira, who was originally from Uganda. The daughter of a former High Court judge and ambassador to the U.N., Judith has had a number of senior jobs in the development field and now works as the deputy director of BreadforLife. She and Abe have three children, and I am the godfather of their nine-year-old twin girls, Edna and Maria, and the unofficial godfather of their younger brother, Emmanuel.

In 2007, Abe and Judith decided to return to Uganda for several years to work in the development or health fields. Although the family was doing well in Canada and all are Canadian citizens, they had a strong desire to give something back to East Africa.

Abe presented his vision of KiBO to a few of us, and the organization is now registered as a charitable foundation in Canada. "Kibo" is a name that is well known in East Africa as the highest of the three peaks on Mount Kilimanjaro. Abe, Judith, and I are very thankful to a number of people who helped get the operation off the ground – John Evans, Brad Badeau (chairman of the foundation), Bill Crawford, June Sommers, and Odette Goodall. Theresa Widdifield, Alan Torrie, and Jim Douglas have joined our group within the past year. We had all known Abe for many years through AMREF or Trimark. Our task now is to create greater awareness of KiBO so it can grow and its growth be sustained in the years ahead.

Abe is giving so much of himself to KiBO and to Uganda. I am hoping that he can find substantial financial support to allow him to replicate, in other parts of East Africa, the excellent learning facility he has established.

Abraham's family background is fascinating, particularly given that four days after his birth, Idi Amin staged a coup in Uganda. His mother, Margaret, who had been a secretary to ousted prime minister Milton Obote, found herself working for Amin for a terrifying fourteen months before escaping with her son to Nairobi. While it is not for me to recount Margaret's captivating life, I do hope she will do so herself one day.

The Toronto French School

When we returned to Toronto from France in 1971, our children already had three years of French schooling, so we decided to enroll them at the Toronto French School (TFS). TFS is now one of the city's top independent schools, but in 1971 it was just starting up and did not have the facilities other private schools enjoyed. However, the quality of education was excellent; the principal and founder, Harry Giles, was a taskmaster. All of our children enjoyed their years at TFS and have maintained friendships with many of the students they met there.

Harry Giles asked me join the board of the school and to act as the treasurer of the Ladies' Auxiliary. The charming woman who kept the books had no concept of debits and credits; she just kept plugging in numbers to make the books balance. Although I am a CA, I had not acted as an accountant for quite some time, so I called my friend, Bill Crawford, a partner at Ernst & Young, to give me a hand. When he saw the mess, he suggested we re-enter all transactions for the year, a painstaking task. I then asked Bill if there was anything else we needed to do before handing over the financial statements. As a good auditor he reminded me that since the year-end for the Auxiliary was March 31, we would require the April cancelled cheques in order to reconcile the bank account.

The bookkeeper dropped the cancelled cheques through the mail slot in our front door. Unfortunately, nobody was home except our golden retriever, who proceeded to tear them to shreds. I spent hours taping the cheques back together.

Almost thirty years later, the school launched a major capital campaign to enlarge and improve the facilities. Sonia and I made a substantial contribution; this school had helped not only our three children, but also, later, four of our six grandchildren.

We also supported the school because, as a relatively young school, TFS did not have a large network of older alumni; it needed support from non-graduates who respected the school's vision and goals.

In October 2001, Sonia gave an excellent address at the launch of the campaign called Building on Excellence. Two years later, the massive construction job was nearly completed and the school had been transformed. I was asked to say a few words at a gala held in the beautiful new surroundings. I recounted some recollections from the period when our children had attended the school in the early 1970s.

Mildenhall (the first new building) was a major improvement over the church basements and other rented locations that had previously served as classrooms. This new facility quickly filled up with students, some even in adjoining houses and portables. There were limited gym facilities and common areas. Everything but instruction took place in the hallways, including gymnastics, games, and lunch.

I was quite involved with the school at that time, serving on the board for a number of years, and at one point was the covert buyer of a house on Lawrence Avenue that was to be used by the school. Sonia would have no part of this clandestine operation, since she knew that the neighbours were already upset with the traffic problems Mildenhall was creating. I arranged to meet the owner, a widow, and her son, on my own. The widow wanted to contact Sonia to see if she wished to buy the curtains, rugs, and some specialty items that her recently deceased husband had designed. I always had to claim that Sonia "was not feeling well."

Finally, the woman's son took me aside and said, "Don't worry, I know how it is; in your family, like mine, the men make all the decisions."

He couldn't have been further from the truth.

At that point, I decided that I would have made a very poor politician. I was no good at modifying the facts.

Harry Giles and his wife, Anna, who was vice-principal, worked well as a team, creating a wonderful centre of learning – out of nothing. They were true visionaries, and we all owe them a great deal for the wonderful school they founded.

I would like to clear up one small but contentious issue that has troubled our grandchildren. At the time of our commitment to TFS, our grandson, Dylan Randle, expressed his dismay that we had helped to fund classrooms instead of the swimming pool or the soccer field.

"Grandpa," he exclaimed, "why would you ever do that?"

Well, I hope Dylan and our other grandchildren will notice that the swimming pool is now housed underneath these classrooms. It was all part of a master plan.

The University of Western Ontario's Faculty of Health Sciences and School of Nursing

As chancellor of the University of Western Ontario from 2004 to 2008, I was incredibly impressed with the talent and dedication of the faculty and staff. This world-class university produces a wealth of exceptional men and women at both the undergraduate and graduate levels.

During that time, Sonia and I became acquainted with many academics, staff, and students, and were impressed by the school spirit and camaraderie on this beautiful and contained campus. We really do believe that Western provides the best student experience among Canada's leading research-intensive universities.

Having grown up in London, where Labatt's was founded, and having attended Western, I felt strongly that I should support this excellent university. In addition, as chancellor, I had learned a great deal about the institution.

There are a number of impressive faculties and affiliated colleges at Western. The relatively young Faculty of Health Sciences (which has thirty-four hundred students) is one of Western's largest and fits in perfectly with our support of education, health, and research. Many of the schools that make up the faculty have existed for many years and are very highly regarded. The School of Nursing, for example, founded in 1920, is one of Canada's first university nursing programs. Another, the School of Kinesiology (1948), is among the most distinguished schools in its field in North America.

Canada is critically short of health-care professionals. Sonia and I felt that the Faculty of Health Sciences needed a higher profile and more recognition, and we knew that Dean Jim Weese and his colleagues were working hard toward that objective. We hoped our financial commitment to the faculty would be of some help.

The magnificent new faculty building boasts state-of-the-art classrooms and research labs as well as a 3D virtual reality theatre (known as an anatatorium), the first facility of its kind in North America, containing simulated hospital and home health-care units, complete with computerized moving and speaking mannequins.

In addition to helping support the construction of the building, we were also pleased to help fund two endowments: the first toward the chair in women's rural health issues and the second for Ontario graduate scholarships. With matching grants from the Ontario government, there will be sufficient revenue to fund eight graduate scholarships annually.

At recent convocations, I had the opportunity to ask individual graduates from Health Sciences about their plans for the future. I learned that most were already working, while others were continuing with their education. Everyone seemed happy and very positive, just the sort of people we want looking after the health of this nation.

In May 2008, we made a further donation to the faculty with a major commitment to its School of Nursing. Choosing which areas of the university to support was a complex decision. As chancellor, I have seen the best Western has to offer. Every faculty is excellent and distinctive, led by dedicated professors and researchers. I have always been so struck by the character, integrity, and drive of all the students. But this opportunity with the School of Nursing somehow resonated immediately with Sonia and me. We know how essential the nursing profession is to our society and how the contribution of these compassionate and confident professionals too often has not been recognized.

At convocation, the nursing graduates appear to walk across the stage with a sense of quiet determination. Maybe it's because they graduate knowing what their next step in life is – whether that's working at a hospital, studying at a graduate level, or working in public health or elsewhere. But I think there's more to it than that. It seems to me that the men and women who go into nursing have a passion for their future vocation. Not all students and graduates have that certainty and purpose at this stage of their lives. When I was a student, for example, I never seemed to know where I was headed. I have a good friend, a few years my senior, who recently told me that he still doesn't know what he wants to do when he grows up!

Historically, nurses have been seen as caregivers *par excellence*, but the term "caregivers" does not do justice to nursing. They are faced with many challenges in dealing with patients in difficult situations. It takes a certain strength of character to do this; I'm not sure I could, so I admire those who can. Moreover, they now deliver much more. They have assumed roles as clinical managers, academic researchers, and health-care professionals in multiple settings. These efforts deserve greater recognition, especially as we face pressures in the Canadian health-care system.

While great advancements have been made in the last ten to twenty years in the nursing profession, it still faces several challenges in Canada. In a country with an aging population that requires more and more nurses, the vocation is experiencing a severe shortage. With more patients and fewer resources, nurses have to do more with less. It is precisely now that we, as a society, need to respect and understand the importance of the nursing profession and encourage motivated and intelligent individuals to consider this vocation.

The Faculty of Health Sciences and the School of Nursing at Western have ambitious plans to attract more nurses to the profession, and Sonia and I were pleased to contribute to this effort. However, while our contribution is monetary, the real gift to society will come from those determined women and men who take up the challenge and take up the nursing vocation. We believe these graduates will provide invaluable services to our community and to our country with their skills and passion. And they will continue to make all of us proud.

Rotman School of Management

Sonia and I are good friends of Roger Martin, dean of the Rotman School of Management at the University of Toronto. In 2008, when the economy was suffering and companies were not hiring, Roger and Sonia came up with the idea of offering a fellowship program that would give up to eight newly graduating MBA students annually the opportunity to pursue full-time work opportunities in the not-for-profit sector.

These fellowships covered half the salary of the MBA graduate for one year. As a result, MBAs can explore new fields of endeavour while non-profit organizations gain access to an invaluable pool of talent. The program has worked extremely well; often the graduate remains with the organization as a full-time employee after the term of the fellowship has expired.

Speaking to a group of graduating MBAs, Sonia remarked that these fellowships are a win-win situation. She said, "In a number of NGOs [non-governmental organizations] in which we are involved [SickKids, World Wildlife, Foundation Fighting Blindness], we have been told how effective the MBAs' participation has been. In addition, we have learned about other local and international NGOs [Right to Play, World Literacy, Frontier College, Climate and Energy Program] throughout the process."

The Centre for Environment at the University of Toronto

Sonia was also instrumental in establishing graduate fellowships, awarded on an annual basis, to support students enrolled in one of the graduate programs at the Centre for Environment. By 2011, more than eighty students had benefitted. The fellowships are awarded to a master's or doctoral student on the basis of financial need and academic excellence.

Honours

IT is difficult for me to write about honours I have received: I don't want to appear boastful. But I've called this section "Honours" because I, along with Sonia, are extremely honoured to have been recognized, either individually or jointly, at formal functions in thanks for our philanthropic gifts. Such accolades can be humbling. While there were several such occasions, I'll describe the ones that stand out as the most meaningful.

ORDER OF CANADA

In May 1996, I was appointed an Officer of the Order of Canada and was invested at Rideau Hall on February 26, 1997, by Governor General Romeo Leblanc. Queen Elizabeth is the Sovereign of the Order, which was established in 1967 to recognize "outstanding achievement and service in various fields of human endeavour." The category I was placed

Proudly receiving the Order of Canada from Governor General Romeo LeBlanc in 1996.

in was Industry/Commerce/Business; however, when the citation was read out at the investiture, it made no mention of business and focused solely on either philanthropy or my association with the arts community. In fact, it said:

> *His philanthropy, both personal and corporate, has supported many organizations, including the African Medical Research Foundation, the Canadian Opera Company and the McMichael Art Collection. By example he has encouraged corporate sponsorship of the arts, committing his own company to serve the public while supporting galleries, artists and theatres throughout Canada.*

At the ceremony, I was seated beside a good-looking, well-tailored gentleman whose long hair was tied in a ponytail. He looked intelligent, was sitting very erect – and was wearing sunglasses. I was puzzled as to what category he was in, imagining that he might be a physics professor. I then discovered that he was Geddy Lee, the lead vocalist in Rush, a heavy metal type of rock band, formed in Toronto in 1968, that has achieved remarkable international success. His category was Arts/Music.

At the dinner following the elegant ceremony, Sonia and I were seated beside Chief Justice Antonio Lamer and his wife, Danièle. Our conversation was lively, as we had a great many friends in common. Danièle Tremblay-Lamer is a judge on the Federal Court of Canada (Canada's national trial court), and the daughter of my very good friend Marcellin Tremblay, who was president of the Canadian Provident Group of insurance companies. Also, Antonio Lamer was a close friend of my sister and brother-in-law, Rusty Lamb, who was a judge on the Quebec Superior Court.

A few days later, my daughter Sheila and her husband, Dominic, held a large dinner party in the house they had just purchased in Forest Hill, to celebrate my Order of Canada appointment. It was a new house with an unfinished basement, so they turned that entire lower level into a colourful dining room. I explained to everyone present, including the older grandchildren, how moving the experience in Ottawa had been.

Nearly everyone at this festive dinner had something to say, and the whole evening turned into a bit of a roast. All of the remarks were funny, flattering, and humbling. It's tough being feted.

FCA

In December 1996, I was elected to Fellowship in the Chartered Accountants Association of Ontario. I have always been very proud to have the CA designation following my name, and to have successfully completed the required exams as well as the apprenticeship program. I was surprised to receive this honour, as I hadn't been a practicing accountant in the business world since leaving Clarkson Gordon in 1962. As well, I had always thought that those with an FCA were either senior partners of the major accounting firms or distinguished members of the profession.

One of those who proposed my name was Brad Badeau, CA, at that time chief financial officer of Trimark. Only recently did I become aware of a letter he wrote that accompanied the nomination form. As you will see, Brad's gracious comments had nothing to say concerning my skills as an accountant.

> We call him the "father" of Trimark not only because he is one of the three founding partners, but because he takes a genuine interest in the well-being of staff members as individuals. In fact, whenever possible, he takes the time to personally greet new employees of Trimark. This extra effort coupled with his ability to put people immediately at ease, has created a cohesiveness amongst Trimark employees which has been key to the incredible success of this company. He has set an exceptional example.

Chancellor – The University of Western Ontario

In March 2004, I received a number of telephone messages from Don McDougall. Wonderfully warm and outgoing, Don had been a good friend of my brother, Jack, who had hired him at Labatt's. Don obtained his MBA from Western and was president of Labatt Breweries of Canada, and senior vice president of John Labatt Ltd., from 1973 to 1979. I had kept in touch with him after he left Labatt's.

I diligently tried to return his calls, but we kept missing each other. When one of his messages said he was calling from a Tim Hortons in Stratford, I thought that perhaps he was calling to see if I would be interested in buying a franchise. (I discovered later that, in fact, he did own some of the franchises.)

Don was the chair of the board of the University of Western Ontario, and the purpose of his call was to ask if I would accept an invitation to become Western's nineteenth chancellor. He said it would be a four-year appointment and that the role was principally ceremonial. I was hesitant to take on this responsibility and told Don that I would get back to him. When I mentioned this call to Sonia, she was ecstatic and stressed that this was a great honour and I must get back to Don with a positive response – right away!

One of the reasons this invitation surprised me was that they were asking someone who didn't even have a university degree to be chancellor of their university. When I was appointed, I was interviewed in the *Western News*, and was quoted in reference to my university years, saying, "I really didn't apply myself and didn't have a lot of guidance. I just enjoyed myself too much. I ended up working for Clarkson Gordon and got my CA. I intended to go back to finish off my few courses at McGill, but I never did it, which I regret. Once I got into the business world, I enjoyed it so much that I didn't go back to university."

The appointment was indeed a great honour, and, as an ambassador of the university, I worked hard to promote it as a leader in learning, both in Canada and abroad. In fact, Sonia and I participated in two Hong Kong convocations as well as many in London. The Ivey Business School has a campus in Hong Kong. The convocation started out just for them, but then expanded to all faculties because so many of the university's graduates came from Hong Kong. The regalia, music, and pomp and circumstance of the Western Convocation in London was duplicated in Hong Kong.

At the president's dinner following my installation on October 28, 2004, I chided both Don McDougall and President Paul Davenport for neglecting to mention a couple of things before I signed on as chancellor. They had correctly explained that my principal function was to grant degrees at as many as fifty convocations. They counselled me wisely about attending board and senate meetings. However, they had neglected to mention that I was expected to deliver the convocation address at my installation, and also that I should be prepared to speak at the president's dinner.

During the summer months preceding my installation, I spent considerable time trying to come up with an address that conveyed something significant and thought-provoking, perhaps even life changing. Not an easy task. As my friend, Dr. David Naylor, president of the University of Toronto, mentioned in his remarks when he was receiving an honorary degree from Western, "There is every reason to believe that, after a few years, no one will recall any of the speeches from their graduation day."

I won't replicate my address to the graduates (see Appendix 3 for speeches), except to say that I pointed out the common element that connects them all, which is the burning desire to do something significant with their lives and to make a difference. I commented on my own life – the successes, failures, and disappointments – and urged them not to worry that many of them were not really sure at that point what they wanted to do with the rest of their lives, because this is perfectly normal.

I encouraged them to listen to people who have their best interests at heart and, in return, to be fair and gracious, and to treat people the way they would like to be treated. I spoke quite openly about my experience in coping with stress when working in Paris. I counselled them to try to lead a balanced life and never to take themselves too seriously.

As chancellor of the university, I had the opportunity to meet many outstanding and charming individuals who were receiving their honorary doctorates. One such individual was Rod McQueen, mentioned in the preface of this book. The convocation ceremony at Western is extremely well orchestrated and I would like to quote excerpts of his impression of the event, which he wrote on his blog:

There was pomp, a brass band, and the pageantry of medieval garb as the official party entered Alumni Hall that was packed with more than 2,000 graduates, friends and family members at the University of Western Ontario. And there I was, wearing a black gown and floppy purple hat with gold tassel, among the faculty in their colourful robes from Canadian universities and such far-off institutions as Oxford.

Monday's ceremony was truly an out of body experience. I've never had such a sensation before, but as I sat on the platform and heard the citation, everything sounded familiar – yes I'd written that book, won that award, or lived in that country – but it couldn't have been me. It seemed like me watching someone who had lived my life. But, it must have been me, right?

Such occasions, when you get to swim in a warm bath of public recognition, don't occur very often in life. You might as well revel in the moment, as I did, but was it really me they were congratulating? Apparently, it was.

UWO Chancellor Arthur Labatt and President Paul Davenport were both delightful hosts and raconteurs. I heard about the 1934 kidnapping of Labatt's father, the first business leader ever held for ransom in Canada. Paul Davenport talked about his love for biking in the Loire Valley and a night school course he teaches on Impressionist painters. Both men are engaging and passionate, two traits we should all emulate.

At the June 2005 convocation, the University of Western Ontario was the first Canadian university to grant Dr. Henry Morgentaler an honorary degree. Dr. Morgentaler is an abortion crusader who deeply divided Canadian society; he has been at the centre of a debate on abortion since 1967 when he testified before a federal government committee that a woman should have the right to end her pregnancy without risking death. He has been arrested a number of times and served ten months in Montreal's Bordeaux Jail.

As chancellor of Western, at convocation.

The decision to grant this degree was extremely controversial at Western. Don McDougall condemned it and posted a strongly worded letter on a website. Paul Davenport wrote an excellent response. He stated that he understood that the decision to grant Dr. Morgentaler an honorary degree went against the values of many in the community, but he added that there had also been an "outpouring of support" from those who favour freedom of choice. Aware of my Catholic upbringing, Paul gave me the option of not attending, but I believed it was my duty to attend all convocations. To not show up would have made a statement that I didn't want to make. Although I remain neutral on the subject, I admired Dr. Morgentaler's tenacity. It's interesting to also note that Paul Davenport gave students the option of receiving their degree at one of the other convocations. Only one out of seven hundred eligible students exercised that option.

At the convocation itself, both the university police and the London police monitored the situation closely. The event was considered low risk, but everyone was apprehensive. Before meeting Dr. Morgentaler, I thought that he would be somewhat stiff and not easy to talk to. He was quite the opposite; I found him a very likable man. He gave an excellent address, which the students enthusiastically applauded. Three years later, controversy arose again when he was awarded the Order of Canada. Although Dr. Morgentaler, now in his mid-eighties, has suffered a severe stroke, he is still carrying on serious discussions with provincial governments concerning his six private clinics across the country.

During my term, the number of graduates was considerably greater than normal because the Province of Ontario had recently eliminated grade thirteen, which meant that students of the "double cohort" group were all graduating together. At one afternoon convocation, nearly eight hundred students crossed the stage and the ceremony ran until six-thirty p.m. I tried very hard to remain just as enthusiastic when shaking hands with the last graduate as I had been with the first to cross the stage. In order to manage the large number of graduates, three are always called up at a time. There was a dean on either side of me, and my job was to shake hands and grant a degree to the middle person. When the names of each threesome were called out, I paid less attention to the names of the first and last students, but listened very carefully for the middle graduate's first name. I was therefore able to address this individual by name. The somewhat nervous graduate would smile at being called by name and was much more receptive to exchanging a few words. My four years as chancellor proved to be an enriching experience. At my final convocation, I was awarded the title of Chancellor Emeritus. This framed plaque hangs proudly on my wall. It brings back many fond memories of Western and of my hometown.

Association of Fundraising Professionals

On November 15, 2007, Sonia and I were selected as award recipients by the Association of Fundraising Professionals (AFP), Greater Toronto Chapter. Each year, the association has a large Philanthropic Awards Luncheon at the Toronto Convention Centre. Looking at the list of previous recipients, I realized we were in good company; it included Ted Rogers, the Ivey family, Drs. Murray and Marvelle Koffler, and the Honourable Margaret McCain.

We explained that our philanthropic focus was on education, health, and research. We mentioned a number of institutions we were supporting and why we had selected them. At the luncheon, I told a story of talking to very bright little guy at SickKids who had had two major operations for a malignant brain tumour. I asked him who had done his surgery and he told me it was Dr. Rutka. I told him that I knew Dr. Rutka and that he was a great surgeon. Then my new-found friend asked if I would like to see his scars. I took a good look at two major incisions at the back of his head and then asked him if he would like to see my scars. He did.

"Isn't this a great hospital?" I asked.

He looked me right in the eye and said, "I love this place."

It brought tears to my eyes.

University of Toronto, Honorary Doctor of Laws

On June 13, 2011, Sonia and I felt privileged to have Honorary Doctor of Law degrees conferred on both of us by the University of Toronto. Sonia has maintained close ties with U of T since she graduated in 1960 with an Honours BA in Science (Food Chemistry). She returned to the university in 1987 and completed an MA in 1990, and a PhD in 1995. She then

The day we received our honorary doctorates at U of T.

initiated and taught a course entitled Industry and the Environment for a number of years, and co-authored two books on environmental finance with Professor Emeritus Rodney White. She is a member of the Dean's Advisory Board for the Faculty of Arts and Science and has served as adjunct professor of Environmental Management at U of T's Centre for Environment.

We were both asked to address convocation, with Sonia going first. We wore bright crimson robes and looked quite presentable. Unbeknownst to us, our presentations were videotaped and posted on YouTube. Although we both tried to deliver some words of wisdom to the graduates, we also aimed to keep things lighthearted. (See Appendix 3.)

For example, Sonia told the stories I described earlier about applying for the master's program in Environmental Studies and being told that a letter from her undergraduate advisors would not be required, as they were all probably retired or expired. And about later, when defending her PhD dissertation, being mistaken as the advisor instead of the student.

As the applause subsided after her excellent speech, I was introduced to the assembly. I opened my talk by commenting on the fact that, coming after her, I felt a bit like Prince Philip – always following the Queen. This line got a good response. I then pointed out to the graduates that it is obvious that Sonia is the academic in the family. I also mentioned that Sonia and Dr. White's books on climate change and carbon trading were published before these terms became part of our everyday vocabulary

I told the graduates that I could go on and on about what an undisputed world-class institution the University of Toronto is, how it's recognized as a global leader in both research and teaching, and how it has by far the largest research budget in Canada, having produced ten Nobel Laureates. I commented on facets of my somewhat eclectic life, its ups and downs, and my successes and failures. I advised the graduates not to be too concerned with the uncertainties that lie ahead, and that we are living in a complex, confusing, and worrisome global environment. Yet we can look at this period as the most exciting and challenging time since the Industrial Revolution. The pace of change is accelerating and the possibilities for their bright generation are endless.

The paths before the graduates are many and I advised them that they should not be afraid of this. As Yogi Berra says, "When you come to a fork in the road, take it." I think he simply meant to never be afraid of a challenge. Successful people tend to have had more setbacks than their more conservative counterparts. They learn resilience – the ability to pick themselves up, dust themselves off, and keep on trying.

I closed by congratulating the students and pointing out that they were celebrating a major milestone in their lives, and that at each turn will come a pressing need to learn new ways of thinking. They should approach problems with an open mind, and temper whatever they do with true compassion for others.

XIV GRANDCHILDREN

WHILE on our African safari, I told our grandchildren that I was writing my memoirs. With pad in hand, I started to collect stories from each of them about their fondest memories of their years growing up.

The first brother and sister team I interviewed were the children of our son, John, and his wife, Diane. The youngest of the group is their son, John Christopher Marshall Labatt, who is fourteen. Christopher and his sister, Kinder, who is sixteen, had returned home to Toronto from France the year before. The family had been living near Aix en Provence and the two completed four years of schooling in the French public school system. Both Christopher and Kinder now attend the Toronto French School.

Christopher told me he was happy to be back in Canada but was sad to leave his friends at the Edouard Peisson public school in Ventabren. He used the term "bittersweet" to express his emotions concerning the family decision to return to Toronto. In fact, when asked how he felt after this move, his favourite answer was "the jury is still out." Fortunately the jury is now "in," and Christopher is thriving in Toronto. During his years in Provence, one major event that stood out for him was the freak snow-storm in the south of France that dumped twenty inches of snow and closed all of the schools for five days.

When he first returned, he found English difficult at TFS. When I asked about his proficiency in French, he said it was pretty good, but still a challenge, pointing out that there were students at the school who had grown up in France and spoke French at home. Although Christopher spoke excellent English, he had received little formal instruction in it. Now, he speaks English, French, Spanish, and even a little German.

Painting of our six grandchildren entitled "Six Cousins" by Phil Richards.
Sonia and I are in the background, in front of our cottage.

The summers spent at his family's cottage at Thunder Beach on Georgian Bay are very important to him, especially the time he spends at Camp Hurontario, which he has enjoyed since he was six years old. He always looks forward to the canoe trips; his favourite so far took him down the Pickerel River. Christopher is very interested in learning about amphibians and reptiles, thanks to the BIO Hut at camp. This interest continues at home with his two pet geckos, Hider and Seeker. Christopher looks forward to participating in the leader-in-training program at camp (a forty-minute boat ride from the cottage) and will likely work there for many years.

Christopher is an engaging and enthusiastic young man who relates particularly well to adults. In 2011, both he and his sister had lead roles in a school production of *Anne of Green Gables*. They were also "web leaders" at TFS. Their job was to help new students at the school become comfortable with their surroundings and meet new friends. Both have also acted as school ambassadors, helping out at school events. Recently, Christopher has taken up the drums, which he plays in the school's junior and senior bands. He also competed in a music competition in the percussion section of the school band, which earned a silver finish.

Kinder Judith Labatt, named Kinder after her great-great-grandfather, John Kinder Labatt, who founded the brewery in 1847, is an excellent student and writer. Kinder settled into life in Provence as though she had lived there all her life, but said she was so happy to be back in Toronto, adding that she "loves Toronto."

Kinder recounted that she suffered a couple of serious riding and snowboarding accidents when living in France. She also mentioned that she had experienced some scary times when their house in France was under renovation and she started to dream of vampires. In fact, she said she wanted to be one, and began writing a novel entitled *The Chosen One*. She e-mailed me three chapters, which I found well written and very interesting. I wouldn't be surprised if Kinder ends up an author, actress, or psychologist.

In 2011, Kinder completed three courses in American Sign Language and plans to take more advanced classes. She has become quite proficient in signing and looks forward to volunteering at the Bob Rumball Centre for the Deaf, when she is old enough. When asked if she made any new friends in the course, she responded that most of her classmates studying sign language are fairly elderly and find it difficult to sign due to the arthritis in their fingers. Kinder's youth and dexterity are clearly an advantage in these classes.

Our daughter Jacquie's eighteen-year-old son, Dylan Labatt Randle, is a very good athlete and excellent student, who graduated this year from Upper Canada College in Toronto. He was elected a steward, which is the new term for a position formerly known as prefect. Dylan's first seven years of schooling were spent at the Toronto French School, but his strongest memories relate to his canoe trips at Camp Ahmek.

During his camp years, he took three long trips, one lasting fifty days. Some were in extremely remote areas of northern Ontario and Quebec and required a considerable amount of bushwhacking. These long trips are carried out using three canoes with six campers and two staff members. He described how, after two weeks "on trip," you can become a bit paranoid due to feelings of isolation.

Dylan had lots of stories. One concerned arriving at a campsite that appeared to have been evacuated in extreme haste, with the trippers having left axes, a camera, open cans of Spam, as well as articles of clothing, soap, tooth brushes – and a rotting fish. In fact, the canoes left behind were from Wapomeo, the girls' camp across the lake from Camp Ahmek. Dylan subsequently learned that, just hours before his arrival at the campsite, all of the "Wap" campers had been taken out by helicopter because one of the group had suffered a severe reaction to bee stings.

Another of his stories pertained to the summer he was a counsellor-in-training at Ahmek. He was on a twelve-day canoe trip, originating from Maskinongé Lake in the Temagami region of northern Ontario. At five one evening, as the group was looking for a campsite, they paddled past an island on which was a small boarded-up cottage. They stopped to take a look; the only sign of human habitation was a child's life jacket lying on the dock. At the back of the house, they found four coffins piled on top of each other, all beside a rusty oil drum. The boys concluded that the owner made coffins for a living. They wanted nothing to do with such a site; they returned to their canoes and continued looking for another place to spend the night.

Later, about two kilometres from that island, they came upon a clearing on the mainland that they thought might be a road. Dylan got out of the canoe and realized it was not a road but some kind of shelter. It contained a half-buried coffin and a headstone with a name chiselled into it.

"We're not camping here!" Dylan shouted to the group.

That year at Ahmek, Dylan and his friend Philip Caldwell won the prestigious Stilson Trophy. Ahmek is basically a tripping camp, and the Stilson is a paddling and portaging race open to campers and staff, comprising 3.3 kilometres in total distance. All of the canoes start from the camp dock and everyone paddles to the Joe Lake portage, a distance of 2.3 kilometres. The contestants, two to each canoe, then grab the canoe and run with it over their heads a kilometre along a sandy road to the finish line at the camp's stables. There were thirty-eight teams competing. Dylan and Philip's winning time was thirty minutes, two seconds. Since 1952, when the race was inaugurated, the CITs have won it only three times. It is usually won by the senior staff members.

Courtney Sonia Labatt Randle, age sixteen, is Dylan's sister. Now in grade ten at Havergal College, she is an excellent student and a congenial classmate. As an athlete, she has focused her attention on rowing and field hockey. Last year, her rowing team did exceptionally well at the Canadian Secondary Schools Rowing Association Regatta, which is open to any collegiate, high school, or secondary school in the world. Their lightweight cox-four won its 2000-metre race by a bow ball (just under a metre, or three feet). Her interest in the sport is now so strong that her choice of a university may well be influenced by its rowing program.

As well as being a model team player, Courtney loves to travel. On several occasions, she visited her Barton cousins when they lived in Seoul and in Shanghai. In 2011, she took a month's community service trip to Thailand and Laos, accompanied by her good friend Rachelle Li from Havergal. Her memories of this trip revolve around elephants. First thing every morning, she put on her constantly wet "mahout" suit (as worn by elephant trainers) and, with a small group, trekked through the muddy jungle looking for, as she put it, "trained" elephants.

These elephants were trained to be ridden. They know how to pick up flip flops with their trunks and to lie down so young folks like Courtney can jump over their ears and onto their necks; then they stand up. There is a video showing Courtney and her friends falling into "elephant poo" water. Courtney assured me that this water is very good for the skin!

More recently, Courtney raved about their family holiday in Chile in early 2012, and her rowing camp in Oak Ridge, Tennessee, which she attended as rowing captain. She applies herself one hundred percent to her school work, while still finding time to maintain her fitness level.

Before Sheila and Dominic moved to England, their twenty-year-old son, Arthur Fraser Labatt Barton, spent a number of his earlier years at the Seoul Foreign School in Korea, then grades seven through eleven at Dulwich College in Shanghai, China. Following this were two years at the United World College of South East Asia in Singapore. Living in these exotic locations was a result of Dominic's transfers by his company, McKinsey & Co., one of the world's largest consulting firms.

Fraser has now completed his second year at the School of Oriental and African Studies at the University of London. At the beginning of his second year at SOAS, he joined the Officer Training Corps. This is a three-year commitment and is open to British, Commonwealth, and Irish students and involves one evening per week and one weekend a month. The first few months are not quite as strenuous as basic training in the army but can be pretty demanding all the same. For students who wish to continue with a career in the army, the next step is forty-six weeks at Sandhurst. In March 2012, Fraser was training with live ammunition. I gather that his fitness level has improved.

In addition to having a strong interest in history and economics, Fraser became seriously involved in student government when at school in Singapore and Shanghai. In Shanghai, he was president of the student council; in Singapore, his title was Secretary of the Boarding House. This title may not sound particularly glamorous, but, as Fraser pointed out, "Remember, Grandpa, Joseph Stalin was *Secretary* of the Communist Party." In addition to his interest in governance, he had a number of lead roles in school plays, both in Singapore and Shanghai. At university, Fraser is continuing to study Mandarin, to build on the foundation established during his days in the Far East.

His recollection of memorable stories revolves around summer vacations and, like his cousin Dylan, long canoe trips at Camp Ahmek. On one such trip in the Kipawa region of Quebec, his group, which had been battling head winds for twelve hours, was exhausted and desperate to find a campsite. On the large lake's lone island sat a derelict cabin that appeared deserted, and from which emanated strange, musty smells. They concluded it must be home to a hermit – or perhaps an axe murderer.

Copper wire was strung everywhere, which the boys thought might be part of a homemade alarm system. A raven was perched in a cage that hung from one of the rafters on the porch. The group decided not to try the door. Because it was very late and they were extremely tired, they pitched their tent nearby.

Nobody got much sleep that night. Early the next morning, just as they were deciding they had better get moving, a motorboat suddenly appeared out of the fog, heading straight for the island. The driver, whose face was covered, was wearing a big yellow rain suit. The moment he saw the trippers, he started speeding up. All they could think of was the fisherman in the 1997 horror film *I Know What You Did Last Summer*. The campers quickly packed up all of their gear and made a hasty exit, paddling as fast as they could. The "fisherman" did not pursue them.

Eighteen-year-old Jessica Alison Labatt Barton is Fraser's younger sister. In 2011, she completed her final year of high school in Singapore at the United World College of South East Asia, the same school Fraser had attended. Like her brother, she had previously attended Dulwich College in Shanghai and the Seoul International School in Korea.

Jessica is a bright girl who worked very hard to achieve top marks. She loved drama and singing and was frequently a leading character in school plays and musicals, both in Singapore and Shanghai. She has been accepted at University College London but took a year off and will start in the fall of 2012. In September 2011, she went to Cambodia and taught English for six weeks before moving to Thailand to teach Geography and lead hiking expeditions. She then returned to London for the balance of her year off.

Having lived in the Far East for nearly all of her life, Jessica was full of stories, but the experience she remembers most vividly was a family camel safari in Outer Mongolia. All they had to eat was meat, sauerkraut, salty camel cheese, and jam. As a result, Jessica, who is a vegetarian, was hungry most of the time. She recounted how her dad, who was wearing new beige shoes, refused to walk through a swamp that was laden with camel droppings. Dominic had already given up on his ornery camel, which had bucked him off on more than one occasion, so he proceeded to walk miles around this swamp in the blistering heat.

Like the nomads in the region, the family slept in yurts during the bitterly cold nights. Jessica still has clear images of the skeletons of small desert foxes that had been devoured by vultures. It is interesting to note that their family trip to Outer Mongolia took place only a week after 9/11, and yet, many of the nomadic people they met en route were fully aware of it and asked the Barton family for their reaction to this terrible event.

~

Sonia and I are so fortunate for our six terrific grandchildren ranging in age from fourteen to twenty. The most enjoyable part of writing this book was sitting down with each of them and listening to their stories and their views of the increasingly complicated world they have inherited. Each of them is quite driven to succeed and their parents should be very proud. Each has moved a number of times and life has not always been easy. I wish, in my youth, I had possessed even half the drive and determination they display.

Memoirs are about the past;
grandchildren are the future.

Of all the places Sonia and I have visited
and all the goals we have sought and achieved,
nothing makes us happier or prouder than our
children and grandchildren.

My words and my deeds may live on in some form,
but only through our family can there
be anything approaching a legacy.

At the party following the annual meeting of the Voting Trust.
I'm in the first row, second from right, between my sister, Mary, and brother, Jack.
Our parents are in the middle of the second row.

Front row, from left: Alan Jarvis, Kay Jarvis, Katherine Grass, Frances Haley,
Margaret Harley, George Brickenden, Mary Labatt, Arthur Labatt, Jack Labatt.

Second row: Honour Cochrane, Verse Cronyn, Barbara Cronyn, Babs Chipman,
Murray Chipman, Bessie Labatt, John S. Labatt, Angela Labatt, Hugh F. Labatt,
Audrey Scatcherd, Colin Scatcherd.

Third row: Doe Cronyn, Barbara Jackson, Kathleen Patton, Jessica Tandy,
Lorraine Russel, Ginny Whitehead, Kay Graydon, Kay Harley, Kay Labatt,
Shirley Brickenden, Ruly Grass.

Fourth row: Hume Cronyn, Shrimp Cochrane, John Cronyn, Alex Graydon, Reg Jarvis,
Dal Russel, Robert Whitehead, John Patton, John Harley, Ernie Jackson.

Appendix 1 – Labatt History

IN this and Appendix 2, I offer the fruits of some of my genealogical research into the Labatt family, which I believe will be of interest to my grandchildren and their descendants. My main historical sources are the family tree that my father compiled in the 1930s, as well as information from the Internet and research by a genealogist. Some information may be imprecise, as some old church records were either destroyed or are questionable in their accuracy. In addition, I have drawn on material from the manuscript by Albert Tucker on the founding of Labatt's and its early days in London, Ontario.

Unfortunately, everyone in my father's generation has passed away. The nine children in his family all had stories about their ancestors; many of these tales had been passed down to them orally. I would have been so pleased if I had been able to learn more about the Labatt clan from them.

The Huguenots

THE Labatt ancestors were Huguenots, French Protestants who were persecuted, with varying intensity, for centuries, up to the time of Napoleon. They were influenced by Martin Luther's teachings in the early sixteenth century, and by John Calvin, a Frenchman who preached in Geneva from 1537 to 1564. As the Huguenot French Protestant church grew, it came into increasing conflict with the Roman Catholic Church and with the French monarchy.

In 1561, Catherine de Medici granted certain privileges to the Protestants, but the peace was short-lived. The next year, the Duc de Guise, who was Grand Chamberlain of France and head of the Catholic

League, was on the way to his estate with his entourage, when he passed near Vassy to attend mass. A scuffle developed with Huguenots who were attending a religious service in a barn nearby. Many unarmed Huguenot parishioners were killed at what became known as the Massacre of Vassy. Thus began the first of the Wars of Religion, which lasted thirty-five years.

There were many assassinations of Huguenots during this period, and on August 23, 1572, an estimated ten thousand Protestants were killed in Paris alone. The governors of the provinces were instructed to do likewise, and in total, one hundred thousand Huguenots lost their lives as a result of the infamous St. Bartholomew's Massacre. The young King Charles IX was reputed to have ordered "the death of all the Protestants of France, so that none would remain to reproach me later." This slaughter wreaked havoc on the remaining Huguenots and devastated France.

Relative peace was established in 1598 following the Edict of Nantes, which granted the Calvinist Protestants of France substantial rights in a nation still considered Catholic. It treated Protestants for the first time as more than mere heretics, and opened a path for secularism and tolerance. However, when King Henry IV was assassinated, in 1610, the Protestants again lost much of their protection. Cardinal Richelieu was obsessed with eliminating all Huguenot communities in France. Freedoms were restricted, and wars against the Huguenots resumed. By 1685, Louis IV believed that years of intimidation and persecution had crushed the Huguenots, and the Edict of Nantes was revoked. The last of the Protestant churches were destroyed, and any assembly of non-Catholics was forbidden.

Prior to the revocation of the edict, there were about eight hundred thousand Huguenots in France. In the face of horrific persecution, five hundred thousand recanted their faith, and, during the next twenty years, about a quarter of a million Huguenots left France. They settled in other European countries, as well as England, Ireland, North America, South Africa, and the West Indies. The émigrés were skilled tradespeople who were forced to leave France with nothing but their vocational skills and their Protestant beliefs.

ANDRÉ DE LABAT

I have traced my ancestry back to seventeenth-century France, to Etienne de Labat (the surname was originally spelled with just one "t"). Born in 1625, he was a lawyer in the Huguenot Parliament in Bordeaux. Through his first wife, he inherited a *seigneury* located near Tonneins, approximately thirty-one miles southeast of Bordeaux.

The youngest of Etienne's children was André de Labat, who was born in 1670 and became Marquis of Clairac, a town just south of Tonneins. He was driven from his Château de Clairac four years after the revocation of the Edict of Nantes; the château was destroyed by the soldiers.

Some of the displaced Huguenots, including André, enlisted in the Protestant armies that fought Louis X1V. André was only twenty in 1689 when he enlisted under the Marquis de Ruvigny, a member of the Huguenot nobility.

André then went to Holland and joined the French army of William (III) of Orange, in which he fought for thirteen years in Holland, Flanders, and lastly, Ireland. He was part of a regiment of émigrés involved in many famous battles in Ireland. He was on the *Mount Joy*, an armed merchant ship, when it broke the siege of Derry. In 1690, he took part in the famous Battle of the Boyne.

William of Orange (King Billy) was the Protestant head of the Dutch Royal House of Orange and was married to Mary, the daughter of King James II. King James was a convert to Catholicism, but his daughter had been raised in the Protestant faith. Although the Battle of the Boyne was a minor military triumph, it was a landmark victory for Britain. It is almost a sacred day for Orangemen around the world, and, in Canada, it is this battle that is celebrated every year on Orangemen's Day, July 12.

After a peace treaty was signed with France in 1697, William was ordered to disband his army. André de Labat, at the age of thirty-four, was discharged with the rank of captain and was given an annual pension of £50, but no land. His regimental commander, the Marquis de Ruvigny, was named Earl of Galway and was given twenty-two thousand acres of confiscated Irish lands. Because most of this land was already occupied, the Marquis was not able to give his veterans free land, in contrast to the way officers later received land in North America.

André married Christina Peppard in 1707. They had a daughter, Marie, and a son, Andrew. He died in 1728 and is buried at St. Mary's, in County Kilkenny. Nearly all of the Huguenots who moved to Ireland joined the Church of Ireland, which is affiliated with the Church of England. André left a long, detailed will, essentially leaving "all his worldly goods and property of all kinds" to his son, Andrew.

ANDREW LABATT

LITTLE is known of Andrew. He lived in a small village to the south of the French settlement of Portarlington in County Laois, then in King's county in Ireland. He had three sons, Samuel, Valentine, and Andrew. Although nearly all of André Labat's descendants had dropped the "de" before their last name, it was probably his eldest son, Samuel Bell Labatt, who formally added a second "t" to Labat, to further anglicize the name. Samuel became a famous surgeon in Dublin and wrote a number of books on the subject of vaccination. He was Secretary of the Cow-Pox Institution, Royal College of Surgeons.

VALENTINE LABATT

OUR branch of the family comes down through Andrew's second son, Valentine Knightley Chetwode Labatt. Valentine married the daughter of Ephraim Harper, an Anglican clergyman. Valentine and his wife, Jane, had seven children, the eldest being John Kinder Labatt, my great-grandfather, who was born in 1803. John Kinder grew up in the town of Mountmellick and attended Sunday school and grammar school under the care of the Church of England.

JOHN KINDER LABATT

MOUNTMELLICK was an agricultural centre, not far from Dublin. John Kinder Labatt lacked the means to attend university in Dublin and decided to move to London, England, around 1830. He made contact in London with an Irish Huguenot family named Claris, and found a clerical job with a timber merchant.

At that time, London was the world's largest metropolis. It was the nation's capital and an international financial centre, with more than a million and a half people. Wanting to break out of his minor clerical job, he discussed his frustrations with two of the Claris brothers, and the three of them discussed immigrating to British North America.

Through the Claris brothers, he met Eliza Kell, the daughter of a senior clerk at the Bank of England, in the spring of 1833. Eliza was only seventeen but had the maturity that comes from being the eldest of three children. In the summer of 1833, her father, Robert Kell, suffered a serious financial loss from a speculative investment and found himself burdened with a debt of £1,150. Those were the days of debtor's prisons, and he stood to lose everything if he were thrown into prison.

Robert encouraged the marriage of Eliza and John, which took place in August. The plan was that John would lead a party of five to a new settlement in Upper Canada. The group would include his new wife, her mother (Robert's wife), her younger brother, and a sister. Robert's annual salary was only £300, and he intended to limit his living costs to £50 in order to be able to pay his creditors £250 annually for five years. He said he would send whatever he could to his family in Canada. Meanwhile, he would live with his sister, Maria, an evangelical who operated a girls' school. She was a spinster and felt a deep obligation to help her brother.

All of these arrangements were made in haste, and the party of five departed from a port near Dover on the *William Osborne*. The ship narrowly missed a major storm by taking shelter in Ramsgate. Robert's letters to his wife showed that he had deep feelings of remorse and guilt for having to send his family four thousand miles away because of his ill-advised speculation. His concern was heightened by the fact that they went to a land that required the clearing of forest before any attempt at farming could be made. Neither his wife nor his son-in-law had any experience to prepare them for the rigours of the frontier.

John K. Labatt and the family of four Kells reached Upper Canada late in the fall of 1833. The journey from England had taken more than two months, but all of the members of the group survived. They landed in New York and boarded a steamship that travelled up the Hudson River to Albany, where they took a canal boat to Oswego on Lake Ontario. Then they crossed the lake to York, which, within a year, would be incorporated as the City of Toronto.

They stopped long enough in York only to establish their claim to two hundred acres located a hundred and twenty miles to the west in the District of London. The final leg of their journey took two more days. The first third of it was by boat to Hamilton, where they transferred to a four-horse coach, which travelled over a rugged corduroy road to London. From London, they went south for about ten miles, heading to St. Thomas. Their two hundred acres were located on a direct line between St. Thomas to the south and London to the north.

Although my father never thought that his grandfather, John Kinder Labatt, was a particularly successful farmer, a great deal of evidence suggests that, in fact, he built up a substantial farming operation over a thirteen-year period. The family survived their first winter without any major problems. Within two years, they had constructed two small log houses facing each other, one for John and Eliza and their baby son, Robert, the other for Mrs. Kell and her son and younger daughter.

Within ten years, John had established himself among the "men of means" on the farms in Westminster Township. He entered his wheat and animals in annual competitions, helped found the first Anglican church at Glanworth, and served in the militia. He supported himself and his family during a difficult period and enabled his father-in-law to pay off his serious debt. When he paid the last installment to the Canada Company on the original two hundred acres, he purchased another farm immediately adjoining his land.

John's partner in attaining this success was his wife, Eliza. Between 1835 and 1844, she bore six children – four boys and two girls. The children all attended an excellent private grammar school in the area. Eliza's mother had returned to England. Everything was going well, but both John and Eliza felt the isolation of the farm, which they had always seen as just a means for beginning a new life. So they decided to move back to England.

In the summer of 1846, John sold the farm for £925 and set out for England with two of his sons – Robert, age eleven, and George Thomas, who was not yet four. The purpose of John's trip was to find a potentially successful business to run in England and eventually bring Eliza and the children closer to her own family in London. In the meantime, Eliza and the four other children stayed with her sister in St. Thomas.

John explored many business opportunities in the Midlands textile trades but did not feel at home with the people he met. He also looked at Ireland but decided against it. As he put it in a letter to Eliza, "People are dying in all directions from disease and starvation, and almost everyone who can get out of the country is leaving for America." If Eliza were to return to England, he was certain that she, too, would find it too expensive for raising a family.

Meanwhile, John's good friend and neighbour in Canada, Samuel Eccles, had sold his interest in a brewery in St. Thomas and had bought the London Brewery on the banks of the Thames River. When John heard this news in a letter from Eliza, he proposed a partnership with Eccles on the condition that his good friend George Claris and Eliza both thought this a good idea. The proposal was satisfactory to all parties, and with his sons he returned to Canada, having put England behind him.

In 1847, in partnership with Eccles, and with some financial backing from the Kell family in England, John purchased the London Brewery.

London Brewery

THE original London Brewery was built by an innkeeper, John Balkwill, in 1828, and was purchased by Labatt and Eccles in 1847. Samuel Eccles was a brewmaster, and he and John had previously supplied barley malt to Balkwill's brewery from their farms at Glanworth.

The partnership continued until 1853, when John Kinder Labatt bought out Eccles and renamed the operation John Labatt's Brewery. According to my father, the partnership fell apart because an American evangelist from Buffalo was touring the farm country near London preaching the evils of drink. Eccles decided he should give up the beer business and stick to farming. The two gentlemen remained good friends and neighbours.

The brewery, which was just a small operation that employed six men, catered exclusively to the London market. The prospect of growth picked up with the arrival of the railway in 1853, making it possible to ship the "product" to Hamilton, Toronto, and even Montreal.

John Labatt

John Kinder Labatt had three surviving sons, the youngest being John, my grandfather. At home, we always referred to him as "John – No Middle Name – Labatt." When John Kinder died in 1866, this son, then twenty-eight, assumed control of the business. John was a keen student of brewing and had apprenticed at a brewery in West Virginia. He returned from there with the recipe for India Pale Ale. Labatt's IPA became the brewery's signature brand. For over four decades, it earned Labatt's many gold, silver, and bronze medals at international expositions around the world.

As mentioned, the growth of the railroads in the latter part of the nineteenth century greatly expanded the market for Labatt's product. Beer could be transported in barrels to bottling agencies in cities hundreds of miles from London. The brewery, which was wholly owned by John Labatt, became very profitable. In the 1880s and 1890s, my grandfather made significant investments in other businesses – agricultural implements, gold mining, and mortgage lending. These ventures did not work out; he lost a considerable amount of money before deciding to concentrate his efforts on brewing. Before his death in 1915, he had opportunities to sell or merge the company but decided to remain independent.

John Sackville Labatt

In his will, my grandfather left the profitable private company, John Labatt Limited, in equal parts to his two sons and seven daughters. In 1900, he had brought his two boys, John Sackville Labatt and Hugh Francis Labatt, into the company. Father had a science degree from McGill University and was a qualified brewmaster, having spent two years at the Brewers Academy in New York City.

John and Hugh Labatt had worked for their father for nearly fifteen years before his death in 1915. At that point, Father became president and Uncle Hugh vice president and secretary of the company. It would not have been easy working for their father. When I was growing up in the 1940s and '50s, we never talked about grandfather Labatt, who had died thirty-five years earlier. He was a dominant individual who was used to running his own show.

My father sent this photo to his sister Dora. He identified our Labatt kin in the accompanying letter and explained the reason for his father's dour expression, typical of siblings to this day.

Dear Dora:

                    MERRY CHRISTMAS!

          Enclosed is a photograph taken
from an old Daguerreotype, which Sydney Mewburn
was kind enough to give me. (Original taken 1863)

          Sitting from left to right are:
Granny Labatt (maiden name, Eliza Kell and Wife
of John K. Labatt, my Grandfather), Uncle Robert
and Granddad; observe the wonderful necktie.

          Standing from left to right are:
Uncle George (Father of the Prescott, Ontario
Labatts), my Father (John Labatt) and Uncle Eph-
raim (Father of the late Colonel R.H. Labatt and
Ephie Reid and Grandfather of Ephie Reid's chil-
dren and of Captain Bob Labatt of Hamilton).

          I have always heard that Uncle
Robert was the best looking of the Family; the
picture, I think, bears this out. Note the
strong face of John K. Labatt. The reason John
Labatt looks so cross is that he just had a dis-
pute with Uncle George. I understand that it had
something to do with how they should stand for
the photograph and that some remark was made about
his being the shortest; George was the youngest
Brother so my Dad, I believe, vented his feelings
on him.

                    With all best wishes for the New
Year, I am

          Your affectionate Brother,

          John T. Labatt.

          C H R I S T M A S   1 9 3 7

In their younger years, both Father and Uncle Hugh had speech impediments. With professional help, Father was able to get rid of a stutter, but Uncle Hugh continued to have a slight stammer. When I heard this story as a boy, I wondered if Grandfather's personality had played a part.

Under the terms of Grandfather's will, the two boys had to obtain the consent of their seven sisters regarding changes in ownership. John and Hugh were very close and assumed joint management of the company. There were never any problems among the nine siblings, and so this appendix ends, where the book began, at the time of my birth when the business was booming.

In our backyard with Sheila, John, and Jacquie ...

... and with the rest of the family.

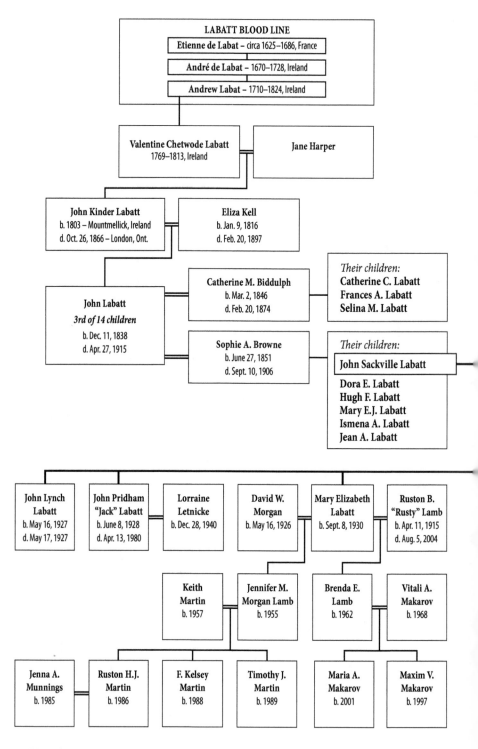

LABATT BLOOD LINE

Etienne de Labat – circa 1625–1686, France

André de Labat – 1670–1728, Ireland

Andrew Labat – 1710–1824, Ireland

Valentine Chetwode Labatt
1769–1813, Ireland

Jane Harper

John Kinder Labatt
b. 1803 – Mountmellick, Ireland
d. Oct. 26, 1866 – London, Ont.

Eliza Kell
b. Jan. 9, 1816
d. Feb. 20, 1897

John Labatt
3rd of 14 children
b. Dec. 11, 1838
d. Apr. 27, 1915

Catherine M. Biddulph
b. Mar. 2, 1846
d. Feb. 20, 1874

Their children:
Catherine C. Labatt
Frances A. Labatt
Selina M. Labatt

Sophie A. Browne
b. June 27, 1851
d. Sept. 10, 1906

Their children:
John Sackville Labatt
Dora E. Labatt
Hugh F. Labatt
Mary E.J. Labatt
Ismena A. Labatt
Jean A. Labatt

John Lynch Labatt
b. May 16, 1927
d. May 17, 1927

John Pridham "Jack" Labatt
b. June 8, 1928
d. Apr. 13, 1980

Lorraine Letnicke
b. Dec. 28, 1940

David W. Morgan
b. May 16, 1926

Mary Elizabeth Labatt
b. Sept. 8, 1930

Ruston B. "Rusty" Lamb
b. Apr. 11, 1915
d. Aug. 5, 2004

Keith Martin
b. 1957

Jennifer M. Morgan Lamb
b. 1955

Brenda E. Lamb
b. 1962

Vitali A. Makarov
b. 1968

Jenna A. Munnings
b. 1985

Ruston H.J. Martin
b. 1986

F. Kelsey Martin
b. 1988

Timothy J. Martin
b. 1989

Maria A. Makarov
b. 2001

Maxim V. Makarov
b. 1997

APPENDIX 2 – LABATT FAMILY TREE

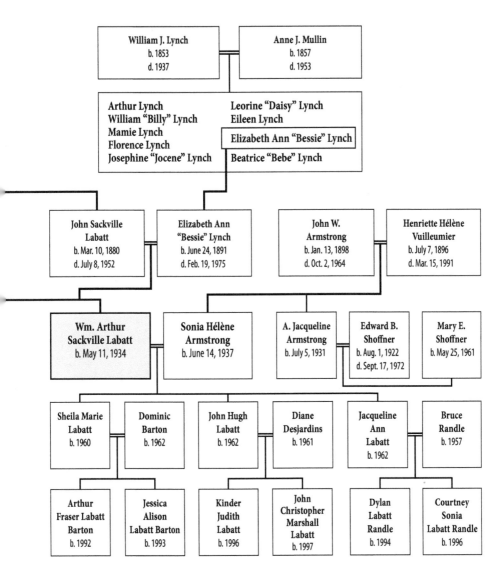

Appendix 3 – Speeches

Speech by Arthur Labatt, at Installation as
Chancellor of the University of Western Ontario
October 2004

Mr. Chair, Mr. President, honoured guests, faculty,
and of course, graduates:

WHEN I was approached by Western to be its nineteenth chancellor,
I was incredibly honoured, and eager to accept for a number of reasons.

This is an institution that has a long and well-earned reputation for
offering quality academic programs. Western ranks among the best of
the major Canadian universities, by providing a learning environment
that fosters intellectual and personal excellence. What started out as a
humble, one-room schoolhouse 125 years ago as the Western University
of London Ontario is now an academic powerhouse and one of Canada's
leading research universities. We should all be very proud.

Western's students and its graduates – including all of you here today
– represent some of the finest minds in the country.

Western boasts a long list of notable graduates who truly exemplify its
motto of "truth and service." People like Roberta Bondar ... and Silken
Laumann. Western has also been home to some of this country's top
researchers and innovators – Dr. Allan Davenport, who built our famous
Wind Tunnel, and Sir Frederick Banting, co-discoverer of insulin.

As your new chancellor, I will uphold the values of this university and
promote its well-being. I can assure you that I will work hard in the next
four years as an ambassador for this great institution of higher learning.

I have fond memories of growing up in London, swimming in the Thames River, going to Springbank Park, to Port Stanley on the L & PS – for those not in the know, that's the London & Port Stanley railroad, which, as my father pointed out, was once North America's fastest electric railroad. These memories remain with me to this day, as does the Western campus, which had a strong presence in my early life.

To my ten-year-old eyes, watching the Western Mustangs play football against the University of Toronto, Queen's, or McGill was incredibly exciting. Johnny Metras was the Head Coach at Western and was a legend in his time.

Mind you, the campus has changed a lot since then … At that time, there were only two large buildings, and a whole lot of grass.

But even though Western has changed in appearance, its high standards and strong values remain the same.

When I was first asked to speak to you, I realized that I was going to have the opportunity to deliver an address that conveyed something significant and thought provoking, and perhaps even life changing. Feeling somewhat daunted, I did what anyone would do in this situation … I went to the cottage.

As I watched my grandchildren build a bonfire one evening, I marvelled at how the fire was the centre of everything. It continued to burn while we sat around it, roasting marshmallows and telling stories, and that's when it occurred to me that all of us have a spark that burns within us and drives us forward.

So to the graduates here today – What is the flame that drives you to succeed?

Although there are many different faculties present at this convocation, there is one common thread that connects all of you – that burning desire to do something significant with your life. To make your mark in the world! To make a difference! That fire within has brought you here today, to the brink of the next great step in your life.

There may be some of you sitting here thinking, "But I'm not really sure what I want to do with the rest of my life." And I can understand that. My own career didn't start out the way I thought it would. But I learned, through a few lessons along the way, that I could succeed.

I'd just like to share a few of these experiences with you.

Because my father died when I was leaving high school, I had very little guidance at that important time in my life. I never quite knew where I was headed.

John Labatt Ltd was founded in 1848 by my great-grandfather. Growing up, I always assumed that one day I would join the family business – and sit in my father's and grandfather's corner office. However, with the death of my father and my uncle Hugh, my older brother, Jack, advised me that it was unlikely that the company would remain in family hands – in fact, by the time I was in my twenties, the brewery was sold.

This was a huge disappointment for me. As time passed, I realized that this was the best thing that could have happened to me. This experience forced me to chart my own course, and discover that I had my own flame burning within. Mind you, my career in business took many twists and turns along the way. I went from accounting, to research, to corporate finance, to sales. Eventually I found my calling in investment management. And it meant so much more because I'd proven to myself that I could attain success on my own – with lots of help from my colleagues.

Now, chances are, you didn't reach this graduation day all on your own steam. You had people who helped add fuel to your fire ... your family, your friends, your professors, and even your fellow graduates. During my own time at Western, I encountered many wonderful people. One in particular, Dr. Ed Hall, was president of Western in the late forties and was a good friend of our family. He set very high standards when it came to teaching and research. His drive for excellence attracted many distinguished scholars and helped Western gain both national and international status.

I think what Dr. Hall said in 1947 still holds true today (and I quote): "We must think in terms of the next hundred years. We must think in terms of this university becoming the greatest university in Canada."

Over the last ten years, our current president, Dr. Paul Davenport, continues to carry on that tradition of high academic standards and quality leadership.

Early in my career, I learned the importance of finding a mentor in one's life. I was fortunate to find two outstanding mentors when I worked at Ernst & Young. One was my manager, Bill MacDonald, who gave me courage and confidence when I was having a rough time with some of the accounting exams. Another was Duncan Gordon, a senior partner who provided wise counsel when I had decided to look at new fields of endeavour, rather than remain as a practicing chartered accountant.

As you move forward, I encourage you to continue to listen to people who have your best interest at heart. In return, be fair and gracious to your colleagues. Treat people the way you'd like to be treated. And never hold a grudge; this can only hurt you in the long run.

Years ago, when I was just getting started, a senior executive told me that finding a good partner in business is as much of a challenge as finding a good spouse. I've been fortunate on both counts: my wife, Sonia, who has been supportive for the last forty-six years, and my twenty-five-year business partner at Trimark, Bob Krembil. When Bob and I founded Trimark in 1981, it was a hands-on, start-up situation – five of us in total. The stock market was at a very low point – CSBs were yielding nineteen and a half percent, mortgage rates were twenty-two and a half percent. In our office, there were telephones sitting on cardboard boxes, order forms with cheques attached with safety pins and filed in shoeboxes and lined up along the window sill.

In starting Trimark, our goal was simply to do a good job for investors – we had absolutely no idea of the growth that would occur over the next twenty years.

Before Trimark, I moved my young family from Montreal to Paris and opened an office for a Canadian investment house. I learned a lesson about stress and how to manage it.

- First of all, there was the difficulty of language and culture. I had grade thirteen French from London Central Collegiate.
- I had to instantly turn myself from a research analyst into a securities salesperson.
- And on top of all this, I had just quit smoking cold turkey.
- If that wasn't enough, I also had to entertain big corporate and government clients from Canada. I was only thirty-three at the time, and, without any warning, the Chairman of the Royal Bank would just drop in to say hello – or on another occasion, I would be asked to host a dinner for the Premier of Nova Scotia. I got to know every maître d' in Paris, and every nightclub act in town. So, in fact, I had a night job as well as my day job.

If you want to keep the fire within you alive, then you have to keep your stress in check – otherwise, it can burn out of control or burn out completely.

And above all, put your family first. Jobs will come and go, but your family is forever.

The message, then, is to try and lead a balanced life. Develop other interests beyond your work. I've stayed active by hiking, canoeing, skiing, etc. And in last ten years, I've taken up golf with a vengeance, but Mike Weir has nothing to fear.

Most importantly, never take yourself too seriously – be able to laugh at yourself. As my brother-in-law (a Superior Court judge in Quebec) used to say, "Have a sense of the ridiculous."

In the mid-'50s, when I joined the working world, North America was flourishing and Canada played a major role in world markets as a supplier of natural resources and agricultural products.

In the past few years, Canada has embraced the new information economy and is becoming increasingly competitive on a world scale. Our future is looking very bright, and I sincerely hope that all of you stay in Canada – because we need you. However, should you decide to pursue opportunities beyond our borders, know that Canadians are highly regarded abroad.

You're very fortunate to have been educated at this wonderful university and in a country that is so rich in opportunity. As you move forward, remember this: Not only are all of you ambassadors for Western, you're also ambassadors for Canada.

It's been wonderful to share with you some of the lessons that have helped me form long-lasting and fulfilling relationships with my peers, my mentors, and my bosses.

Take the time to reflect on what it is that motivates you. It's not easy – and sometimes it changes as you mature and your horizons widen. When you think you have found your calling, nurture it and keep it burning.

So to the class of 2004, I salute you! You should all be extremely proud of yourselves and grateful to have attended this fine institution. Today marks a significant milestone in your life. Use your education as a springboard and build on it. Look forward to the future with confidence.

I wish you well.

Speech by Sonia Labatt, upon receiving an Honorary Doctor of Laws degree from the University of Toronto June 13, 2011

Chancellor Peterson, President Naylor, distinguished members of the platform party, graduates of University College, families, and friends:

I can't tell you how overwhelmed Arthur and I felt when we were informed of the great honour that has been bestowed on us today. We are most grateful. And coming from my own alma mater makes it even more momentous and meaningful.

When thinking about what I would say to the graduates today, a friend of mine suggested that I relate the length of my comments to the dress code that was in force in 1960 when we graduated, when we made sure that our skirts were long enough to cover everything, but short enough to still be interesting.

In the next few minutes, I will try to stick to these principles as I share with you some key points that I learned from my academic involvement.

My first point is about the importance of continuing to learn. My own experience at this fine institution spans fifty-five years, from my first year in 1956 as an undergrad in Honours Science at University College, to my present association at the Centre for Environment. But like many things in life, this journey has not followed a direct route. In fact the theme of my continued learning saga could well be titled "The Road Less Travelled."

When I graduated with my BA in Food Chemistry in 1960, I was awarded a fellowship to continue my studies in the U.S. But I was married at the time, so therefore did not accept the offer. In the following years, Arthur and I enjoyed raising a family, travelling extensively, and living in various cities, including Paris. As more time passed, however, I continued to feel that my education was incomplete.

So in 1987, I decided to return to the U of T to take a master's degree in Environmental Studies. Coming back to university after a twenty-five-year hiatus can be daunting – and here is where I learned my second point: to recognize the humour in parts of my journey.

- On applying to pursue a master's degree, the Geography department would normally have required a letter of recommendation from my undergraduate advisors. "But I suppose," suggested the department chair, "that your professors are either all retired or more likely all expired by now."
- Also at that time, Simcoe Hall rejected my student number for having too few digits. I advised them to look back twenty-five years, and lo and behold, there I was.
- After defending my PhD dissertation in 1995, my advisor Virginia Maclaren (who hooded us today) and I went to the Grad School offices to sign some official documents. There I was handed the advisor's document and Virginia the student's one, since I was visibly the more senior at the table. This was quickly corrected, but as you can see, not as quickly forgotten.

So I suppose my second point is: If you follow this non-linear road, remember not to take yourself too seriously, and just roll with the punches.

When I returned to the world of academia in 1987 I had developed a great interest in the environment, a subject matter, by the way, for which there were no courses in 1960. Also by 1987 I had absorbed some understanding of the business and financial worlds. Thus I was able to bring together two areas of knowledge that I had gained since 1960.

Persevering through the challenge of continued learning has awarded me a number of opportunities. I was able to:

- Examine corporate environmental and carbon management
- Establish new courses
- Teach and
- Co-author two books

Each of these stepping-stones presented a challenge, since I had not done any of them before. But the satisfaction I experienced on completion was well worth it.

Thus my next message is that one should accept meaningful challenges as they present themselves, because many challenges are accompanied by great opportunities. Or as Albert Einstein has so aptly put it, "In the middle of a difficulty lies an opportunity."

I believe that higher learning is critical to Canada's future. It makes us, as individuals and as a country, more competitive and prosperous and not to mention – more interesting. And it opens up the potential for original thinking.

And we all need people and institutions to think differently. Take, for example, how we look at water as a resource.

Historically "water" has been perceived as

- A common good
- Collectively owned
- Shared by all

However, today we are witnessing an increased scarcity of water, creating

- Environmental refugees in Africa
- Water-diversion proposals in China and elsewhere

At the same time, businesses and the public sector are becoming involved in its management, using

- Strategic thinking about supply and demand
- New technologies to improve quality, access, and availability all of this in an attempt to assess water-related risks across different geographies and sectors. Innovative thinking is essential in such a complex situation.

So now, turning to today's accomplished graduates, you may not have all the answers today but your experience here at the U of T has given you:

- The tools to develop a vision
- The ability to view a challenge as an opportunity
- The capacity to think differently

All these qualities are important as you venture out on paths that others may not take.

If I can leave you with one more consideration, it is to look at today as a stepping-stone to further education. As you can see from my experience, you can do it all, but you don't have to do it all at once.

So graduates, I congratulate you all. And wish you well, whether you take the road more – or less – travelled.

*Mr. Chancellor, Mr. President, Principal Bashevkin, Dean Gertler,
members of the platform party, ladies and gentlemen – and – most
importantly – Graduates of University College:*

SONIA, coming after you, I feel a bit like Prince Philip – always following
the Queen.

As you can see, Sonia is the academic in the family. We had been
married for two years when Sonia graduated in 1960. And what I learned
very quickly is that food chemistry has nothing to do with knowing how
to cook. But she did know when food had gone bad!

Sonia also learned a great deal at the Centre for Environment. She
co-authored a book on climate change and carbon trading long before
these terms were used in everyday conversation. In fact, these words were
so foreign to some that, at the launch of the book, one of my banking
friends said to me, "What does Sonia know about carpet trading?"

To all of the graduates, first, let me say – congratulations. You have
worked very hard and you must be so proud to have earned a degree from
the University of Toronto. U of T was established almost two hundred
years ago and has half a million alumni living around the globe – you are
truly associated with a prestigious university.

The University of Toronto is an undisputed world-class institution and
is recognized as a global leader in both research and teaching. It has by
far the largest research budget in Canada – and has produced ten Nobel
Laureates. Many famous discoveries have emanated from your soon-to-
be alma mater. Insulin in 1921, the first artificial pacemaker in 1950 – and
also the discovery of stem cells in 1963 – all profound discoveries – and I
could go on and on …

I am extremely proud to have been awarded an honorary degree from
this incredible institution, and I thank the University of Toronto for this
honour.

When I was asked to say a few words to you – the graduates – today, I realized that this was an opportunity to convey something thought provoking, profound, and, maybe even life changing. Feeling somewhat daunted with this responsibility, I did what anyone would do in this situation – I went to the cottage for the long weekend.

While there I recalled watching our grandchildren build a fire and I marvelled at how the fire was the centre of everything. We sat around roasting marshmallows on the fire and telling stories and it occurred to me that all of us have a spark, a flame, a fire that burns within us and drives us forward. It is that fire that led you to U of T, helped you persevere – and will ensure that you prevail (and prosper) in the future.

So to the graduates here today – What is the fire that drives you to succeed? Arts and Science is a huge Faculty and the interests of its graduates are wide ranging, but there is one common thread that connects all of you – that burning desire to do something significant with your life. To make your mark in the world! To make a difference.

Some of you may be sitting here thinking, "But I'm not really sure what I want to do with the rest of my life" and I can certainly relate to that. My career didn't turn out the way I thought it would. My father died when I was finishing high school, at a time in my life when I needed considerable guidance. I never quite knew where to start or where I was headed.

The Labatt brewery was founded by my great-grandfather in 1848. Growing up in London, I assumed that one day I would join the family business – and perhaps sit in my father's corner office. The death of my father – and within a very short period the death of two of my uncles who succeeded him as president – alarmed my father's seven elderly sisters. They were major shareholders in the brewery, and their investment advisors had counselled them "not to have all your eggs in one basket." My older brother, Jack, advised me that it was unlikely that the company would remain in family hands – in fact, by the time I was in my early twenties, the brewery had been sold.

This was a huge disappointment for me. However, as time passed, I realized that this was the best thing that could have happened to me. It forced me to chart my own course, and discover that I had my own little flame burning within. My career in business took many twists and turns. I had plenty of ups and downs – successes and failures. I went from accounting, to research, to corporate finance, to sales, and eventually to investment management. With lots of help from friends and colleagues – and a lot of luck – everything has turned out for the best. As my mother said to me shortly before she died, "Arthur, you have lived a charmed life" – this is so true!

We are living in a complex, confusing, and worrisome global environment. Yet one can look at this period as the most exciting and challenging time since the Industrial Revolution. The pace of change is accelerating, and the possibilities for your bright generation are endless.

As you move forward:

- Listen carefully to people who have your best interests at heart.
- Be fair and gracious with your colleagues and even with your competitors.
- Treat everyone the way you'd like to be treated.
- Give of yourself without expecting something in return.

Today you are celebrating a major milestone in your life – at each turn will come a pressing need

- To learn new ways of thinking
- To approach problems with an open mind
- To temper whatever you think – and whatever you do with true compassion for others

Congratulations to each and every one of you.